THE ART OF ROCK AND ROLL

THIRD EDITION

THE ART OF ROCK AND ROLL

Charles T. Brown
Saginaw Valley State University

 PRENTICE HALL, Englewood Cliffs, New Jersey 07632

Library of Congress Cataloging-in-Publication Data

Brown, Charles T.
    The art of rock and roll/Charles T. Brown. — 3rd ed.
      p. cm.
    Discography: p.
    Includes bibliographical references and index.
    ISBN 0-13-044892-3
    1. Rock music — History and criticism. 2. Rock music — Analysis,
appreciation. I. Title.
ML3534.B76   1992
781.66 — dc20
                                    91-31870
                                         CIP
                                       MN

Acquisitions Editor: Bud Therien
Editorial/Production Supervision: Margaret Antonini
Cover Designer: Bruce Kenselaar
Prepress Buyer: Herb Klein
Manufacturing Buyer: Patrice Fraccio
Editorial Assistant: Lee Mamunes

Portions of this book were taken from *Music U.S.A.:
America's Country and Western Tradition*, by Charles T. Brown,
published by Prentice-Hall, Inc.

 © 1992, 1987, 1983 by Prentice-Hall, Inc.
A Simon & Schuster Company
Englewood Cliffs, New Jersey 07632

Printed in the United States of America

10 9 8 7 6 5 4 3 2

ISBN 0-13-044892-3

Prentice-Hall International (UK) Limited, *London*
Prentice-Hall of Australia Pty. Limited, *Sydney*
Prentice-Hall Canada Inc., *Toronto*
Prentice-Hall Hispanoamericana, S.A., *Mexico*
Prentice-Hall of India Private Limited, *New Delhi*
Prentice-Hall of Japan, Inc., *Tokyo*
Simon & Schuster Asia Pte. Ltd., *Singapore*
Editora Prentice-Hall do Brasil, Ltda., *Rio de Janeiro*

To the memory of my son, Andrew

CONTENTS

PREFACE

This third edition treats rock and roll as a serious art form, tracing its development from the time African slaves were first brought to the American continent. We trace the significance of Afro-American musical forms through the nineteenth century, the history of jazz, and finally the formal naming of rock and roll in the early 1950s. We define rock and roll as a phenomenon that comes from people and their cultural roots; we do not see it as isolated from society.

Although this book is not highly technical, it does propose a method for analyzing music. If it is properly applied, anyone reading this book should be able to develop techniques for intelligently listening to music and then making some legitimate statements about it. This is the goal of any text dealing with music, to teach a model for musical appreciation.

Different forms of rock are treated in chronological and topological order. We have attempted to show the interrelationship between attitudes of society and the music that was produced, either as a reflection of those views or in reaction to them. Musicians discussed are representatives of movements in rock.

We believe that rock and roll is a significant form of American music and that its study will yield valid conclusions about American life. We further believe that rock and roll has dignity, technique, and complexity which would provide a good basis for the further study of music. Therefore, the subject has been treated with respect and with the seriousness it deserves.

In the third edition, we have added major chapters on music of the 1980s, rap, dance music, alternative/neo-punk, and an update on heavy metal through thrash, speed, and death styles. We have added new analyses of compositions from 1984 to 1990 and given more credence to MTV and its impact. The author worked hard to maintain the nonencyclopedic nature of the original book, so if your favorite musician is still left out, please understand that this book is essentially designed as a text for people who can complete its material in one semester.

ACKNOWLEDGMENTS

This list may seem long but these people have all helped me to become what I am (which allowed me to write the book), or they have helped me to write the book by correcting me. In this list are teachers, colleagues, students, and a few professional musicians who have been important to me. I would like to thank the following people: Ashley Alexander, Joseph Arbena, Bill Barnett, Gerard Behague, Matt Betton, Larry Biehl, Mike Brush, Jack Bruske, George Buelow, Barbara Doriean, Tom Ferguson, Ron Free, Joe Freyre, David Gilmour, Irving Godt, Jeff Hall, Mike Hanley, Tom Hearron, Donald Johns, Alan Kagan, Bill Kehoe, Kirker Kranz, Robert Lauden, Bill Lee, Kenneth Mack, Brian Malone, Walter May, Curt McCray, Eric Petersen, Barry Rankin, Robert Reynolds, Johannes Riedel, Kurt Schwertsik, Tim Smith, Clark Terry, and Robert Yien. A special word of thanks goes to Rick Hall and Justin Ivey, who assisted me greatly with the heavy metal material in the second edition, and to Brad Lewis, who helped me update that material for the third edition.

I would also like to thank my mother, Esther Brown, for allowing me to become a musician over the ranting of my father; my wife, for having patience; my children, for their musical taste, and my students who have tried to keep me "hip." Lastly, I would like to thank Bud Therien and Margaret Antonini of Prentice Hall, for their kindness and their faith that there is a market for this kind of book, and for allowing me to write a better and more thorough third edition.

CHAPTER 1

ELEMENTS
OF ROCK

This particular study of rock and roll is aimed at a wide audience, and therefore most of our discussions will be nontechnical in nature. Everything in this book should be understood by anyone who reads the material, listens to the music, and then spends some time thinking about the relationship between the two. In some ways, a vast knowledge of music might prove to be inhibiting; it has been my experience that musicians with long years of training in classical models sometimes bring certain biases to a discussion of "popular" music.

ASSUMPTIONS

We will begin with several assumptions:

1. Rock is a legitimate art form, primarily fostered in the United States.
2. Its roots are in folk, jazz, and pop music.

3. It is just as valid to study rock and roll as European classical music.
4. Simple musical analysis of selected compositions is a primary tool for understanding musical evolution.

I hope that anyone reading this book will come to understand that these statements are true. However, it is important that they be taken as true from the beginning of this book to understand the text properly.

Assumption 1

There are many definitions of an art form:

1. An artistic creation with lasting social impact
2. A creative act that is understood by a literate audience
3. Anything an actor, painter, musician, dancer, or other artist does that he or she considers art.

However, our definition of an *art form* is as follows: *a creative act that springs from the artist's experience as it reflects or reacts against society.* This definition differs slightly from the others in that it is culture-bound, a perspective that will run throughout the text. Sometimes art is a clear reflection of society; sometimes it is a vague reflection of society; and at other times it reacts against society. If we view art in this way, we will include more activities as artistic than if we were to follow any specific models. I hope we can find examples of music for what we will call art, but at times we will have to begin with contemporary rather than older models.

Rock and roll was fostered in the United States, in the sense that it took shape in this country and that most rock musicians were in fact born here. Although clearly we will be talking about European and African influences on the development of the form, the early rockers were from the United States, and more importantly, they were part of our culture. The matter of African influences on rock and roll will be taken seriously, but it is imperative to understand that these were Afro-American influences. That is, certain African musical traits exist in many popular forms of music in the United States, most notably jazz and rock.

Acculturation is the process by which a certain people are influenced by a foreign culture. Although this process was a forced one for early Afro-Americans, the net result was the same. They were changed from their original culture to one that was a mixture of U.S. influences and African roots. This process is well documented elsewhere, but it is important to point out here that acculturation was rather complete. Although Afro-Americans retained certain African traits, culturally and socially, their lifestyles changed, and thus they became a mixture of past and present. An analogous situation is the mixture of Spanish and Indian roots in Mexico. Although there are clear differences in the process, the desires of the people and the physical setting of both the contemporary Mexican and the contemporary Afro-American are the result of acculturation.

Given our definition of an art form, it is relatively easy to accept rock and roll as an example of it. As will be thoroughly shown in the following pages, rock and roll comes from an older tradition that developed in ways similar to other forms of music that eventually became art forms (even under the most conservative of definitions). Following our earlier definition, rock has had lasting social impact. It continues to influence an increasingly larger segment of the population. Older rock songs have become models for a particular era in rock or "concert" pieces. Rock and roll has more meaning to specific audiences than to nonunderstanding ones — a primary definition of literacy, although some will quibble with this use of the word. It is a musical form that has meaning for an audience conversant in that particular form of communication (that is, through its elements). Many of our important rock musicians considered themselves artistic, thereby satisfying the third definition of art. Finally, the working definition of this book is satisfied by a more complete understanding of the relationships among the accomplishments of rock musicians of different eras — accomplishments that spring directly from their life experiences. All the rock musicians discussed in this book will illustrate by their music that they are consciously reflecting their views of society and their experiences. Therefore, rock is an art form.

Proving that rock and roll is legitimate is perhaps more difficult. Legitimacy in music (as one example of art) is normally earned by lasting power. It is something that comes from survival over years, and unlike children, artistic forms do not earn it simply by birth. Rock and roll has had difficulty in establishing this quality, especially when we consider how many people were against this particular form of communication.

Although we will not dwell on negative views toward rock, there is a significant, although shrinking, group of people who do not accept rock and roll as even being music. Some of them have written books and articles pointing out the many evils of rock. It has been called a Communist plot, anti-Christian, and antiestablishment. Although it is highly doubtful that the Communists had anything to do with it, the last two claims are at least partially true. Rock and roll was a form of rebellion in its beginning; and in its evolution, some rock musicians have always tried to be antiestablishment (Bill Haley, Elvis Presley, Frank Zappa, Alice Cooper, and others). However, this is the nature of an art form, in that art often attempts to react against society. When it does, it is usually condemned by someone. Rock and roll was criticized during the McCarthy era; it was also blasted during the 1960s; and it continues to create some negative views today. This fact does not negate its legitimacy as an art form; it merely suggests that as a legitimate art form, it is controversial.

Like any art, rock and roll has many forms, some of which are not socially acceptable to the entire world. However, some of its forms are acceptable on a mass scale, and that acceptability can be seen in rather diverse performances — symphony concerts, half-time shows, commercials for television and radio, and Muzak. No working musician could survive without an ability to play rock songs at wedding receptions, concerts, or public performances like the circus or the Ice

Capades. This fact establishes firmly the legitimacy of the art form; that is, it is utilized and necessary.

Assumption 2

The roots of rock and roll can be found in the basic popular forms of music in the United States — folk, jazz, and pop. Although this assertion will be shown more thoroughly in chapter three, it must be understood here that rock and roll did not simply happen in the early 1950s, devoid of earlier influences. That simply does not occur with anything, much less with art.

Since art springs from life, the musicians who played the music that became known as rock and roll must have had experiences that caused them to play a certain way. Musical patterns in melody, rhythm, and harmony (to be explained later) are shaped over time and through the hardest part of being a musician — practice. Most of the early rock patterns came from some older tradition, the blues, for one. These patterns — from folk, jazz, and pop — were used to produce a new sound, and although it was different, it was basically derivative.

Early rock musicians came from similar social backgrounds. They started playing in rural areas and moved to the larger cities as they became better at what they were doing. They followed the same pattern as earlier jazz musicians from New Orleans, in that they moved north to spread the style of their music and to make more money doing it. Because early rock musicians did not generally have access to sophisticated marketing techniques, they followed rather traditional patterns of expansion, primarily through increased opportunities for public performance.

The roots of rock and roll can be traced in two ways:

1. Style elements, or the characteristics of the various styles of music that ultimately would blend to form rock and roll
2. The actual technique of playing jazz, folk, and pop in comparison to that of playing 1950s rock and roll.

The point is that the actual lifestyles of the blues musician and the early rock musician were fairly similar. Moreover, the basic musical techniques of early rock and roll and its antecedents were similar as well.

Assumption 3

This whole book questions the value judgment that music should be taught solely through the European classical tradition. Although my training is primarily in that tradition, it is my conviction that it is a mistake to assume that music should be taught only through classical models.

In a paper entitled "American Music Education Foundation in Jazz: A Historical Perspective," Dr. Reginald Buckner suggested that America has never really developed its own system of music education (one that is nonderivative) and that jazz should be its musical foundation.[1] Although thoroughly agreeing with his premise, we could argue that American popular music, or the music of the people, should be the basis for our music education system.

We could hypothesize that music should be taught first from the oral tradition of folk music (by extension, jazz and rock as outgrowths of the folk system) and then as an imitation of classical models. Dr. Buckner further shows in his paper that other countries have done just that. The systems of Johann Heinrich Pestalozzi, Carl Orff, Zoltan Kodaly, Béla Bartók, and others have based their music education on the concept that we should start with our own cultural experiences before using other models. Of course, this is a philosophical argument, but it is quite compelling.

A more practical argument is that people generally feel more comfortable working from the known to the unknown. Also, there is a tendency for people to keep up a course of study if they are enjoying it. Some would argue that we should learn the best from the beginning (that is, the classics), but we must question that judgment. What makes one form better than the other?

The general aim of this book is to affect audiences who would not be influenced by the more specific approach (that is, the classics), although it is hoped that this experience will lead to a desire to know about this music as well. By studying rock and roll, technically and socially, we can gain an appreciation of how music works as a system of communication. Many of the advantages of studying music can be made clear through this study, and those bits of learning can easily be applied to other learning activities.

Our conclusion is that rock will prove to be a valid means of producing competent musicians and that its performance demands the same kind of diligent artistry demanded in any musical form. Therefore, we contend that rock is a valid way in which to study music in general, and that starting with rock for our first musical study is just as valid (and perhaps more so) as starting anywhere else.

Assumption 4

Of all the assumptions, this one will place the greatest burden on both the reader and the teacher of a course in rock and roll. We must develop a form of musical analysis that adequately describes what we are hearing and studying. If we do not take the effort to analyze music, we would not be engaging in a study of it. Rock and roll may be other things, but its most important quality is that it is music and should be studied as a musical form.

The next section of this chapter will define those elements with which we are concerned. The reader will need to learn definitions, because music for the beginner is a foreign language, and it will then be necessary to learn some skills (see chapter two) in order to use the definitions. It is our contention that anyone will be able to learn this skill, and without it much of the book will be meaningless.

[1] Reginald Buckner, "American Music Education Foundation in Jazz: A Historical Perspective," presented at the National Association of Jazz Educator's Convention, St. Louis, Jan. 14–17, 1981.

Music is a nonverbal language (with the exception of the text). The body language of a performer, the way he or she dresses, and the stage presentation are forms of nonverbal communication that most of us can deal with rather easily. However, dealing with the various elements of music and those nonverbal communicators seems to be more difficult. Therefore, we will develop techniques for translating what we hear into words.

A system of analysis is simply a model of some structure—architectural, musical, or anything else. We would like to be able to generalize and say that rock from a certain era has common characteristics or that early Beach Boys has a certain style. We do this through musical analysis or through a definition of stylistic traits. The easiest method is to take notes on what we hear and then to compare the notes for two or more songs of the same period. The methods outlined in this book are simple (although they can be made more sophisticated as one's ability to analyze grows), and anyone can learn to follow them at some level. This book will teach some common vocabulary for analyzing songs, but the results will be highly personalized.

By simply performing the tasks called for in this book, we should achieve the skills necessary for analyzing music. However, like any study, it would be highly advantageous to go beyond the tasks of this book and analyze many more songs. Such practice would produce more knowledge and more sophistication in musical analysis. In order truly to appreciate the tremendous variety of musical styles, we must immerse ourselves in the music, through analysis and listening. Rock and roll is in this respect no different from Mozart, Palestrina, or Shankar.

METHOD

We will treat rock and roll as a chronological study because this system allows us to give brief overviews of society in different periods and then to illustrate how the music of a particular period either supports or contradicts societal views. Each of the chapters treats a specific historical period, a particular group or set of groups as a model for a style, or a specific form of evolution.

ELEMENTS OF MUSIC

Nonverbal Communication

Music communicates through organized sound, which is traditionally defined in terms of beat, harmony, melody, and lyrics. All the elements of music except lyrics are nonverbal and therefore are difficult to translate into words. We will define them and then suggest ways by which we can know each of the elements individually—apart from other elements of music.

We must begin by dealing with elements of music as independent qualities, realizing full well that in actual performance they seldom exist separately. However, we must isolate them at the beginning in order to understand what each element does. It is a matter of blotting out the other elements in order to understand clearly what one element does within a musical context. After practice in listening to one thing only, we can then proceed to an analysis of how different elements interact.

Melody

Melody is an organized set of notes consisting of different pitches (high or low sounds). The melody of a song is what we would be singing if we substituted the syllable *la* for all the regular syllables. Melody can be much more complicated than this definition indicates, but it is easiest to think of it as the up and down motion of the lead singer, without accompaniment. There are also other types of melodies used in rock and roll, but we should concentrate at first on the lead singer — Elton John or Diana Ross, for example. Melody often makes the difference between a boring song and an interesting one, although generally melody alone will not make a good song. "One Voice" by Barry Manilow is pure melody at the beginning — a rather unusual example.

Various melodies are used by rock groups: the main melody (sung by the lead singer), background melodies (sung by a vocal group or the other instrumentalists), and bass melodies. It would be wise to concentrate on the lead singer and the main melody of the song, and only after we have the skill to pick out that melody should we turn our attention to backgrounds or bass melodies (also called bass lines). Fortunately, 1950s rock and roll consists mainly of lead melody, which will allow us to build our listening skills gradually.

Rhythm

Aside from being the most misspelled word in the music vocabulary, rhythm is relatively easy to understand. It is simply those beat patterns that underlie most forms of communication. Many things in life are made up of pulse, or beat — the heartbeat, traffic lights, business cycles, and eating habits. Many rhythms are recurring or reiterative, in that they follow a consistent pattern, like the tides or the clicking of railroad car wheels as they go over the ties. Rhythm is made up of pulsations that last various lengths of time. It is basic to poetry and to language — long and short syllables — and defines the time framework of communication.

In music, the basic beat pattern, or rhythm, tells us something about the emotional feel of different kinds of songs. A slow piece has different rhythms from a fast one; a waltz (three-beat feel) has a different beat pattern from a bossa nova. If we can perceive differences in rhythms, we can make some determinations about different kinds of music (strong beats, triple feel, double feel, slow and emotional, and so on). In chapter two we will discuss some different ways to describe rhythm and beat. However, at this point, although it will not be necessary to write out rhythms in standard notation, we should develop some personal way of describing differences. Eventually, we will be able to describe beat patterns in fairly precise terms.

Rhythm or basic beat is easiest to hear by listening to the drums and counting at the same time. Especially in early rock and roll, the beat pattern is very simple and will often be supported by the other instruments. In fact, the beat pattern may be the same throughout the entire song. Clearly we must listen for the beat and try to count aloud at the same time. When the counting and the music seem to coincide, it is simply a matter of writing down the repeating patterns we have heard. We can use dots and dashes, numbers, or descriptive words (see chapter two).

Harmony

An understanding of harmony probably requires a prior knowledge of melody, that is, if we wish to perceive harmony in an actual piece. However, we can define harmony before actually hearing it. Harmony is the simultaneous sounding of two or more different notes at the same time. The most obvious examples are all the strings on a guitar (although it will be more pleasing if someone shows us how to hold our left hand), the sounds of a chorus, or blocks of notes on a piano. Perhaps the best way to understand harmony is through a teacher's or musician's example.

Once we develop a sense of what harmony means apart from a rock and roll piece, we can begin to listen for it. The easiest place to hear it is in the background melodies sung by a vocal group or in the instrumentalists backing up the lead singer. In order to make appropriate selections, we must distinguish between songs that use unison background melodies (that is, everyone singing the same pitches, or notes) and those that use blocks of sounds for background.

Harmony serves a very important function in rock because it provides the texture of the total sound. In the 1950s the movement from one harmonic texture to another was fairly simple. However, in the later styles harmony became rather complex. Harmony often delineates one style from another, and there are even some groups that distinguish themselves from others on the basis of their harmonic practices.

Lyrics

Of all the elements of music, lyrics are by far the easiest to understand because they are verbal and usually in English. Since lyrics are in a common language and since we have all dealt with the meanings of words, we can probably become quite sophisticated in our analysis of lyrics right from the beginning. In fact, many readers will analyze the music in relationship to the lyrics, which is a valid and logical way to begin musical analysis.

Although we will not attempt heavy literary analysis, lyrics normally fall into patterns, or verses, and the music will usually be consistent with these lyrical patterns. Unless we are listening to a purely instrumental piece, we can analyze the structure of the lyrics and then talk about how the music supports it.

At first we should concentrate on the lyric sung by the lead singer and treat the background singers as a separate group. Quite often the background vocalist will simply repeat some phrase sung by the lead singer, answer the lead singer, or sing the refrain. Less often the background singers will sing a part of the song while the lead singer is resting. We should start by figuring out if there are repetitions of parts of the lyric, usually called a refrain, and if the main lyric falls into verses. Generally, lyric analysis is the task of writing down repetition schemes. We could also write down the scheme of the interaction between the lead singer and the background singers. When we do this on several songs by the same musicians or from the same era, we begin to see consistent patterns.

Another fruitful area of lyric analysis is a value judgment on how good or how trivial the lyric is. Although we may not be able to make these judgments on other elements, we can certainly do so on the lyric. If the lyric does not seem to make much sense, we can make an assumption about the intended audience and the purpose of the song. This is an important activity when we try to connect music with society.

Performance

We include the performance in our definitions of elements of music because it often will tell us quite a bit about the purpose, function, and impact of a certain song. In defining this element, we recognize the significance of the performance and its effect on the audience. For what kind of situation was this song intended? Was it recorded, and if so, was it recorded with good equipment? Were the musicians under stress when this song was performed? What did they have in mind about its impact, or who should the audience be? Was the song designed for a black or white audience, in the North or South?

These questions are not normally considered elements of music, but we include them here because they may be as important as analyzing the drumbeat. Especially in rock and roll, which began as an oral art for live audiences, these types of questions may be paramount in understanding the cultural setting of the musician and the audience for which the songs were intended.

SOCIAL SETTING

Reflection of Values

One of the basic premises about music in general is that it reflects the values of society. Rock and roll, then, must reflect societal values at all periods in its history, and it will be our job to illustrate that assertion throughout the text. By using the elements of music, we can begin to make some assumptions about how rock and roll reflects its society (however important that may be in various eras). The lyric will state the general intent, and the other elements will support its philosophical content.

. . . folk song . . . exhibits the general characteristics of a genuine people's art in class societies. Folk art serves the interests of the common people;
its subject matter arises out of their everyday life; it is practiced by the people
as participants and not merely as spectators; its individual exponents spring
from the people themselves.[2]

We will attempt to work from both directions, occasionally defining the views
of society at a particular point and illustrating how specific songs reflected or
reacted against that view. At other times, we will analyze specific songs and consider how they influenced society. In any event, our specific premise is that music is
a reflection of its society and that it serves as an opaque mirror of the values of the
society.

Rebellion and Escapism

Rock and roll was first a new form of music — really a modified version of
rhythm and blues — but it quickly took on an attitude of rebellion, at the beginning
for a relatively small group of people. As the form developed, it became a stan-
dard-bearer for youths, and, significantly, a symbol of their independence. This
role created the antiestablishment image of rock and roll, although there were
certainly elements of early rock that were noticeably antiestablishment in comparison to other forms of music. As a form of rebellion and escapism for youths, early
rock and roll could be marketed for that specific clientele, and this helped to shape
its substance. Some would argue that these same elements have allowed rock to
continue to stand apart from other musical forms.

Although there is clearly some validity to the argument that rock and roll is a
separatist movement, this view must be seen in the context of its history. At times it
has prospered from rebellion (early 1950s, mid-1960s, the late 1970s), although at
other times it has prospered from mainstream involvement (late 1950s, early
1960s, early and mid-1970s). We must see rock and roll as a diversified art form,
where rebellion and escapism are significant aspects of its variety. However, there
is a healthy tension between the need to make a social point (that is, to rebel) and to
communicate on a mass level.

IMPLICATIONS

In the chapters to follow we will discuss various influences society has had on the
development of rock and roll, and we will also show that rock has induced a quicker
acceptance of certain attitudes. Although there are many areas of influence, some
that should be singled out are politics, religion, class struggle, changing mores, and
race.

Politics is the most obvious force that rock musicians rebel against and most
particularly at those times when there was a conservative in office (Nixon and

---

[2] Louis Harap, *Social Roots of the Arts* (New York: International Publishers, 1949), p. 127.

Agnew) or when politics caused trouble for youths (Vietnam). If politics is expanded to encompass social structure and economics, we can see that the implications of political decisions will always be rallying points for folk art, of which rock and roll is a part. Many of our explanations of what society is thinking at a certain point and how rock music reflects that thinking will be focused on political activity, lack of activity, or the direction of politics in a particular age.

Religion influences rock and roll in that many rock musicians have religious feelings when they perform, or they communicate religious values through their performances. Of course, gospel music was an important part of early rock and continues to be at the heart of soul music. More importantly, rock music in general develops its own sense of morality, and this is often viewed as religious, even when it is sacrilegious. The Who in *Tommy* take on Messiah-like views; the Beatles in *Yellow Submarine* imply rather strongly that they have been sent by someone to save the world from the oppressors. Cult worship of a sort is very much a part of rock and roll; and this aspect has caused some notable religious leaders to condemn the music, both for its seeming immorality and for its competition with more traditional religious views.

Class struggle is a noticeable part of rock's history, specifically that between youths and the older generation. This difference in world view, expressed openly in rock lyrics, is a constant theme, which makes rock the language of youth. Certain theorists have contended that rock and roll is the language of Marxist politicians, who see it as a form of lower-class confrontation with the establishment. Whether or not that theory is true, rock and roll does promote change.

Changing mores are reflected in rock's lyrics and in its stage antics. This is most certainly a chicken-and-egg kind of argument, but it is obvious that moral values have changed in the last thirty years (roughly the time span of rock and roll). The sexual revolution and other moral equivalents have been expressed in rock and roll, which in turn has influenced other modes of communication. In this way, rock and roll has been influential in creating a language to express changing views.

An understanding of the interaction of white and black society is paramount in understanding the development of rock and roll. It began as truly a black art form and owes much of its technique to black musicians, who codified the style. In chapter three we will show how rock was derived from Afro-American blues forms and give due credit to its black roots. The story of black songs paying off for white musicians enlightens us about the continuing suppression of black people within a white business society. Of course, the interesting thing is that race continues to be an issue, even if some of the sting has been taken out.

SUMMARY

This first chapter sets forth some premises for the book, defines in basic terms some of the major elements of music, and outlines our view of music as a reflector of society. The chapters that follow will carry us through the history of this art form, discuss some of the major artists, and, most importantly, outline a basic technique by which the information can be made more meaningful. Although we will be neither encyclopedic nor exhaustive, we will cover the significant points of development and prove our first premise, that rock and roll is a legitimate art form.

LISTENING

The first recommended listening assignment will be at the end of chapter two.

CHAPTER **2**

LISTENING SKILLS

WHY LISTEN?

Through extensive listening and application of analysis, we can define not only the social impact of a rock group but also its musical style. Although each of the suggestions in this chapter has worked in the past, it is not necessary to use all the suggested techniques; and they should certainly not be used in exactly the way they are presented. Although we will try to give enough examples of how a technique could be used, the purpose of this chapter is to outline ways in which the individual can create his or her own system of analysis. In short, you must create your own system or it will not be as meaningful.

Some suggested guidelines for analyzing music will be presented in the form of questions we can ask while listening to a piece of music. After listening and questioning, we should be able to write down some notes on the composition and then make a structural model. It cannot be stressed too much that we should form our own logic according to our own order (by perhaps omitting some of the questions or by creating different ones) and then decide what sort of model we want to create. Moreover, we should try several different schemes at first in order to see which one is most productive. By the time we have completed fifteen or twenty pieces, we should have a workable and personal model for musical analysis.

Although we could have produced several examples of a complete analysis of selected rock compositions, we have chosen not to do so for some of the following reasons:

1. Providing models would remove responsibility from the reader for this all-important activity. (He or she might be tempted to copy the style and avoid creating an individualized model.)
2. Not everyone reading this book will take analysis seriously.
3. Analysis should properly be separated from the reading of the text; then the reader can integrate the text material and his or her own analysis, either with or without a teacher.

Concentration

It may seem silly to mention that we must pay attention to what we are doing, but that turns out to be a crucial issue in this chapter. Fortunately, we are already well trained in listening, because we have to be able to listen or we could not survive. However, let us examine for a minute what we concentrate on and what is normally treated passively. We concentrate on or listen to material that we think is important — a lecture, a news report on changing tax laws, a police officer telling us we have made a mistake. In school we learn how to take notes on significant material and how to organize our notes into meaningful logic so that we can memorize the information. However, there are many types of communication on which we do not concentrate fully.

There are also many types of blocking behaviors, most of which are associated with either unneeded or unwanted information. We tend to block out authoritarian information if possible, as well as the bantering of children when we have decided they are not our responsibility; adults block out teenagers, and so on. Unfortunately, the kind of music that this book is about is often given little real attention. Many of us tend to use popular music as background sound, perhaps even doing our homework to the sound of the Beach Boys.

At least for the purposes of this study, we must change our attitude toward rock and roll and give it the same kind of careful attention that we would to material we consider essential to our existence. Unfortunately, much of the music we will hear during the progress of this book is exactly the same kind of music we might have used for background, either in our homes or while driving our cars. Even though we may continue to hear similar examples in our daily lives, we must heighten our sensitivities for analysis by treating that music differently. Listening assignments for a music class are its most important task, and you must do them with the same concern and attention you would give to math problems.

The crucial behavior in good listening is concentration, and for this we must block out any interference. In some ways, listening to music properly is like effective studying. We should be in a relaxed setting, be rid of background sounds, and be paying careful attention. For some, it will be difficult to concentrate on that which we may have formerly treated passively; but this change is absolutely imperative if we are to succeed in musical analysis, which in turn will lead to a more complete understanding of the true nature of rock and roll. Even when the song may not be exactly what we like, we must treat it seriously and analyze it fairly.

One of the early premises of this book comes to mind, that rock is a legitimate art form. We must assume this to be true and complete our listening assignments without previously conceived bias. Our purpose will be to analyze a number of compositions of different periods, the long-range goal being stylistic models for each of the types of music studied.

Dissecting What We Hear

Now that we have established the necessity of concentration, we should proceed to its various levels. We must be able to listen with a purpose in mind, which is to remember what we have heard. Each person will handle this task somewhat differently, but there are some general guidelines to help us achieve results.

The first thing to decide is what we wish to use as a reference point. Most people feel that lyrics are fairly easy to analyze for reasons presented earlier. In early rock tunes the lyrics are very simple and will be easy to summarize or even write down completely. Seldom did the record jacket give the complete lyrics in the 1950s, but in later years the complete lyrics may have been printed on the liner notes. However, we may decide another musical element is easier to hear the first time through a song. Whatever we decide, we must consistently use one element as our structural device, at least for the first fifty songs.

Clearly, we will have to listen to most songs more than once. After a time we may be able to analyze a song the first time through, especially if it is rather simple. But at first we will need to listen to a song three or four times before we can hear enough to make a respectable analysis. On the first time through, we will get a general idea of what the song is like, what it is about, and what kind of sound it has. Using whatever structural device we have chosen (for most of us, the lyrics), we will write down whatever we hear the first time. If we can successfully block out other elements, we might try to take notes while the song is being played. However, we must clean up our notes afterward, similar to the way we would rewrite a term paper before handing it in.

As we continue to listen to the same song again and again, we will add new information, basing each item on how it fits with our main structural device. If we chose lyrics the first time through, we will try to figure out how the background vocalists and instrumentalists fit with the lyrics. Do they emphasize certain words or phrases? Do they play all the time? We will try to sort out the instruments and figure out what they do and what their function is. If there are instrumental solos, we will write that information down — their character and where they fit in connection with the lyric repetition scheme.

This is an excellent place to start counting beats. Many people will be able to feel the correct rhythms without technical assistance. We can look down at our feet and see if they are instinctively tapping out the beat pattern, or imagine ourselves dancing to the music. Beat can also be figured out by taking our structural device, finding its repeating phrases, and subdividing it until a beat pattern emerges. It really does not matter if we all have the same number of beats per section, only that the sections that are equal in time have the same number of beats. We may get half the number of beats as someone else, which only means that the other person is subdividing one more level than we are. Although this may sound complicated at first, virtually everyone catches on to it after enough practice.

After we have done whatever we feel we can, we will write it all up as a description of that particular song. We will try to find out some information about the group and the performance. Then we will listen to the song again and see if we recognize in our description all the things we hear. If we think our analysis fits what we are hearing, we have done the job correctly. We can of course share our analysis with someone else, but we should not be intimidated by the fact that the other analysis is different. We might want to question our analysis in order to improve it, but remember that our purpose is to create a technique that is personal and meaningful to us. *If we feel good about our results, we must not change them.*

We should be able to see that good listening is the key to good analysis. What we are trying to do is translate the nonverbal communication into a verbal model (or one based on symbols that could be verbalized). Concentration is essential so that we pick up as much as possible, but once we accomplish the act of analysis a few times the process becomes quite simple. Analysis is like anything in life: It will become easier and more sophisticated as we do it. Practice invariably yields improvement.

LYRICS

The easiest way to analyze a lyric is to write down all the words and then figure out if there is a verse structure, that is, repetition of music and various verses. If there is a set of words (usually shorter than a verse) that is repeated several times during the whole song, it should be called a refrain (or some similar word or symbol). We should also note whether there are words that are consistently sung by background singers and whether they are repeated in any recognizable pattern. Although it is easiest to analyze lyrics by writing down all the words, it is often unnecessary, especially if the song is short or very simple in lyric structure.

In 1950s music it is often possible to use letters or symbols that stand for parts of the lyrics without writing down the words at all. For instance, songs normally start with a verse, so one could simply write down *V1* when the singing begins (verse 1). Quite often, the refrain will follow each verse or sets of two verses. When the refrain occurs, we will write down an *R* because the refrain will normally be the same throughout the song. On rare occasions there will be two refrains, in which case we can use *R1* and *R2*. Several standard forms of composition are the following: *V1, R, V2, R, V3, R . . . R* and *V1, V2, R, V3, V4, R . . . R.*

We do not have to use these particular letters and numbers. We could use stars and hearts, short words, or whatever; but the point is that this is a shorthand for analyzing lyrics. We want to develop a system for modeling the structure of the lyrics that will work consistently. We may be able to arrive at the point where we do not need to write down the words at all, but simply do it by listening.

MELODY

Soprano—Lead Melody

As has been described earlier, the lead melody is the organized set of pitches that fits with the lyric of the song. There are sometimes background melodies that have background lyrics, like *do-bop-do-bop* or other phrases. However, the first important task is to be able to sort out the lead melody from the background lyrics. Some people are capable of simply hearing the main melody the first time through. Others must listen for the main lyric and figure out the main melody by ignoring the words.

We should spend some time practicing this task. Also, we should *not try a complete analysis while we are working on one element.*

The lead melody is sometimes called the **soprano melody,** which means the highest melody, although this term is perhaps unwise since many lead melodies are sung by men, who are not sopranos. In any event, the only way we can learn to pick out the lead melody is through practice and having someone check our answers.

The next job is to find some way to talk about the lead melody. Descriptive words are often adequate, such as "it jumps around a lot" or "it is smooth." Descriptions like "it's pretty" or "I hate it" are not very useful. Descriptions that talk about the shape of the melody or its contour are useful. Musical notation is of course the most precise way to describe melody; however, we could use a line chart of the melody or some words that describe its up-and-down motion. If the melody has jumps in it, we should use words that clearly say that; if it is smooth, then it does not have jumps in it. Whatever system we use, it should describe in our own terms what the main melody sounds like. It is to be hoped that someone else could understand from our description that it does truly represent the melody being analyzed.

Bass Melody

The bass melody has not been discussed yet, but it is surprisingly easy to pick out once we have mastered the task of hearing the lead melody by itself. The bass melody is normally played by an instrument rather than sung, although there are some bass voice solos in novelty tunes. Obviously, what we have to do is focus our attention on those particular sounds and try to listen solely to them.

The bass line is halfway between melody and rhythm, or beat; it is usually played by the bass guitar (when present) or by the piano. It is usually reiterative, in that it does the same thing over and over, and it always fits the basic beat of the song. In 1950s rock, the bass line is usually played on all four beats of a fast song, and it is mostly a melody of jumps. It follows the blues progression (see chapter three) in many cases. In any event, it is a low-sounding part, it is repetitive, and it is rather continuous. Later examples of bass lines in disco or funk/rock/jazz of the 1970s will be more complicated. But early rock bass lines are very simple and should be relatively easy to isolate. Their function is to serve as the foundation for the instrumental ensemble, which is of course primarily an accompaniment for the singing.

Inner Voices and Backgrounds

These melodies are the hardest to isolate from the ensemble because they are in the middle of the texture. Even a trained musician will have trouble describing the inner voices unless they do something obvious. If the inner voices (between the lead melody and the bass melody) are background figures, it is usually easier to hear and describe them. If they are simply part of the vocal texture, it is difficult to say anything about them except just that.

If the inner voices are instrumental or if they do the same thing as the instrumental parts, they can be tied to our description of the instruments (next section). Although we should always try to describe everything, the inner voices, unless they are unusual, will present a challenge. Most students will simply say that inner voices are in harmony or that they are background figures.

If there are noticeable background figures, responses to the main lyric, or repetitions of it, these should be noted. The simplest way is to write down the words of the background figure, indicating that background voices sing these words. Sometimes the rhythm of the background figures is repeated by instruments alone, and although it is a subtle thing, it would be nice to mention that. Lastly, 1950s music is very easy when it comes to this type of analysis, and we should be as accurate as possible when the music is easy, in obvious preparation for when the music will become more complicated.

Instruments

As this is the first mention of instruments in rock and roll, we really should realize that although rock and roll is vocally oriented, it would not be rock and roll without the instruments. It is the instrumental ensemble that gives rock its character and of course the beat. The standard instrumentation for rock and roll uses guitars (six-string and four-string bass) and drums. In different eras, the piano, saxophone, and other instruments are necessary. In the 1950s there were generally piano, guitar, drums, and saxophone. It would be very useful to be able to tell the difference among these instruments.

The function of these instruments is rather straightforward. The drums provide the beat, and our exercises in hearing rhythms and counting beats will rely on our ability to sort out the sound and pulsation of the drummer. The guitars provide continuous rhythm, occasionally solo lines. The bass guitar plays the bass melody, and the piano (when used) will provide rhythm, bass melody, and sometimes solos. The saxophone plays background figures and solos, usually at a specified time in the composition.

Although we could do an analysis based totally on lyrics, we could also base it on the instrumental functions. Perhaps we should try to use the instruments as the organizing function, if for no other reason than to sensitize ourselves to their roles and significance. The best analysis includes both the lyrics and the instruments, and we must reach conclusions about the interrelationships.

RHYTHM AND HARMONY

We should apply the logic of the previous section on melody to the function of rhythm and harmony. We would not expect many readers to use either rhythm or harmony as their main structural device, but this is not to imply that these elements are less important. They are more technical in nature and harder to verbalize and therefore should probably be treated in second-level analysis.

However, rhythm is the most important definer of this kind of music, and without certain rhythmic phrases, it would not be rock and roll. If we could pick out the major rhythm figures, while counting the music, we could analyze the music in terms of the development or lack of development of those rhythmic phrases. This would be somewhat difficult for the reader without technical training, but certain figures could be identified and discussed (see the following section).

Harmony is perhaps easier and definitely should be considered for analysis. A particular example is when the vocal group uses passages in vocal harmony to emphasize certain words, quite often the refrain or the end of a verse. Sometimes in slow songs, harmony will be used for one section of the song to set it off from others. Of course, harmony also defines changes in basic background figures (such as the blues progression, to be discussed in chapter three) and as such must be considered.

Both rhythm and harmony determine the relative complexity of a composition. We must become aware of changes in rhythm and/or harmony because they indicate changes in the song. Although we may not be able to describe in technical terms what the rhythm and/or harmony is doing at any particular point, we should be able to tell that there are changes at specific places.

MODEL FOR ANALYSIS[1]

The following questions and suggested tactics outline some of the activities that could be noted in a composition, all for the purpose of providing the material necessary to write up our own analysis. However, these are merely suggestions and should not be taken as exhaustive. We must create our own system in order to be successful.

Part One

1. What is the lyric repetition scheme?
2. What instruments are used and how do they function?
3. Are there any instrumental solos?
4. Is the instrumental accompaniment continuous?
5. If there are changes in the accompaniment, how do the changes fit the lyric scheme?
6. Where do background vocals occur in relation to the main lyric?
7. If there are refrains (vocal or instrumental), do they have something unique (low bass voice, novelty lyric, or some special quality)?
8. What is the predominant rhythm pattern?
9. Are there changes in harmony usage and/or pattern?

Part Two—Counting

1. How many counts does one verse take?
2. How many counts does the refrain take?
3. Figure out the number of counts in the entire piece and then divide the piece into sections and indicate the number for each section.
4. Within each section, figure out which counts receive strong accents or heavier pulsations.

Part Three

1. Describe the melodies.
2. Describe the harmonies.
3. Describe any important rhythms.
4. Describe lyric content (qualitative).
5. Define the performing situation.

[1] See Appendix B.

6. Write up the structural model.

7. Write a short description of the musical style.

Checking Results

Once we have analyzed a song of a particular group, we should check it with someone else to see if it makes sense. Then we should listen to another song by the same group that sounds basically the same — in the 1950s there were many similar songs — to see if the second song has the same structure. It is quite useful to build up a stock of standard analyses in order to use them again. All we have to do is mark the deviations or the differences.

We should trade our analyses with other people. Often by seeing how someone else approaches analysis, we can modify or strengthen our own skills. We are not cheating by checking our results with other people. The most important thing is to learn how to do it, and it does not matter how many people help. Eventually, we will develop our own technique and will not need help at all.

We should talk with some musicians about the way they structured their songs when they put them together. Eventually we will be able to tell whether or not a song is well structured. Most successful songs were intelligently structured, or they would have died at once.

LISTENING (SEE DISCOGRAPHY)

Bill Haley and the Comets

Early Elvis Presley

The Coasters

N.B. In all of the listening assignments, the selection of pieces is left up to the teacher and/or the reader. The important thing is to use the system rather than to select a particular song.

CHAPTER **3** _____

THE SOURCES
OF ROCK

SLAVE MUSIC

Although we might properly term this section the history of African music in the United States, we actually begin with a discussion of slave music, because that is exactly what it was. Black people were forced to come to the United States, thus alienating them from the environment or bringing about forced acculturation. The difference between free acculturation of a race or society and forced acculturation is quite significant; we must first recognize that Africans had little choice in their environment, and free interchange with white society was not always possible.

The slave routes brought Africans to the New World through various ports, primarily in the southern United States, the Caribbean, and several places in Latin America. The slaves brought directly to the northern part of the United States traveled a different cultural path from those brought through the Caribbean. The kinds of music that developed from different cultural experiences is a study in itself (the bibliography at the end of the book provides excellent source material on this subject).

Most of the slaves imported to the New World came from West Africa, which brought about some continuity in the basic tribal experiences of the acculturation process. For our purposes we will examine some of the kinds of music that were staples of the slaves and were carried over into the nineteenth-century antecedents of the blues as they influenced early jazz and later rock and roll. In passing, it would be interesting to trace the influence of tribal roots in popular music in other American cultures, such as Brazilian cult and popular music (see the bibliography).

The first slaves were brought to the United States in the early part of the seventeenth century, and it is important to understand at this point that they were Africans and not Americans at all. As Western Africans, they would go through a long process before they became what we can truly call black Americans, or Afro-Americans.[1] LeRoi Jones, or Imamu Amiri Baraka as he prefers to be called, traces the process of becoming Afro-American in a most convincing way. He points out that the original black slaves did not see themselves as Americans, but rather as captives. From this perspective, they did not immediately begin the process of free acculturation.

The original slaves viewed themselves as alien in this foreign land and preserved the idea that they would be returning to Africa. Also, they had to perform certain tasks on a schedule established by those in power. They did not give up their language, their view of the universe, or any of their customs (except those eliminated through punishment). There are analogies with other groups brought to the United States (such as the Orientals brought to build the railroads in the nineteenth century), but these are weak at best. The Indians of Latin America (most particularly, Mexico) were acculturated rather freely, but they were the native population. Africans were alien in the land, they were not acculturated freely, and their roots were thousands of miles away.

In some sense, the most significant way of showing the slow process of acculturation for Africans would be through their use of language. Only when they began to tell their life stories in some form of English would they become truly Afro-American. Slave tradition relied heavily on African languages, or more properly, the people spoke two languages. Everything of substance was said in an African dialect; English was used for less substantive things, but also for survival.

Secular Tradition

The process of change in musical tradition for African slaves began quite early in the United States, primarily because they were spread out somewhat more thinly here than in other parts of the New World. Although there was a continuation of pure African traditions, the slow process of acculturation began as soon as there were American-born slaves, and that change was most apparent in secular music.

[1] LeRoi Jones, *Blues People* (New York: William Morrow, 1967).

The only place where African slaves really saw themselves as part of this alien land was through the work they were forced to perform. And although the work was performed for different reasons and with weak motivation, it was done in a manner similar to that which would have been used in a tribal setting. As Africans quite naturally sang to help in the process of work, this became the focal point for change in their musical culture.

It is important to understand at this point that Africans do not necessarily recognize music as an art form, separate from life in general. To them, music is a part of living, and aside from certain religious events, it is not a separate experience. It is done in conjunction with life — with work and with daily activity. We are not trying to conjure up the image of the happy slave singing while enjoying hard work in the field, because this was not the case. There was a tremendous amount of misery involved in this forced labor. However, the fact that slaves did sing is true, although they sang because it helped them accomplish the work and avoid the misery. Although their motivation for working in a tribal situation might have been stronger, hard work was necessary here and their culture had trained them to sing while they were doing it. Later discussions of the blues will rely heavily on the patterns set up in work songs and the message of misery in the lives of black people, whether African or Afro-American.

The similarities of certain life experiences are the cornerstone of acculturation. The reason that some acculturation first took place in secular music is directly linked to the similarities between the secular experience (that is, work) in both Africa and the New World. Because of the massive dissimilarity between religious experiences (the African religious system was very different from those in this country), acculturation within religious music and traditions would occur much later.

Work songs were basically chants, first in African languages and then in English with African words thrown in. **Chants** are simple phrases repeated over and over, and the phrases are usually quite short. They are very rhythmic in the sense that they usually have a short melodic phrase (three or four notes) and a reiterative rhythmic pattern. For example, "Song of the Volga Boat Man" is a work song, although it is quite different from African ones. Many children's songs have aspects of work songs, as do the chants of cheerleaders at football games. There are many fine sources for work songs of African slaves, and although certain characteristics survive in the blues, the actual rhythms or pitches of these early predecessors are far from rock and roll.

A trait of early African work songs that is significant for later developments is the scale, or the melodies. The songs usually had three to five different notes, and the scale was not a Western one by any sense of the word. It normally contained a flatted third degree, giving it a sense of plaintiveness. Some critics have referred to it as pentatonic, although the important point for us is that the scale degrees used in the melody later appear in what we will call the blues scale. A pentatonic scale is made up of five notes; an example would be C D E G A. The concept of scale is explained later in the section on the blues. These songs were quite simple, which should not be taken as an overall indictment of African music. The fact is, obviously, that work songs were sung during work, and it is probably unfair to expect Italian arias from people who are digging trenches.

It has been fairly well established that the music was performed mainly in unison, with everyone singing the same melody. However, there was a leader who sang one phrase, with the entire group responding to him or her. This *call-and-response* pattern is definitively African and has been retained in the blues tradition and in gospel music. Leaders, or *callers,* were very important in slave society, which is a direct implantation of the social structure of the tribe. The call-and-response pattern is the most often mentioned characteristic of African roots in black music in general.

Another type of secular music practiced quite far back in the history of slave music was the field holler. A *field holler,* or *cry,* was simply a message that was supposed to travel some distance. It could be a name, a simple command, or an expression of emotion, and it was usually voiced in an African dialect, which the white slave owners could not understand. As usual, it was functional, although occasionally it took on another meaning. It was short, sung in unison or by one person, and was rhythmically simple. Special characteristics of a field holler, which will be significant in our later discussion of blues style, are:

1. It often used notes bending to produce a sad feeling or a brief slowing down of the melodic pattern.
2. It often used slides between notes, or drop-offs (the pitch is held and then is slid downward over a wide range).
3. It was usually more complex at the beginning and ended with a long held note.

Field hollers established many of the patterns that would later become staples of early blues.

Religious Music

As previously stated, acculturated religious music occurred much later in the history of the slaves because there was such a massive difference between the philosophy of African religious concepts and the philosophy of Protestantism as it was practiced by whites in the United States. Generally speaking, African religions are animistic or naturalistic, in that they are polytheistic (many gods), and each god generally corresponds to some phenomenon in nature (water, fire, animal spirits, and so on). The *Loa,* or natural objects that have power or spirit in them, each deserve respect and appropriate rituals to appease or satisfy their needs. This kind of system does not correspond very well to anything contained in the kind of Puritan Protestantism of colonial America. Interestingly enough, there are significant parallels between Roman Catholicism and animistic religions that were used quite effectively in places like Mexico. However, there was no parallel in the

United States, and our Puritan forefathers probably would not have used them even if they had existed.

By virtue of this disparity, there was little way black people could be woven into the fabric of religious experience, and for a few centuries they were left on the outside as heathens. There were, of course, early attempts to convert American-born slaves by taking them away from their parents and raising them as Christians, but the differences in culture were so vast that this activity had little influence in creating a black Christianity.

However, like everything else in the slave's environment, white religious music became influential by the end of the eighteenth century, by which time the idea of returning to Africa must certainly have been waning in the blacks' view of reality. By 1780 or so, Christianity had a pretty firm hold in the slave community, and its practice was occurring at the same time as that of certain African traditions, although later these would be dropped. However, there was at least one notable difference between the black-oriented Christian service and a comparable white service — the spiritual. Most common sources indicate that the spiritual was essentially a Christian hymn with a strong rhythmic beat imposed on it, in the singing style and in the accompaniment.

Although the slaves' secular musical style was hardly influenced by the white's style, the religious style of Protestant slaves most certainly was influenced by European tradition. Interestingly, there was an easing of Puritan values around the turn of the century, and certain taboos against emotion in religious experience were beginning to be thought of as old-fashioned. The beginning of the nineteenth century saw many changes in the United States, and certainly the move toward expressiveness was most significant from a cultural point of view. In other words, the philosophy of white religious experience was shifting to the point where it could be consistent with certain aspects of the black experience. Therefore, free acculturation was finally possible, even though the *Emancipation Proclamation* was still quite a few years off.

The *spiritual* was basically a Protestant hymn, with even phrases and standard European structure (for an explanation of structure, see the later section on the blues). What were added to make it a black experience were the rhythm of work songs and the call-and-response pattern of African tribal music. Instead of everyone singing the song straight through, the minister would sing one phrase, which would either be imitated by the congregation or followed by another phrase sung by the congregation. The singing was still in unison, without harmony. Hand-clapping and foot-stomping accentuated the rhythmic feel of the composition. The piano player would also add rhythmic figures in back of the singing. The result was a rhythmically alive composition, which made for a very different kind of performance from that in white churches. This free adaptation of a white style probably caused the growth of black Protestant sects, particularly in the South.

Gospel music (the religious blues) is a direct descendent of these spirituals; and at least the style of performance can be considered a direct antecedent to both jazz and rock and roll, although these are secular traditions. The separation between secular and sacred is usually quite thin. Although it exists quite clearly in black attitudes toward music, both in the past and in the present, there are many stylistic traits shared by both.

VAUDEVILLE

The significance of this particular form of entertainment is normally left out of a discussion of early sources of jazz because it is such a potpourri of musical styles. Vaudeville loosely defines the music and entertainment of traveling shows of people, somewhat like county fairs. A vaudeville show could consist of everything from plays, musicals, and boxing matches to full-scale concerts (like that of the Germania Orchestra of the 1850s). When vaudeville performances were musical, they were primarily symphonic, or they consisted of just folk songs. However, from this very important tradition came the minstrel show, which was an insulting comment on the black population. However, it was entertainment, and as such it was important to both small towns and large cities.

The important point for us is that vaudeville provided the first opportunity for folk songs (some of which contained black themes) to be institutionalized (like a recording industry without records). Many of the traditions of vaudeville would be used later in black vaudeville circles, which fostered boogie-woogie, ragtime, Dixieland, and what will later be defined as urban blues.

Although vaudeville is less important as a source for jazz and rock, it is highly significant for performances, that is, the style of presenting music as a live experience. Without vaudeville, these popular musical forms might have remained regional arts, or even more, styles of one town. Vaudeville produced the first means for mass communication.

EARLY JAZZ FORMS

In this section we will discuss some early jazz forms (as they are commonly defined), with the purpose of showing that they are really part of the development of rock and roll as an extension of jazz development. Most of these forms resulted from relatively free acculturation of black and European styles, although this statement may be debatable.

Cakewalk

Many of the early black minstrel shows (that is, minstrel shows in which the performers were black) were parodies of the minstrel shows first started by whites. White vaudeville performers would put on blackface (shoe polish or coal soot) and imitate black people. This imitation was later reimitated by black performers (even to the extent of using blackface). One very important part of the early development of black performing style was that blacks were constantly putting on their audiences — either laughing at themselves or at the whites who imitated them.

The cakewalk was a European square dance. People walked around a square with different numbers painted on it, and when the music stopped whoever was standing on the right number won a cake. This dance was traditional at church socials and is still performed in white traditions in parts of the Midwest. Black tradition developed a dance step in the form of a cakewalk, but its intention was to parody the stiff way whites walked and danced. As a parody it was successful in black circles and was probably the first truly Afro-American dance step. It enjoyed success on the scale of the twist, and it was danced by blacks and imitated by whites.

Ragtime

Ragtime was a piano style developed around the turn of the century. Its significance in the history of jazz is well accepted. (Its history is well documented in source material in the bibliography.) It is clearly a black art form with definite European influence.

Ragtime is composed music, although it originated in oral or unwritten tradition. It usually has four main themes, which are divided into four sections of music equal in length. The general style and sound of the music are quite complex. Ragtime has the following features:

1. A left hand based on chords, which are broken up differently on each beat (commonly in a four-beat phrase)
2. A melodic right hand with complex figuration
3. Uneven accenting between the two hands (syncopation).

Next to the black-oriented songs of Stephen Foster in the mid–nineteenth century, ragtime was the most published music from a black tradition until the 1940s. Although most of the black composers who played ragtime made little money from it, it was mass communication for both blacks and whites.

European influence is obvious in the sound of the music, the structure of the composition, and simply the fact that it is composed. Black influence can be heard in the rhythmic patterns (the syncopation). Ragtime is one of the best examples we could find of an acculturated art form. Scott Joplin and others clearly put together the influences of the European tradition with the black American experience. The result is not just European music; it is Afro-American music.

Stride

Stride is a style of playing the piano. James Johnson, considered to be the father of stride piano,[2] Willie "The Lion" Smith, and Thomas "Fats" Waller were early exponents of this particular style. Some later pianists who played stride piano

---

[2] Paul Tanner and Maurice Gerow, *A Study of Jazz*, 4th ed. (Dubuque, IA: W. C. Brown, 1981), pp. 59–62.

(at least at times) were Art Tatum, Oscar Peterson, Duke Ellington, and Count Basie. Stride piano has influenced many piano players, some of whom still play it today.

Stride is a direct outgrowth of ragtime in that it uses a basic rag (or ragtime melody) as the foundation for improvisation. *Improvisation* is the act of making up additional music, based on some theme or some part of an original theme. Ragtime usually involved improvisation in live performances, and some of its performers wrote down the music in a composed form, that is, a slightly modified version of the live performance. Therefore, it should be viewed as notated improvisation.

Stride is based on a concept of theme and variations—the pianist plays the basic theme (the rag melody) and then does one or more variations on it (improvisations). Stride piano is faster than ragtime in tempo, more flamboyant, and more intense in feeling. As the stride piano style developed, musicians used any theme available—from pop music, Dixieland, or the blues—and stride piano players became parts of instrumental ensembles (and later leaders of big bands, such as Ellington or Basie). Jelly Roll Morton is the best example of a flamboyant solo stride pianist who later put together a full band (Dixieland in his case). Stride was probably the most important style for a pianist until the 1940s.

Dixieland

Dixieland is very easy to define in general terms, although a definitive definition would take another book (and then some people would argue with it). Dixieland is basically a musical style that developed in New Orleans in the first twenty years of the twentieth century and then moved to other cities in the United States, where it developed styles with noticeable differences. It is basically an instrumental style, requiring more than one instrument.

The standard Dixieland band of the early twentieth century in New Orleans contained a trumpet (cornet), clarinet, trombone, banjo, tuba, and drums. This was an instrumentation drawn from street bands or marching bands. The rhythm section, consisting of banjo, tuba, and drums, was the rhythm section of the street band (no piano was used until ragtime and Dixieland combined). The cornet played the melody, the clarinet a countermelody, and the trombone an elaborated bass line. Each of the melody instruments played solos in the variations that followed the presentation of the main melody.

The standard form of Dixieland was theme and variations, the melody being presented first and then the solos by the different melody instruments (backed up by the rhythm section). The melody was presented again for a conclusion. Although Dixieland may not be too significant in the history of rock and roll, some of the techniques of the solos can be heard in the evolution of rock. The important point is that it solidified the concept of a rhythm section that provided the background for the melody.

The rhythm section eventually substituted a piano for the banjo and a string bass for the tuba and increased the role of the drummer to provide true rhythmic interest (at first all three rhythm instruments played on every beat). The expansion of the role of the rhythm section and the resulting complexity of its intermixing are significant examples of what happens in rock and roll. Therefore, Dixieland is important to know about, both as a part of the development of jazz and as a model for rock and roll.

Boogie-Woogie

Boogie-woogie is another piano style that began sometime in the mid- to late 1920s. It is a very interesting style of playing because it has some similarities to stride piano in its intensity, but since it is somewhat more precise, it is easier to define.

Boogie-woogie was a black style associated with a circuit of black musicians who traveled from town to town to play for parties, often "rent" parties, where the musician would play for people who needed rent money. *Boogie* is a term derived from *bogey,* meaning spirit. *Woogie* is the name of the pieces of wood that tie together railroad tracks. Because many of the boogie-woogie piano players rode the trains (usually under the train), they were closely associated with the railroad ties. The clicking sound of the train can be heard in the long-short rhythmic pattern of boogie-woogie.[3]

In boogie-woogie the left hand plays a set pattern on the piano (usually with a feel of eight beats to the measure) and the right hand plays short melodic figures (sometimes called *riffs*). This is a form of theme and variations and is usually based on the blues progression, in twelve-measure phrases. It is freely improvised music, like stride piano, and many of its exponents have had major influence, although they made very little money from playing it. Boogie-woogie is the first obvious influence for rock and roll, and its patterns can be clearly heard in 1950s rock.

THE BLUES

The Pattern—Blues Progression

We have avoided using standard musical notation, but we must now define a musical scale in order to teach the blues progression. We will deal mainly with the underlying structure of the blues rather than with the complexity of its possible variations. The following technique will teach a simple blues progression. If the reader wishes to go further, many fine publications on the blues are listed in the bibliography.

A musical scale is a set of notes leading from one to another. For our purposes we will use the major scale of Western music, based on the following notes: C, D, E, F, G, A, B, C. This set comprises one octave and can be counted in both ascending

[3] Milton Stewart, "Polyrhythm and Its Role in the Development of Structure in Boogie Woogie," presented at the National Association of Jazz Educator's Convention, St. Louis, Jan. 14–17, 1981.

form (going up) and descending form (going down). A simple example of the latter is the song "Joy to the World" (the traditional form, not the rock song).

Joy to the world the Lord is come

C	B	A	G	F	E	D	C
8	7	6	5	4	3	2	1

"Joy to the World" is one of very few songs that use a complete major scale in the opening eight notes. You will notice that we are talking about the melody without considering how long each of the notes is held. If we have not yet understood what a melody is, here is an example. The pitches themselves, without the words, form a melody, in this case a descending major scale.

The letters represent the notes as they could be played on a guitar or a piano. The numbers represent the scale degrees, which could be used to describe the different pitches in the scale and the relationships among them. For the remainder of this book, all descriptions will be based on these pitches (C to C).

We should stop and do some exercises now before going on to the next paragraph. Someone should play the scale both up and down on a guitar or a piano, or someone could sing it. We should sing the notes up and down by ourselves, using both the letter names and the numbers.

After we have understood the definition of a scale, we can see that individual notes are used to create melodies. Individual scale degrees also serve as the foundation of the melody as harmony or chord tones. For instance, the first note of a scale, in this case a C, is called the tonic of 1. An F would be the 4 chord or sub-dominant, and G would be the 5 chord or dominant chord. The relationship among the 1, 4, and 5 chords (based on those scale degrees) is pivotal to understanding rock and roll, especially its structure.

We will be using a standard explanation of the blues, although there are many variants. For our purposes, we must master one model or pattern. After that we can discuss variants in relation to our basic model, similar to the way we used one basic element and tied our analysis of compositions to that.

A **progression** is a set of occurrences that happens more than once. It should not be confused with progressing from one place to another, although that is a meaning of the word also. In music, progression usually refers to a set of chord changes that occurs over and over, serving as a basis for verses of a song or for improvisation. We will first set up the blues progression, explain a method by which to count it, and then repeat it many times. *This progression must be fixed in long-term memory.*

The basic blues progression normally consists of twelve measures, each of which has four pulsations. To produce a measure we simply clap our hands four times, keeping the beats even. We can use the second hand on a clock, if we wish, to keep the time even. Next, we sing some note at the same time that we clap our hands, for instance, C, C, C, C or 1, 1, 1, 1. We have produced one measure with four notes. Next, we might want to produce two or four measures; usually a musical phrase will have four measures.

The blues progression consists of twelve measures of four beats each, which follow a certain pattern of scale notes. If each measure has four beats, one will have forty-eight beats, or pulses, in one progression of the blues changes. Using both letters and numbers, we can represent the blues progression as follows:

CCCC/CCCC/CCCC/CCCC/FFFF/FFFF/CCCC/CCCC/GGGG/
FFFF/CCCC/CCCC//

or

1111/1111/1111/1111/4444/4444/1111/1111/5555/4444/1111/
1111//

It could also be written this way, so that only the beginning beat of each four-beat measure shows the scale degree of the progression:

C///C///C///C///F///F///C///C///G///F///C///C///

or

1///1///1///1///4///4///1///1///5///4///1///1///

A suggested way to practice the above is to clap and sing: the scale degree first on all four beats, and then only on the beginning beat of each measure. We should practice with both letters and numbers so that they are meaningful to us. However, as we use this system more and more, we will begin to use only the numbers. Before proceeding, we must be able to use the numbers and follow the progression. Then we must sing more than one progression and clap at the same time, and last, find some blues recordings and sing the progression along with the recording.

Development

The term *blues* is used in a variety of ways to describe very different phenomena. It can be used to describe a feeling of sadness or frustration. Certainly many of the early work songs illustrated such feelings and also some of the note patterns, that is, blues-like melodies. However, this is not the same as the blues progression just defined.

The term can also be used to describe certain notes that exist in singing but are not part of the major scale previously given. There is a blues note halfway between scale degrees which, when used, gives color to a melody. Sometimes certain scale notes will give a melody the sound of African tribal music, in a way that does not correspond to European scales at all (the blues progression we have shown is based on European, or Western, scales). Actually, there are some notes on the piano that are not described by this scale. The black notes on the piano are in between the scale degrees given (which are all white keys). The note between A and

B is a black note called B-flat (or B♭) because it is a half step below (or flat of) B. A note halfway between B and B♭ is a blue note. The note halfway between E♭ and E is another common blue note. Putting the blue notes into a scale, we would get a blues scale that is used extensively in blues melodies:

C E♭ F F♯ G B♭ C

Although this concept is not imperative to an understanding of the material in this book, it is important to understand that there are some melodic tendencies in blues songs that are incorporated into rock and roll, especially black-oriented rock.

The blues can also describe a feeling in a song, or it may be part of the title, when in fact the song does not follow a blues progression. This of course confuses the issue still further, but for our purposes we will talk of blues songs that follow the basic twelve-measure progression given previously.

The history of the blues is significant, especially as we slowly work our way toward rock and roll. Early blues was rural blues, in the sense that it was performed by rural musicians in rural settings, usually as a solo (accompanying him or herself on the guitar). It quite often followed patterns that were marginally like the blues progression presented in this book. Early blues forms had eight-measure lengths, ten-measure lengths, twelve, thirteen, fourteen, sixteen, twenty-four, and other odd lengths. Some were influenced by European dance forms and others were simply produced spontaneously. The only overriding consistency was that they began as simple songs and then were improvised, both in lyrics and accompaniment, to fill out the remainder of the song. Improvisation is probably the most important trait of the blues.

Primitive blues was the primary form throughout the nineteenth century. Classic blues (as defined by LeRoi Jones in *Urban Blues*), the form that followed primitive blues, was the acculturated blues form. It was still not urban blues in the commercial sense, but it did begin to solidify the style and move toward a standard blues form.

By the beginning of the twentieth century there were significant blues singers and instrumentalists who were influential in both the blues and in most other forms available: Bill Broonzy, Leadbelly, Lightnin' Hopkins, Ma Rainey, Ethel Waters, Bessie Smith. Some later musicians in this same development are T-Bone Walker, Billie Holiday, Ella Fitzgerald, and B. B. King. Interestingly, some of these singers continued to employ eight-bar blues forms as well as the more standard twelve-measure phrase. The point is that each of these musicians influenced other blues singers and eventually rock and roll. Even when they used progressions that did not follow the twelve-bar pattern, they used one to five changes and blues melodies.

Rural to Urban — The 1930s

In the 1930s the blues took on a different character because of basic changes in society. Instead of being performed mainly for rural audiences or an imitation of rural audiences (Dixieland blues), the blues had become a vehicle for city blacks. In

Leadbelly *(Photo by Playboy Records and Music; used by permission of Ginny Cartmell and Creem Magazine Archives)*

the 1930s a counterculture to the white big-band era continued the popularity of the blues, but this time in a different setting.

Many black musicians developed big bands analogous to the white ones, and they were eventually quite competitive with their white counterparts. However, the blues singer continued to have great importance in an all-black circuit, which eventually fostered *rhythm and blues.*

The history of rhythm and blues is told in Arnold Shaw's *Honkers and Shouters: The Golden Years of Rhythm and Blues,* and he very acutely points out between the lines that rhythm and blues did not just start in the 1940s and end with rock and roll. It has a history intertwined with the history of rural blues, assisted

B. B. King   *(Photo by ABC Records; used by permission of Ginny Cartmell and Creem Magazine Archives)*

greatly by the boogie-woogie renaissance of the late 1930s and firmly established by singers like Robert Johnson and Joe Turner.

The style of these two musicians in particular illustrates the change brought about in the 1930s: The blues became stronger, angrier, and more like what is found in early rock and roll. Rhythm and blues is simply the addition of strong rhythm to the blues. It usually has elements of shouting, a characteristic that will later become a significant part of rock and roll.

Rhythm and blues probably was born the first time the blues was sung with accompaniment; some might say that black spirituals of the nineteenth century were incipient rhythm and blues. In any event, the history of the blues became the history of rhythm and blues in the 1930s, and it was precisely then that rural blues as such became more urbanized.

The difference between rural and urban blues is primarily one of culture. The urban dweller's problems differ from those of the rural dweller; he or she develops different artistic communications. Turner's blues form was called the *jump blues,* in that it was filled with terms like "rock 'em," "shake it," and other utterances that would become part of the rock vocabulary. Jump blues was undoubtedly the beginning of rhythm and blues, if it did not occur earlier; and jump blues was the beginning of rock and roll as well.

RACE RECORDS

The final stages in the prehistory of rock and roll are found in the last part of the 1930s (the boogie-woogie craze) and in the 1940s. It is certain that a major reason for the emergence of rock and roll in the 1950s was the creditable market built up for race records (as recordings for the black community were called) in the 1940s. Significantly, although it may seem inconsistent, this era was blessed by the start of the removal of the color line between musicians.

Notable white musicians like Artie Shaw and Benny Goodman helped to remove the stigma about black and white musicians performing together — Billie Holiday with Artie Shaw and Teddy Wilson and Lionel Hampton with Benny Goodman. Although there continued to be distinctively black organizations — Basie, Ellington, and eventually Louis Jordan (the king of the black performers) — there also was relatively free interchange of ideas, and certain black styles began to slip into white organizations, if only by way of theft.

Race records, indies, or sepias (whatever they were called) were primarily rhythm and blues recordings aimed at black audiences. As black financial status began to build up in the war years (even more so after the war), there began to be a market for race records. Rhythm and blues was a staple of these small record companies, and there was a sizable if not millionaire status market for the recordings. Many of the rhythm and blues artists who eventually became significant in the 1950s (although perhaps not rich) paid their dues in the 1940s by making recordings for these small companies.

At first the most interesting kind of recording was essentially boogie-woogie. By the mid-1940s the form became an imitation of the white crooning tradition (the main leader at that time was Frank Sinatra), in which Nat King Cole was probably the most popular ("Mona Lisa," from 1949). All these recordings were sophisticated city songs designed for an urban audience. The significance of rhythm and blues, both as a continuing tradition and as a commercial art form, must be understood as the beginning of rock and roll. Although rhythm and blues is not rock and roll, the latter would not have existed without the former.

COUNTRY BLUES

Too little is made of country music's influence on rock and roll, probably because of an unwillingness on the part of "hip" writers to accept the significance of white influence on early rock musicians. Much is made of the black singing style of Bill Haley and more particularly Elvis Presley, and we will certainly give due credit to their predecessors and to Haley's and Presley's black influencers. However, we must recognize that each was also influenced by country, or country and western, music.

Country music has two distinct styles — one is Southern and the other is Southwestern. The Southern style is the rural blues of the white culture of the rural South. It is characterized by simple folk songs dealing with everyday feelings, accompanied by simple rhythmic and melodic instruments. It is devoid of unusual syncopation. The Southwestern style is slightly later in development (post-1930s) and is steeped in northern Mexican and cowboy life. It uses slightly more interesting melodic figures and more intense rhythm. This form is sometimes called *Western swing* and tends to be instrumental in style when it is not singing about little dogies and/or horses (see Bibliography).

The Southern style of country music has been most influential in shaping early rock, in combination with the black influences already discussed. The basis of this music is the isolation felt by poor whites in the South, and in this sense it shares some of the desolation of early black music. Although very much watered down in comparison to the earthiness of rural blues, it has some of the same singing techniques, in particular, sliding and flatted notes. Many Southern country tunes are based on blues progressions, although the words are clearly oriented toward white problems, in some ways similar to black problems. That these two styles (black rural blues and Southern country blues) have influenced each other is probably debatable, but they have both influenced early rock. Clearly, the term *rockabilly* (which many people use to refer to early rock and roll) comes from putting together rock and roll and hillbilly.

SUMMARY

We hypothesize the following:

1. All the following movements were significant in providing material for the beginning of rock and roll:
   black work songs

spirituals
cakewalk
ragtime
Dixieland
stride
boogie-woogie
primitive blues
classic blues
jump blues
rhythm and blues
urban blues
country

2. Black singing style was most influential in the early history of rock and roll.

3. Most early rockers were rhythm and blues musicians and/or country musicians who were influenced by rhythm and blues.

4. Rock and roll can be defined as a song with a specific instrumentation and beat.

The evolution of music toward rock and roll began at least as early as the nineteenth century, because the roots of jazz are also the roots of rock and roll. The blues, developing as a form of jazz and as an art form in its own right, combined with jazz in the 1940s to provide the artistic material from which rock and roll came.

The marketability of race records in the 1940s provided the financial incentive necessary to induce musicians to develop a particular form that was a successful hybrid between white and black styles. Black musicians were the first rock and roll musicians, although it took white musicians to legitimize the form and to make it financially lucrative.

Once the form was solidified, it was possible to have free interchange between white and black musicians; the development of free acculturation on the part of Afro-Americans became a reality, at least in the music business. *Rock and roll then became the art form of racial interaction,* analogous to what happened in jazz (but interestingly enough, not until the same time).

Rock and roll came from a combination of blues, country, and jazz elements of the 1940s but certainly did not instantaneously appear in 1951, as some have suggested.

The purpose of the following chapter is to define rock and roll precisely.

LISTENING

Blues selections from the *Smithsonian Collection of Classical Jazz History of Rhythm and Blues,* Vol. 1

Other blues examples from the discography for chapter three

CHAPTER **4**

EARLY ROCK—
PRE–BILL HALEY

DEFINITION OF ROCK AND ROLL

The definition of rock and roll changed throughout the history of the art form. When the term was first used in the early 1950s, it stood for a specific type of song (which our definition still includes). As rock and roll progressed in the 1950s, the term began to include music from the pop field and slow rhythm and blues tunes. By the 1960s many types of music that would not have fit into the definition in the 1950s would be included.

Our definition has four parts:

1. Rock and roll uses certain rhythmic devices.
2. Its lyrics and jargon came initially from the jump blues, rhythm and blues, country, or some combination of these.

3. Many pieces use a blues progression or a variation of it.

4. The basic style of performance is continuous shouting by the singer and continuous playing by the instrumentalists.

Perhaps the most important defining quality of rock and roll is the beat, or the rhythmic devices. Without a substantial change in rhythm, rock and roll would simply have remained one of its ancestors. Rock is different from swing style (big band and/or pop music) in that it is divided into equal subdivisions of beat. In swing, beats are divided into long and short subdivisions. Rock also tends to accent loudly beats two and four, punctuated by the drummer, in a four-beat measure. Most of the other types of music accent beats one and three. Generally speaking, the tempos, or the speeds, of songs which were turned into rock were changed to fit the general speed of rock songs. Therefore, there were specific tempos and rhythmic models for rock and roll.

Lyrics and subject matter were drawn almost completely from black blues, white country, or a combination of the two. Only later were pop music and, for that matter, even slow songs accepted as rock and roll. Rock and roll songs at first were rather limited in scope and were developed for a relatively small audience. Many of these songs used blues progressions, if not the one given in this book, at least something fairly close.

The style was vocally oriented and usually featured one soloist who shouted at the audience. The instrumental ensemble (made up mainly of guitars and drums) played continuously in back of the lead singer. The instrumental ensemble in early rock quite often emphasized beats two and four, which further supports the position that rock and roll is different from other music primarily because of the beat.

TYPES OF SONGS

Shouting

Many of the early rock tunes were rhythm and blues or jump blues. They used the blues progression, and the tempos were relatively fast. The lyrics were virtually shouted over the band background. This style of singing was made famous by the two musicians covered in chapters five and six, Bill Haley and Elvis Presley, but it was earlier musicians who perfected it. Joe Turner, Leadbelly, Johnnie Ray, Fats Domino, Ivory Joe Hunter, Little Richard, and others were musicians who performed in the shouting style, which was directly derived from rhythm and blues. This was the predominant style of early rock and the foundation for the careers of the famous rock musicians.

Many of these fast rhythm and blues tunes from the 1940s and early 1950s, some of which would be called rock and roll, used a backup band of five to six musicians — the Louis Jordan band, for example. On top of this constant playing, the singer would go through many verses of the song, each verse covering the span of one progression of the blues. This music was most definitely urban blues as opposed to the rural blues so significant to the early history of jazz. And it was quite different from the kind of pop music cultivated by the white population. It had little of the subdued emotion generated by the white population, and it most certainly retained the earthiness of black blues. It was at times sexually blatant, and it used the call-and-response pattern associated with Afro-American music.

Although the band played constantly, it also responded to the phrasing of the singer through background riffs, or simple melodies drawn from the lead melody. These background riffs served to answer the main singer and to reinforce the basic rhythms of the composition. As the singer ended a phrase, the instruments always filled in the empty spaces (those places where the singer was taking a breath). These riffs also served as the basic accompaniment figures when the singer was singing. This riff orientation was present in rhythm and blues, and it was also present in big-band style (although perhaps more so in black big bands).

One of the important traditions of the jump blues from the late 1930s and 1940s was improvisation, usually by the tenor saxophone. This style of playing, called *honking* or *wailing*, ultimately developed into a particular style of rock and roll saxophone, significant in the 1950s and then again in the 1970s. Improvisation by the saxophone player usually occurred in the center of the song to give relief from the constant singing. Ultimately it became a stylized function of a fast rock song. Although there are many tenor saxophonists noted for this style, we should certainly listen to Rudi Pompanelli, the saxophonist with the Comets; King Curtis, who played with Lionel Hampton and backed up the Coasters, Aretha Franklin, and others (he also recorded "Soul Twist" in 1962); and musicians more known for their contributions to jazz, like Sonny Rollins and John Coltrane. With the exception of Rollins, most of these tenor saxophonists were large men who projected strength through their instruments. This strong way of playing did emancipate the tenor saxophone from its role as the sweet instrument (the way it was played in the big bands). In fairness, Charlie Parker had quite a bit to do with emancipating the saxophone, but we should also give credit to the honking style of rhythm and blues.

Ballads

Ballad singing was also important in early rock and roll, although our theory is that ballads were seldom considered to be a part of the form, a distinction that was held for the shouting kind of rhythm and blues tune. Ballads were the real stock and trade of pop music, and whether the ballad was essentially a big-band tune, from the rhythm and blues tradition, or from country and western, it had a better chance for "crossover" popularity than did the shouting tune. For this reason, many musicians performed ballads, for both contrast and the real possibility of reaching larger audiences.

Although the history of ballad singing can be traced very far back in European music, the most significant starting point for a pop ballad is the crooning tradition in the United States. The first real pop culture crooner was probably Rudy Vallee in the 1920s and 1930s. The man who made "I'm Just a Vagabond Lover" famous sang through a megaphone (prior to amplification) and was essentially a big-band vocalist. But the significant point is that he held captive those people who heard him, and he had a profoundly emotional effect, especially on women. Vallee was a sex object before people used that term. Although he never directly influenced rock and roll, nor for that matter even liked it, he was influential in that he became a model for other crooners, singers with charisma.

Frank Sinatra was the crooner of the 1940s, and without a doubt he was the most important crooner of all time. He was the darling of a large majority of the women in America, and interestingly enough he still is. Although primarily a big-band vocalist, Sinatra was the most copied crooner of that era, and many black musicians of the late 1940s and early 1950s acknowledge indebtedness to his style. Some might argue that Bing Crosby, Dean Martin, and others should be included here, but the point is that Frank Sinatra was important because of what he represented and his longevity in that image. There were some black crooners of the late 1940s, like Cecil Gant, who clearly patterned themselves after Sinatra; they were called sepia Sinatras or black Sinatras. Nat King Cole is another good example.

Although the first vocal style of rock and roll — shouting — was based on the blues, the ballad was almost by definition never a blues song. We cannot give a model progression for a ballad because each one is different. The harmonic progressions were simple during the 1950s and the dominant part of most songs was the lyric. Background singers were used either to sing in harmony with the main singer — as responding units using nonsense syllables — or to sing the melody with the lead singer. The ballad was not part of the mainstream of rock and roll until the mid-1950s, enjoying its greatest success between 1956 and 1958; it was considered to be just pop music before its inclusion in rock and roll. However, to discount its importance to the ultimate popularity of rock and roll would be like taking the heart out of a living human.

Novelties

The third kind of rock and roll song is a novelty tune, that is, a song with some gimmick that makes it catchy. Novelty tunes have always been important to a popular tradition, for example, the cakewalk or tunes like "Pennsylvania 6-5000" or "Chattanooga Choo-Choo," both by Glenn Miller. Although they are often short lived, some of them last a long time, if for no other reason than nostalgia.

Novelty songs have been important in the prehistory of rock and in the mainstream of rock as well (most notably in the 1950s style). Boogie-woogie songs were significant in the 1930s and 1940s, performed by both black musicians and white big bands. One of the first big rhythm and blues tunes as a novelty was Stick McGhee's "Drinkin' Wine Spo-Dee-O-Dee" from 1949. Other examples are "Splish, Splash," all the twist tunes, and the monster songs like "One-Eyed, One-Horned, Flying Purple People Eater." "My Baby Loves the Western Movies" was an interesting example of crossover novelty (from country and western), although its commercial success certainly belies any musical taste.

STYLES OF SONGS

Rhythms

The rhythms of these kinds of songs can be quite easily classified by type. The shouting style usually uses rhythm and blues rhythms, which are consistent with the fast tempo of the songs. The rhythms are usually riff-oriented and are quite often derived from the long-short rhythm of boogie-woogie, with an underlying set of accents on beats two and four. This characteristic drum beat of 1950s rock in the fast tradition began to emerge in the late 1940s. The beat pattern eventually became standard for rock drummers in fast style, but with one change: Beat two was further subdivided into two equal half beats.

Beat one	nonaccented	O
Beat two	both halves accented	XX
Beat three	nonaccented	O
Beat four	accented	X

The rhythm of ballads is usually more oriented toward simple straight accompaniment, and there is seldom anything tricky or distinctive. Up until the mid-1950s, most ballad accompaniment was simply continuous and very light in texture. By the mid-1950s one of the rhythmic styles for background ballad accompaniment (played by both the piano and the drums) was a subdivision of the four main beats into three sections each, which gave the measure a feel of having twelve beats, with emphasis on one, four, seven, and ten. We will see examples of this type of tune during the discussion of 1950s rock ballads.

The rhythm of novelty tunes is probably the most diversified and is frankly the most interesting in the 1950s style. Musicians used standard swing rhythm for novelty tunes in the late 1940s; this rhythm was derived directly from big-band drumming. By the mid-1950s novelty tunes employed many different rhythms, even within one song. Rhythm was also used for special effects, like banging on the drum to indicate knocking on the door. Novelty tunes depended on a large number of tricks to fill out the song and to provide as many catchy ideas as possible. Certain novelty effects in the use of the bass voice (for instance, by the Coasters) took on rhythmic significance.

Progressions

The shouting style basically uses the blues progression, although there are occasionally shortened versions of it or a gospel structure (see discussion of Ray Charles). The progressions are repeated many times, and the harmonies are not too hard to follow, even for an untrained ear. Most of the harmonies of fast songs have to be simple because they go by so quickly. In fact, fast songs are the one place where progressions are not extremely complicated, even as rock and roll evolves over time. There simply is not time to get very fancy, so the progressions are kept simple and the words and/or the texture is emphasized.

The ballad style has many different harmonic progressions, some simple and some more complex. Interesting harmony is sometimes used to emphasize particularly emotional parts of the lyric, but more often than not the progression is simply a foundation for the all-important lyric. In ballads, there is a tendency to have one main melody for the verses, with a refrain or bridge section to provide contrast. Although clearly we would like to be able to follow all the progressions in music, knowing each one of the chords in each ballad is not too terribly important in estimating the significance of the form. The importance of the ballad is in its emotionality, its impact, and its influence on the public, which is normally not harmonic.

Novelty tunes use simple progressions, and about half the time they are blues or modified blues. The other 50 percent of the time they are folk song progressions. Again, the harmonies are occasionally used to emphasize novel aspects, but more often than not these novel aspects can be explained in terms of the words or special effects, without resorting to harmonic analysis.

Backgrounds

The background figures (both vocal and instrumental) can be best categorized after listening to some examples of these different types of music. Although many of the background figures by singers are sung with nonsense syllables, they usually fit the context of the song. Background figures by instrumentalists are normally riff-oriented, taken from the main vocal. In fast songs these riffs become the motivating force for the entire composition and often become the entire piece toward the end (see Ray Charles, "What'd I Say?"). Background figures are based on rhythm and blues in shouting songs and in some novelty tunes. Ballads use lush, smooth background figures, and novelty tunes use whatever works. Generalization past this point is difficult, and background figures should be determined on a song-by-song basis.

CAPSULE VIEW OF THE 1950s

It is important to realize that the 1950s were generally a time when most Americans felt reasonably secure, although the existence of the Cold War and the creation of bomb shelters might tend to argue against that position. Relatively speaking, people prospered in the 1950s. Our involvement in the Korean War was thought to be successful from the point of view of national image. We saw ourselves as *the* world power, which had led the fight for democracy. When Dwight D.

Senator Joe McCarthy   *(Used by permission of Folkway Records)*

Eisenhower was elected president, we entered a period in American history where everything was all right, everyone was getting richer, and tomorrow would always be better than today.

During this era there was a strong feeling of patriotism. Of course, this was a carryover from the end of World War II, but we retained the feeling throughout the 1950s that ours was the best country in the world. We derived a certain sense of security in having Eisenhower as our leader and national symbol, in some sense the grandfather that we all desired. He was a great military leader; he represented anticommunism; and he would be able to provide good government for the people. Richard Nixon was appreciated for his involvement with Joe McCarthy in their fight against communism, most particularly in the House Un-American Activities Committee (HUAC). Our control over Nikita Khrushchev and the subsequent softening of the post-Stalin era made us feel that we were truly in power. In short, these were prosperous times, with a baby boom and more house ownership than ever before.

The economic solvency of many Americans was especially gratifying, and the postwar inflationary period that was predicted did not take place in the 1950s (we would have to wait for that). Although middle-class America felt prosperous, there were some elements of American society that seemed ripe for change, if not revolution. Some of these depressed groups were youths, blacks, and the lower class.

The history of the black movement in the United States is significant throughout our discussions, but the most jarring changes were to take place during the 1950s. By the 1960s civil rights legislation would be taken seriously and finally consummated during Lyndon Johnson's administration. However, the seeds of discontent were sown in the late 1940s and the 1950s. Blacks had fought on the side of America during the wars. When they returned to the United States, they discovered quickly that they had been important during the national crisis but their position had not changed in peacetime. Afro-Americans demanded a place in American society. They would not be going back to Africa, even though there were some later movements that would suggest this plan still had validity.

The promise of economic success led many blacks to assert their power in the 1950s, and at least some of this drive came from the fact that white society notoriously became rich by imitating blacks. Possibly the best example was rhythm and blues and ultimately rock and roll.

The young population in the 1950s is also a relevant factor. The growing affluence of young people as an offshoot of parental affluence created a real market for their interests. Although it can be clearly shown that they were just as conservative as their parents in the early 1950s, it can also be hypothesized that this would be the first time they had the free time (because of the peace and their financial solvency) necessary to pursue their own interests. The change in attitudes about communism and war would come somewhat later, but the rebellion of young people in terms of expressing their own values started early in the 1950s.

Lower-class Americans followed a similar pattern in that they wanted some of the affluence themselves. The labor union movement became strong in the 1950s, even during a Republican administration. This constant push on the part of the have-nots to become the haves was a source of rebellion; still fomenting, it could not be stopped once it started. Therefore, the economic prosperity of the 1950s, the feelings of security, and the resulting attitudes of not worrying about tomorrow provided the opportunity for the lower class to begin asserting itself.

MARKETING

Because of the cultural situation, rock and roll became a focal point for rebellion, and it must be understood in that context. In some senses it still is a focal point, although it has reached mass-communication levels in its present state. In the early 1950s a midwestern disc jockey named Alan Freed supposedly coined the term *rock and roll* as a replacement for *rhythm and blues.* He did so to make rhythm and blues more acceptable for broadcasting, especially as he had started running rhythm and blues shows at the Cleveland Arena. Rock and roll (at least its origins) most certainly was a conscious attempt to capitalize on the true marketability of music as a symbol for particular groups in society.

White youngsters had already developed a taste for black rhythm and blues, and the rock and roll revolution was certainly the result of a conscious desire to broaden that audience. As a marketing technique, the invention of the term was very important. It separated the music from the racial connotations of rhythm and blues; it was something new; and it could be promoted as the music of youth. It is not clear whether it was an exploitation or simply a fad. The point is that it worked.

From 1948, when the Orioles sang "It's Too Soon to Know," there was an available formula for slow ballads (see chapter seven). There were more "bird" groups than you could possibly feed at the record store, and they basically followed one pattern of performance. The shouting style was also firmly established, and it had many talented practitioners. When rock and roll, as a legitimizing term, was invented, there was a vast amount of music that would ultimately be called by that name.

Early marketing techniques were primitive in comparison to later models (Elvis Presley and the Beatles, for example), but marketing was precisely what made this splinter movement into a multimillion dollar business. The stories of individual record companies, radio stations, and significant entrepreneurs of rock and roll provide information about individual progress (see the bibliography).

Of course, rock and roll was not immediately popular or acceptable to the entire population of the United States. There were many people for whom it was a profoundly uninteresting phenomenon, a Communist plot, or just completely decadent.

The rock performer was seen as a symbol of pain, frustration, and rebellion. He or she was also viewed in adulation and as an interpreter of the dreams and desires of the population to which rock spoke. The reactions by those who were not part of that image were understandable, if perhaps overstated. As indicated earlier, there are still people today who view rock as nonmusic, with little redeeming value, or as just plain junk.

Our basic position is that rock and roll was formally named in the early 1950s and that conscious techniques were used for these early songs. The elements of rock and roll were firmly established by 1951, and the performances of songs in this genre provided the models for success. However, it took a catalyst (or more precisely a charismatic character) to serve as a focal point for the art form.

LISTENING

History of Rhythm and Blues, Vol. 2

CHAPTER 5

BILL HALEY
AND THE COMETS

BIOGRAPHY

Bill Haley was born in Detroit in 1927. In the early 1940s (as a young teenager) he began playing country and western music; he was a relatively good guitar player. He toured with his band for six or seven years and then gave up music for awhile, taking jobs with radio stations. At the end of the 1940s he began shaping his band, the Comets (previously known as the Four Aces of Western Swing, and the Saddlemen) in a new style, which was a mixture of pop, country and western, and rhythm and blues.

Haley represents in his career precisely what was discussed in the last chapter. He put together various forms of music that were popular for different segments of the society in the late 1940s. When he began to emphasize rhythm and blues elements in his music, he quite naturally retained some of his country and western roots, which is why much of his music was also called rockabilly.

In the process of making the transition to a white version of rhythm and blues, which culminated in 1951, he listened carefully to its popularizers in the 1940s, in particular, Louis Jordan. Haley copied the beat pattern of the jump blues and some of the performing antics of Jordan, who was really a consummate performer. When Haley finally renamed his group Bill Haley and the Comets, he had a clear view of what he wanted to do with his music and how he wanted it performed.

Haley's major contribution to the development of this form was probably in what he did to the lyrics of rhythm and blues tunes. He took the sexually obvious lyrics and changed them so that they were not quite so obvious. He really did not take the meat out of the lyrics; he just covered it with a disguise. In essence, he made the lyrics of rhythm and blues relatively acceptable to white audiences.

He also worked out elaborate stage routines, many of which were quite acrobatic. Although he himself did not move much, his musicians were known for assuming incredible poses while they were playing; for instance, the saxophone player would lean back and play with his instrument almost parallel to the floor. These stage techniques were already well known to black performers, but white performers were not used to this kind of motion. It did not go over well with people who were accustomed to the relatively staid performances of big-band musicians or groups like the Mills Brothers or the Andrew Sisters, but it went over very well with young audiences.

By 1951 Haley was ready to go out on the road again with his new group; they had a new style and a completely worked out routine for performing it, neither of which was radically changed in later performances. It is important to realize that Haley was one of the few significant musicians in the history of rock who really did not change over the years. Virtually everyone else grew up with the times, including Elvis Presley, but Haley performed the same way in the 1970s that he did in the mid-1950s.

Haley's significance in rock was that he did it first in the complete sense of the word. He was not original, although he felt that he had invented rock and roll. He simply put together available elements at the right time and had the good sense to get them before the public. As a white representative of what black musicians had been doing for some time (and in many ways better than he ever did it), he was the catalyst necessary for rock and roll's success.

In 1951 he did quite well with a tune called "Rock the Joint." In 1952 he made "Crazy Man, Crazy," and in 1954 he made a cover of Ivory Joe Hunter's "Shake, Rattle and Roll." Also in 1954 he made "Rock Around the Clock." The film *Blackboard Jungle* came out in 1955 and was aimed at a young audience. Its story of teenage decadence and alienation was backed up by soundtrack music by Bill Haley, at the beginning, "Rock Around the Clock." This film really catapulted him into the limelight. In 1956 he made a film called *Rock Around the Clock,* which was an international success. After that he made another film entitled *Don't Knock the Rock,* in which he was overshadowed by another performer. Little Richard seemed to be a better rocker than Haley, which put a dent in Haley's significance.

Bill Haley and the Comets *(Used by permission of Michael Ochs Archives, Venice, California)*

However, Haley continued to make popular recordings, for instance, "See You Later, Alligator," "Corinne Corinna," and "Green Door."

Haley was quite popular in England, where he first toured in 1957. As his popularity was beginning to wane at home (due to competition with Elvis Presley), England was still virgin ground. The people loved him there in 1957 and again in 1964. Although the Beatles and the Rolling Stones have not admitted to being influenced by Haley, they certainly must have been. His particular blend of musical styles was precisely what English rockers would do in developing their own unique style.

From the late 1950s on, Haley was a relatively minor figure on the rock scene, although he always evoked feelings of nostalgia and importance as the first big name. After all, he was not a terribly good musician to begin with, but he did perfect a model for rock and roll. Other musicians would do it much better, but Haley was the first white man to do it at all. He continued to put out single records and an occasional album. He played concerts; his fan club was alive and strong; and whenever there was a rock and roll extravaganza, he would usually be included. His performances were very consistent, but as other people surpassed him, he seemed to be only a poor comparison. When he died in 1981, the obituaries were short; however, they all included the fact that he started the whole thing called rock and roll. As we have seen, this may not have been true, but he was the first to codify it and to be successful at it.

MUSICAL STYLE

The musical style of Bill Haley and the Comets fits the model definition of rock and roll, and in the 1950s it was a revolutionary concept. What Haley did was to put together a white rhythm and blues band; somehow he managed to use just the right elements in order to be successful as a white imitator of black music. It is highly questionable whether he would have been so successful had he only imitated, without changing, the black style.

Haley explained on the album *Bill Haley Scrapbook* (Kama Sutra 2014) that his band was working as a country and western band in the 1950–1951 era and that it was expected to perform country and western music. Although he eventually played in a style called rockabilly, his guitar playing retained a country sound. However, his band would occasionally include a rhythm and blues tune with country instrumental arrangements. A close examination of that album, and in particular the song "Rock This Joint," will certainly illustrate this point.

This particular song is a rather straightforward blues tune, with many repetitions of the blues progression. It is fast and clearly in the shouting tradition of rhythm and blues. In a short section (the first four measures) of singing at the beginning of his progression, Haley sings by himself with stop-time chords by the band. That is, he sings a little bit, and then there is a chord or two by all the musicians. After this short section, the band comes in and plays continuous background while he finishes the blues progression. The first part is from rhythm and blues and is the call-and-response pattern derived from African tribal music. The second part is straight country and western in back of a blues lyric.

With the exception of one rhythmic figure, which will be mentioned later, everything in the background instrumental figures is country and western. The bass player usually plays a walking bass pattern without noticeable accents on all four beats. The drummer plays a straight swing-time drum pattern. The guitar solos are in country and western picking style, not at all like some of the great guitar rockers of the 1950s — Chuck Berry, for instance. The saxophone solo is melodic and sounds different from standard saxophone solos in the mid-1950s. In a live performance, they might look like rock musicians, but their playing style is not rock-oriented.

There is one significant rhythmic figure present in "Rock This Joint." The following example has the rhythmic beats for two measures in numbers and small x's below the numbers that correspond to where the instruments play:

```
1 2 3 4 1 2 3 4

x x     x x
```

For lack of a better explanation, this is a rhythmic riff, that is, a pattern that can be repeated over and over. This particular figure was used in a number of other traditions, for instance, in boogie-woogie, but it is also used throughout Haley's music and is central to the background accompaniment of "Rock This Joint." This riff happens to be a staple of 1950s rock and roll, and a number of musicians used it. It is appropriate that Haley used it in 1951.

The musical style of Bill Haley included these elements:

1. Rhythm and blues lyrics (watered down)
2. Basically country and western instrumental playing
3. A stage routine designed to entertain and captivate the audience.

One can analyze most early Haley tunes (and the later ones as well) in terms of the definition of rock and roll given in chapter four. Therefore, his music can be used as a model for 1950s rock, in which, of course, he was quite successful.

POPULARITY

The issue of popularity is one we will have to tackle at some point. We have already stated that just because something is popular, we need not assume that it is therefore automatically nonartistic. The real question is why certain music succeeds and other music does not. The first matter is success based on style; the second is success based on nonmusical issues.

Bill Haley put together a model of performing, based on his experiences of what popular music was. He combined elements of rhythm and blues — which he believed to be significant as a form of communication — and country and western. He also clearly understood that audiences would respond to visual entertainment. In essence, he applied logic to the production of a model for communication.

If artistic accomplishment is measured by the appropriateness of the ability to communicate ideas, popularity can be one measure of the relationship between art and its audience. We contend that the model of performing created by Haley was an appropriate one for communication because it took into account the perceiver and his or her needs.

One reason Haley's music was popular was that it used styles that were proven communicators for certain classes and types of people. By putting together models from different styles of music, he created a larger audience, which would relate to the new style as a combination of other styles. In essence, the music itself could communicate artistically to a certain population because that population already understood the elements of the new style, at least parts of them.

However, the interesting thing is that even though there were good reasons for this style to be accepted, it was not without controversy. The reaction against rock and roll, and in particular Bill Haley, intensified the significance of this particular form for those people for whom it was designed. The story of rock and roll is often told by who is against it rather than for it.

Although Haley enjoyed mild success with his early recordings, especially "Shake, Rattle and Roll," it was not until the movie *Blackboard Jungle* came out that his audience gathered in his favor. There were so many critical statements made about Haley and rock and roll in 1955 and 1956 that he became an overnight sensation. Although we believe that the music itself should have guaranteed its success, it was the reaction against it that insured its popularity.

In particular, Haley's stage antics were thought to be crude. The white establishment did not accept entertainers who moved around a lot, unless it was someone like Spike Jones or something slapstick. Bill Haley moved his legs; Elvis Presley was to move more. Even though the lyrics were quite watered down from the original songs, they were still perceived as evil. Many people thought the music was simply bad, and therefore they condemned it on that basis. As the music was a protest movement of sorts, this kind of reaction helped its popularity immensely. If it irritated our parents, it had to be good.

We have to understand that because the 1950s were prosperous, young people had a tremendous amount of free time. The attitudes of the majority were not acceptable to younger people, and many of them rebelled against these attitudes, although they may not have realized they were doing so at the time. When the press began to take up the cause and attacked music as a part of a Communist plot, youth rallied in reaction. Haley and Presley might have lived their lives out as minor pop singers had the establishment (and occasionally the police) not decided that such singers were bad for the youth of our nation.

Therefore, we propose that part of Haley's popularity came directly from his rejection. Middle-class America still yearned for the days of the big bands, which died more for financial reasons than anything else. This new kind of popular music did not fit their image of what music should be, and besides, it was "dirty." As every generation is probably destined to rebel against the previous one, the young people of the 1950s rallied in favor of rock and roll — partly because their parents hated it.

NOSTALGIA

It is appropriate to deal with nostalgia here because Haley's popularity arose directly from a group that wanted something of its own. This same group would eventually see Haley as a re-creation of its youth. Nostalgia is significant for every form of music once it becomes older than ten years. As previously stated, Haley did not change his style over time. Therefore, all he had after his burst into popularity was the nostalgia for that particular sound.

Psychologically, nostalgia comes from the desire to reestablish contact with our past, usually from our youth. We all have yearnings from time to time to live the way we once did. Rationally, we cannot succeed, but music is an obvious way to remind us of the past.

It is not uncommon for people running high school reunion parties to hire a band that plays in the style popular at the time of graduation. In the 1980s reunion committees hired big bands or 1950s rock bands. The big-band revival, which started in the mid-1970s, is based on nostalgia, as is the popularity of Sha-Na-Na and other 1950s groups.

Nostalgia does not involve music just from the 1940s and 1950s. It is also present in devotees to the early Beach Boys, those who hoped for a reunion of the Beatles (sadly now impossible), and even those who want a return to the folk-rock of the early 1970s. Nostalgia will always be present, if for no other reason than the psychological one.

As society becomes more and more complex (and some say more depressing), nostalgia for the past will continue to grow. The continued popularity of Bill Haley can certainly be explained in terms of this phenomena. Haley's fans (even more so after his death) will continue to like his music for some of the following reasons:

1. It is simple and can be understood on an emotional level.
2. It represents the 1950s in all of its optimism (even though it was a rebellion against some of its attitudes).
3. It contains elements of commonly understood communication.
4. It is not sad or depressing.

One of the most important things about 1950s music is that in comparison to contemporary music, it is uncluttered with deep messages, and especially, sad messages. Communication in general in the 1950s was optimistic and not complicated, and rock and roll is a reflection of this style.

We must not make too little of the fact that 1950s music was happy music. Although people were singing about the human emotions of pain, anguish, and frustration, it was not the frustration found in the 1960s and 1970s. We still trusted people in the 1950s, even if we should not have.

Bill Haley, then, represents his era, the 1950s, and all the optimistic things about those times. By continuing his style into the 1970s, he allowed us to recapture some of those golden moments when everyone was rich, happy, and optimistic about tomorrow. The nostalgic feelings created by Haley's music are potent ones, and they are one of the reasons why he enjoyed continued success.

THE DEATH OF ROCK AND ROLL

This may seem to be a strange place to bring up the possible death of rock and roll, but it has been a continuing story since the 1950s. Many people felt during the last half of that decade that rock and roll was just another passing fad. At first it was probably wishful thinking on the part of conservatives, who really never liked it in the first place. However, by the early 1960s it was a real concern because of a momentary lull (before the Beatles) in the speed and quality of the music's evolution.

The argument was taken seriously by a number of conservative columnists and radio announcers; naturally Bill Haley was one of the first rock musicians to be interviewed. He frankly admitted over the years that he was never really sure how long rock would last; but by 1964 he was completely convinced that it would survive, if only because there were other musicians who would add things to the form that would make it last. He cited the contributions of Elvis Presley and later of the Beatles; over the years he gracefully gave credit to many other performers. If Haley and the style of his music were the entire history of rock and roll, it probably would not have been as significant; Haley contributed part of the history, however, and it was up to others to originate other variations.

Rock and roll did not die in the 1950s because it was a vibrant form and because its detractors motivated the fans to support it. Rock in later generations did not die because it kept changing with the times. It continues to speak in the language of the present, and its definition keeps getting bigger, bringing in more and more varieties of music.

LISTENING

Bill Haley Scrapbook

CHAPTER 6

ELVIS PRESLEY
AND MEMPHIS ROCKABILLY

1. "Heartbreak Hotel"
2. "I Was the One"
3. "I Want You, I Need You, I Love You"
4. "You Ain't Nothin' but a Hound Dog"
5. "Don't Be Cruel"
6. "Love Me Tender"
7. "Any Way You Want Me"
8. "Too Much"
9. "Playing for Keeps"
10. "All Shook Up"
11. "That's When Your Heartaches Begin"
12. "Loving You"
13. "Teddy Bear"
14. "Jailhouse Rock"
15. "Treat Me Nice"
16. "Don't"
17. "I Beg of You"
18. "Wear My Ring Around Your Neck"
19. "Hard-Headed Woman"
20. "I Got Stung"

21. "It's Now or Never"
22. "A Mess of Blues"
23. "Are You Lonesome Tonight?"
24. "I Gotta Know"
25. "Can't Help Falling in Love"
26. "Rock-a-Hula Baby"
27. "Return to Sender"
28. "Where Do You Come From?"
29. "Anything That's Part of You"
30. "Good Luck Charm"
31. "She's Not You"
32. "Devil in Disguise"
33. "Bossa Nova Baby"
34. "A Big Hunk O'Love"
35. "Stuck on You"
36. "Little Sister"
37. "Surrender"
38. "Ain't That Loving You Baby"
39. "Viva Las Vegas"
40. "I Feel So Bad"
41. "Kissing Cousins"
42. "One Broken Heart for Sale"
43. "A Fool Such as I"
44. "Wooden Heart"
45. "Crying in the Chapel"

This list represents Elvis Presley's gold records, awarded for selling one million copies each. During his career he sold more than 400 million records. In this chapter we will try to illustrate some of the reasons for his enormous success. It is our contention that Presley was a truly unique talent in the history of pop music and that he had some particular technical abilities that made him stand out from the rest of the performers of the 1950s.

Although Bill Haley was an important musician in the history of rock and roll and stood as a national symbol for this particular movement, Presley had musical and personal qualities that far surpassed Haley's. Presley had that important and rare personal quality called *charisma,* and his mere presence was awe-inspiring. We will walk a careful line between saying that the situation produced the possibility of his tremendous success or that he caused the situation and made the success. In any event, without Presley rock and roll might not have lasted at all.

BIOGRAPHY

Elvis Aaron Presley was born on January 8, 1935. Vernon and Gladys Smith Presley were poor by anyone's standards, and when their son was born in Tupelo, Mississippi, they lived in a two-room house built by Vernon Presley. The family farmed the land on which the house stood; the land was barely capable of sustaining crops, but at times the Presleys had to live solely on what they could grow. During World War II Vernon worked in a war plant, which raised the standard of living of the Presley family to poor, just above indigent.

There were several important influences in Presley's early life in Tupelo, important in the sense that they can be traced throughout his career and in his music. He was raised in a strict manner, and his entire family was quite religious. He was raised as a Southern Baptist and this was important to him over the years. The second major influence was his mother—her love and her seeming ability to remain optimistic in the face of impending disaster. Certainly he was also affected by being poor.

Musically, Tupelo was a mixture of styles and ethnic backgrounds—English, Scotch, Irish, French, and African—coupled with Southern hillbilly and the nature of a small hick town. Tupelo was not a cultural mecca, but like many small

Elvis Presley *(Courtesy of RCA Records)*

towns it may have had more character than large ones; its musical character was significant in Elvis Presley's style.

The basic story of his life in Tupelo is one of poverty, although he was given the basic necessities of life — shoes, clothing, and food. His mother provided for her family as much as possible from their meager existence, but they did not have very much. They had to stuff cloth and other items in the holes in the walls during the winter to keep out the cold, and obviously both parents went without in order to provide for their child. Presley lived a simple life; he did not have many of the advantages of children in the 1950s and later. Of course, this particular kind of background would have an effect, and it should be clearly understood that his rise to fame and fortune was always bittersweet for the entire family. Unfortunately, Gladys Presley did not live long enough really to enjoy it.

When Presley was nine or ten years old his father bought him a guitar for $7.75. Although this amount may seem minor to us, it was a major extravagance at that time, given their circumstances. Presley had already shown a great interest in music, and those around him knew he had a good voice. However, there was never any intention of his becoming a professional musician. He used the guitar as a diversion, listening to the radio and picking out tunes. Various sources are rather unclear about his real talent at this time, although it is known that he never had any formal musical training. Elvis Presley was a product of what he heard, his environment, and an awful lot of luck.

In 1948 the Presley family moved to Memphis, Tennessee, in quest of more opportunities for Vernon Presley. Biographers of Presley have tried to make something of this move in terms of his development as a musician, but the Presleys moved to better their lot in life and their son prospered for it.

Presley attended L. C. Hume High School and ultimately graduated in 1953. Other than having a strong interest in music, he was a mediocre student. Certain personality traits began to emerge at this time. L. C. Hume was predominantly black, and Presley was a big white boy. His only claim to fame in high school was his hair, which he spent hours on and which probably irritated his peers. He performed in a school talent show, and according to contemporary accounts, he became a minor hit because of his emotional style of performing. Also, he had an impact on the girls in the crowd, although certainly not at the level that would occur later.

It is truly amazing that facts about his early career are so clouded, especially because these events were happening in the 1950s, but this underscores the fact that Presley was not being schooled as a professional musician. He was just an average kid trying to get through high school. He had competed in a singing contest at the Alabama-Mississippi fair in 1945 at the suggestion of his school principal, and he won with a favorite song of his mother's called "Old Shep." Sometime between 1953 and 1954 he made a demonstration record of "My Happiness" and "That's When Your Heartaches Begin." This record, made for his mother as a present, cost Presley four dollars. Although it normally would not have led to anything, in this case it did.

At some point in this book, we really should discuss the probability of achieving success as a professional musician, especially big success. The chances are one in a million. Like many heroes of success stories, Presley was at the right place at the right time. He did not have professional training, he had no contacts, and he received no assistance from important relatives or friends. No one should rationally assume that he or she will be as successful as Presley was. Of course, that will not stop people from trying, but most people who try to follow in Presley's shoes will end up with sore feet.

Probably the most important person in the development of Presley as a marketable item was Sam Phillips. Phillips was in the process of beginning a small record company, ultimately named Sun Records. Although most small record companies die shortly after birth, Sun Records went on to become one of the most significant small companies of the 1950s, launching the careers of Jerry Lee Lewis, Johnny Cash, and Elvis Presley, among others.

Of course, demos are one of the means by which an unknown performer can become recognized, and record companies have set up full-time businesses for creating these records. In the 1950s small record companies would make demos for a small amount of money, and these short production items would help to cut the overhead costs of the company. The demos were basically designed for the performer only, and there was no promise of putting them out on the market. Today, demos can cost up to $10,000, although unfortunately the results are usually the same; the performer is left with a record and nothing else.

The record Presley made was not sold, but Phillips was impressed with the basic sound of his singing voice. Presley later said that this recording sounded like "somebody beatin' on a trash can lid," but something about his voice influenced Phillips, who told Presley that when his company got started he would contact him.

In the meantime, Presley had graduated from high school and had taken a job as a truck driver. He had worked as an usher at a movie theater, and the move to driving a truck was a natural one for him because he was interested in cars and mechanics. He made thirty-five dollars a week, and this was in 1954, although his financial picture would change quickly over the next two years. Phillips did contact Presley later in that year and Presley cut his first real record.

Phillips helped Presley form his first musical group—the Starlight Wranglers, which included Scotty Moore on piano and guitar and Bill Black on bass. Obviously, this was basically a country and western group in the Southern tradition, and frankly it was not very successful. Both Moore and Black were significantly better musicians than Presley. However, Phillips kept them together for an eventual recording, and they spent quite a bit of time at the Sun studio.

Apparently without guidance, Presley sang a song called "That's Alright, Mama," originally done by Arthur "Big Boy" Crudup, an important rhythm and blues singer. In the same session at the Sun studio, Presley suggested another tune called "Blue Moon of Kentucky" by Bill Monroe, a white singer who was known as the father of bluegrass. These two songs were put on a record, which sold over seven thousand copies locally. The sale was accomplished through the help of a local disc jockey, Dewey Phillips, no relation to Sam. Although a minor success by national standards, this recording can be credited as Presley's real beginning.

A point that should be made here is that Presley had departed from the original intention of the musical group formed to back him up. He was singing black blues in an unmistakably black style. He sounded like a black singer with a country and western instrumental style. Although his judgment of the record as being "trash can" music may have been accurate, it was the combination of his voice in a black style with Southern instrumental accompaniment that would eventually become his personal mark of success.

At this time another disc jockey entered his life. Bob Neal took over as his manager and renamed the group the Blue Moon Boys, which was taken from "Blue Moon of Kentucky." Neal had many contacts in the area, and he began to book the group at dances and auditoriums. Neal and Presley began to create Presley's image, particularly his singing style and stage presence. Frankly, he was not terribly successful during that year although he was beginning to earn as much as $200 a week. Although there were continuing difficulties over his black image, his obvious sexuality, and his nonconformity, Presley was becoming a sex symbol and not without true impact. Neal was careful as a manager, although not as successful as Presley's next manager would be. He built Presley's career slowly and by the end of 1955 was grooming him as a national star. He arranged for an audition for the "Arthur Godfrey Show," which was unsuccessful.

During the summer of 1955, Neal began to feel pressure because of his commitment to Presley, and the increasing involvement of Colonel Tom Parker did not help (Parker had been involved in making some tour arrangements for Presley). Parker was a very successful manager of musicians, including Eddy Arnold and Hank Snow. Although Sam Phillips was most influential in the beginning of Presley's career, it was Parker who made him really big. Parker took over toward the end of 1955 and turned an emerging career into a monumental one.

Parker arranged for a release from Sun Records, selling Presley's contract to RCA Victor. He obtained an appearance for Presley on the "Jackie Gleason Show" with the Dorsey Brothers, the "Steve Allen Show," and eventually the "Ed Sullivan Show." Parker also pulled off one of the most significant marketing tricks in the history of rock and roll; he signed Presley for movies. Parker's concept was a package deal. Presley would do the movies and then they would release the songs from the movies, first as singles and then ultimately as albums.

When Presley released "Heartbreak Hotel" in January 1956, he quickly got his first gold record, and the television appearances, concerts, movies, and recordings became one gigantic package. Parker engineered the whole thing, and Presley became a multimillionaire as a result. The press certainly helped, especially the press that talked about Presley's sexuality, from both a negative and a positive perspective. The fact that Presley was condemned by many people probably did a great deal to enhance his "aura" and charisma, as we discussed in an earlier chapter.

In 1958 Presley was inducted into the army, and in a stroke of masterful image-building, he accepted induction without complaint. Whether or not he actually was patriotic, this gesture endeared him to people who previously condemned him. In a sense he legitimized himself in the eyes of his detractors, who still might not like his music but had to appreciate him as a symbol. After all, Presley was accepting his role as one of the people and also as a symbol for youth. It also took him off the market for a while, which actually insured his success after a two-year absence. Fortunately, Parker had plenty of Presley material to work with during this hiatus.

During basic training in the United States, Presley returned home to be with his mother, who had become sick. The illness was diagnosed as hepatitis, and there was every expectation that Gladys Presley would recover. However, she suffered a heart attack and died in July 1958. Presley was deeply affected, as his mother was probably the most important person in his life. During 1957 he had purchased a large mansion, Graceland, in Memphis, and the rest of his family returned there. Presley went to Germany for his military service, but there is no doubt he was deeply troubled that his mother was not alive and enjoying Graceland, which certainly must have been purchased with her in mind.

While in Germany Presley met Priscilla Beaulieu, who would eventually become his wife in 1967. When he met her she was still a teenager, and Presley had her brought to the United States, where she lived with his family and went to school. It seems that she led a very sheltered life and that Presley was grooming her as a wife and mother, almost maintaining her until she became of age. This is one of the hardest things to understand about Presley; however, he did love Priscilla and their child, Lisa Marie.

Returning from the service in 1960, Presley was immediately thrust back on the American scene in a movie called *GI Blues* with Juliet Prowse. His career was certainly significant in the 1960s, although it was mostly tied to movies, which became the focal point of the marketing package. At least until the Beatles became popular, Elvis was still the hottest property around. He began gradually to stop giving concerts and making appearances, reserving most of his time for Graceland (with his new family and a new stepmother), recordings, and movies.

For the rest of the 1960s, Presley was seldom seen in public and seldom performed for live audiences. From the late 1960s until his death in 1977, his performances were mainly in Las Vegas, where he continued to pack the house. The so-called declining years became filled with stories about his obsessions — weight, drugs, and battles with reality. He most certainly was a vibrant personality until the end; however, the naive simplicity of his early career was gone. He had become an extremely complex and rich middle-aged man.

We are tempted to say that Presley did not evolve with the times, but a careful listening to his recordings from the end of his career would suggest the opposite. Retained in his music were country and blues roots, but the instrumental backing was constantly updated. He used contemporary music where it fit, and his performances made use of modern technology — additional musical resources and contemporary subjects. Although Presley was tied to his background, he changed as his background changed. His last performance in Las Vegas was exciting and filled with energy.

MUSICAL STYLE

The following comment by Carl Wilson of the Beach Boys says quite a bit about Presley's music:

> His music was the only thing exclusively ours. His wasn't my mom and dad's music. His voice was a total miracle, a true miracle in the music business.

This comment was made right after Presley died, but it sums up what could be said about his music from the start. All of the elements of his style added up to music that was exclusively for youth. It is important to realize that he was successful because he became identified with the needs of youth, regardless of what their parents thought.

Like Bill Haley, Presley combined elements of white and black culture, but his singing was primarily black in style. His first recording was of tunes by blues singers who had influenced him — one black and one white. Many of the elements of those early records could be analyzed in terms of the original sources. His vocal inflections, his choice of rhythmic accents, and the instrumental ensemble must be understood in relation to the particular combination of elements in his individual style.

In fact, many of his early problems in achieving success were tied to his musical style. He was a white country and western performer who sang rhythm and blues. Most disc jockeys would not play his records because they could not play blues tunes in a country and western format, or they could not play country and western tunes in a blues format. He was caught in the middle.

Lyrics

Most of Presley's tunes had watered-down black lyrics, at least at the beginning. Although some of the tunes were written by white lyricists, for instance, "You Ain't Nothin' but a Hound Dog" (originally a black rhythm and blues song by Big Mama Thornton and later adapted by white lyricists), the content and structure of the lyrics are very much like black rhythm and blues. At first Presley recorded two basic types of songs — shouters and ballads. The shouters used blues progressions (or modified blues progressions) with call-and-response technique. The ballads had slow rhythm and blues formats. Later Presley's ballad style would be more influenced by white tradition, in particular, by hymns. He was a crooner in the black tradition who later expanded his vocabulary to include songs from a white tradition.

The lyrics were usually fairly simple, and they were consistently emotional. Until the 1960s, they seldom contained references to the leisure-class rich (for example, rock and roll parties and foreign places). Obviously, his movies had a great deal to do with lyric choices, but these were not natural choices for Elvis Presley. The lyrics followed very simple structures—the blues progression in short lyric patterns in the fast tunes, and simple song structure in the ballads. All Presley's songs were lyric-dominated, and his voice and the words were the most important qualities, even when he was using nonsense syllables or gutteral sounds as emotional expressions.

Vocal Tricks

Probably the most significant part of Presley's talent came from his voice. He had one of the most naturally gifted voices to come out of the history of rock. He did not have any formal training, so his voice was developed through listening and imitating, but it must be understood that he had a natural ability to sing. His vocal range was quite large—from baritone to deep in the bass range—and he used the entire range to communicate effectively a large number of emotional feelings.

He made extensive use of *vibrato,* a wavering of the pitch designed to color the note or to make it sound fuller and more emotional. Unlike many musicians, he used vibrato with a great deal of sensitivity and variability, a most important quality in good music. When a particular passage called for a straight tone, he would do that. When it called for a heavy vibrato (very wide and punctuated), he could do that also. He had ultimate control of the vibrato, and he either naturally used it well or learned to do so.

He also made extensive use of *vocal slides,* beginning a pitch and dropping it off at the end (or sliding up to a note), for example, in "Love Me Tender." As you might recall, vocal slides were a predominant feature of work songs and field hollers and early blues and gospels. The vocal slides were used in conjunction both with significant lyrics and with nonsense words. Some people have characterized these vocal slides as sexual utterances.

Presley also used a technique employing a glottal stop. The glottis is a flap of skin that cuts off the breathing function during swallowing. It allows the singer to control how the musical note ends or begins. By cutting off the note in a certain way, he or she can produce a strong sound for an emotional or accenting effect. Presley made extensive use of this technique for emotional or sexual purposes. In fact, some people have said he could make women faint simply by moving the glottal flap.

Presley had a marvelous ability to move back and forth between full voice and soft voice. He used musical contrast to the utmost, which for strictly musical reasons is quite effective. However, he also used it for audience response. By softening his voice for certain passages, he could create a personal effect, which made the women in the crowd feel that he was singing directly to them.

Another characteristic of Presley was the contrast between his straight singing voice and shouting. This is clearly a gospel technique and relates rather interestingly to the call-and-response technique discussed in earlier chapters. He could

Elvis Presley *(Courtesy of RCA Records)*

change in the middle of a song from one style to another, thereby enhancing communication with the audience. Fortunately, all these techniques worked on records as well.

These vocal tricks and others produced a total and consistently interesting sound. Presley was a very involving performer, and even without his physical movement, he was captivating. Although this could be debated, his movies probably would not have been successful because of plot alone. They were clearly vehicles for Presley to show off his singing and his body.

Stage Presence

Normally when we discuss a particular singer we will include the background musicians and their impact on a performance; however, in Presley's case the background musicians probably did not have very much to do with the effect. The stage presence was the presence of Presley alone. He was called the "King" because he commanded everything all by himself. Bill Haley could not do that, but Presley was able to hold the audience's attention in a decisive way.

His stage movements were designed to fit what he did with his voice, and they must be understood in this connection — they are significant as part of the package. These movements consisted of general body movement; the shape of his mouth; and movements of the head, hips, and arms. Each of these movements came naturally to Presley, although clearly he used them more and more as they worked.

Presley's movements, quite natural during fast tunes, almost cost him his career at first. People did not like those contortions in a white singer. But as he gained acceptance, the motions became part of his image. He just generally moved at the right times. When he wanted to make a point in a particular song, he stopped moving. That told the audience it was time to pay attention.

Presley had a natural sneer; that is, the right side of his mouth was quite often a little more open than the left. When he was singing a strong vocal line or when he was portraying a tough or a hurt image in a film, he naturally went into the Presley sneer. It was an effective and natural act, and it worked.

He was called "Elvis the Pelvis" because of the way he worked his hips. This movement, which was most certainly natural, conveyed an obvious sexuality (whether or not he meant it to), but it was also very rhythmic and accented the beat of the song. He seldom used the hip movement in slow songs because the songs did not need it. He did use hip movement or pelvic thrusting in slow songs for emphasis, but again the key point is that he used the movement to enhance the feeling of the song.

He also used his head, hands, and arms to emphasize particular aspects of a song, to reach out for the audience. His performances were very visual, but it was the combination of his movement with his singing that made them so captivating. He would at times project the image of a folk singer for songs like "Are You Lonesome Tonight?" or for religious songs. He was a master at using body motions to communicate, and he showed this mastery by occasionally using no motion at all.

Religiosity versus Sexuality

It is tempting to treat Presley as if he were all body and no mind, but an objective view of his life would suggest that he was a fairly complex person. He came from a humble background, and at one time he was content to be a truck driver and part-time musician. He loved tinkering around with automobiles and he later showed that he had an obsession for material things. He obviously needed to be loved, handling some of his power and charisma rather poorly. However, he gave of himself to others, and in so doing, showed that he had real human concern. In fact, his financial advisors often feared that he would give away everything.

It is also easy to dismiss each of Presley's acts of charity, patriotism, and reverence as part of the big package designed to sell the star. However, a careful look at some of these will reveal that they usually happened when he was not being controlled by someone else. And even when they were advantageous to his career, this part was an afterthought rather than a motivation.

To trace his religious feeling it is important to return to the First Assembly Church of God in Tupelo. His mother had a great deal to do with his religious upbringing, regularly taking him, even as a baby, to church with her. Although we can be skeptical about this story, it is reported that by the age of two he could carry a tune without being able to sing the words of the hymns. His mother supposedly had a good voice, and she certainly must have sung hymns around the house; Presley would not have sung these songs throughout his life had it not been for his mother. It is hard to presume that he did not believe in the messages of these songs, even if at times he may not have necessarily reflected on them.

But Presley was also sexual, both in action and in singing. Although his singing style would suggest a preoccupation with sex, some of his actions in the early years would argue against that view. In the early 1950s he had a desire to be seen with women, his ultimate goal being to marry the right one. His relationship with Priscilla, at least until he married her, appears to have been relatively puritanical. He seems to have used sexuality as a cover story rather than as an end in itself.

Presley started out as a simple country boy, and during his rise to power he retained many of his country roots. He commented on being able to buy indoor plumbing and cars, in fact, just being able to buy anything at all. His was a classic example of *nouveau riche*, newly acquired wealth. For a period, he retained all the old values. Even in the 1960s he would often get underneath cars and tinker with them. We can see many of those country roots in his singing and in his life, and remnants of them in his lifestyle, even when he went to excess.

Religiosity and sexuality, then, should be seen as two extensions of his personality and beliefs. They are not contrary attitudes. They express the same dichotomy as white country and western and black rhythm and blues. Elvis Presley put both pairs together — musically as well as philosophically.

Style Development

Style development is normally thought to be the province of "serious" artists. However, rock musicians go through stylistic changes just like other artists, and these should be taken seriously. It is precisely this kind of continued change that makes rock and roll vibrant.

Elvis Presley did not change as much over the years as did the Beatles or the Beach Boys (chapters nine and ten), but he did go through some different periods: the first between 1952 and 1958; the second, 1960 and 1965; and the third, 1965 and 1977. Each period, or stage, could be defined in terms of stylistic traits, and there is variability among the stages.

Stage 1 (to 1958) can be characterized as the formative period in which Presley combined the elements of his musical environment and came up with the basic package. He clearly combined black rhythm and blues with white country and western (Southern style), established his basic stage presence, and marketed himself as a singer and performer. In this style he was a model of 1950s music and could be analyzed in terms of our definition of rock and roll. He was emotional and somewhat simplistic. Although the technical level of his performances was good, there was little sophistication in the background music or the recording techniques.

Stage 2 (1960 to 1965) is basically the movie period, in which his singing was the focal point for a somewhat larger audience. His singing remained basically the same although the background became greater. The instrumental ensemble was enlarged (using studio musicians as a backup group), even though the ensemble shown on the screen was still a rock and roll band. However, the setting of the performance was extended to real life experiences, if we can call singing on a beach in Hawaii a real life experience. The stage had been extended to the world, and this must be seen as a definite change in style; he had become broader in scope.

Stage 3 (1965 to 1977) is usually overlooked in discussions of Presley because of the troubles he had during these times. However, this last part of his life contains some of the best examples of his use of advancing technology and a real updating of musical materials. Most of the songs were the same, and there was a great deal of nostalgia in his late performances. However, even when he sang an older song, he usually made a change in the musical background. Advanced technology was used to make the background sound bigger, similar to the way the Beatles used larger musical resources in their later albums.

A careful listening to his last album, *Elvis in Concert,* will illustrate the last point. He used a big band to back up these performances from a tour in June 1977. From the very beginning of the record, the presence of the large ensemble changed the basic sound of a Presley performance. That is, although his voice was still the most important thing, the addition of the big band changed the overall sound. The theme song was an up-tempo simple riff composition that was really not rock and roll at all; it was show music. There was a brief performance of an arrangement of the *2001* theme, which went back into the riff to introduce Presley. It was a very effective stage device, but more significantly, the big band continued to be important in all the songs on the album. It provided a contrast with a rhythm emsemble, used for backing up Presley's singing; the band, and at times a backup vocal group, was used to fill in the empty spaces. Guitar solos were typically country and western in orientation.

The most interesting thing about these very late recordings is that even Presley changed. If we listen carefully to a song recorded in 1977 and then to the same song recorded in the 1950s, we will notice some changes in vocal inflection and range (he seemed to be weak in the upper notes in 1977), but more importantly, there were at times differences in rhythmic feel. Whereas earlier tunes reflected country accenting, there was a definite funk or disco feel in his later ones.

It is a subtle but very important point. Presley was influenced by other musicians and the prevailing way of making music. If you listen carefully, you can hear where those influences changed his style.

On a general level, the later music also had a kind of vibrancy, which some of his earlier material did not. The difference was made primarily by the addition of more musicians, better musicians (that is, studio players), and advancing technology. Even the microphones used in these later recordings were infinitely better than those from the 1950s.

Impact

By being successful, Presley opened up markets for other musicians and served as a symbol for the development of marketing techniques, for technological advancement in electronic equipment, and for the significance of a charismatic character. We had heroes in the United States before, but the magnitude of Presley's stature was probably larger than that of any other performer. He was also important in that he combined white and black elements, thus creating an amalgamated art form.

The marketing techniques used to accelerate Presley's impact were not new; they were based on previous models that had been successful on a large scale. However, these marketing techniques had a multiplier effect because of the cash flow available in the 1950s. The significance of Colonel Parker is major: He was the guiding force behind the creation of an entertainment complex, first through performances, then television, and finally movies.

It is noteworthy that Parker used so many resources for creating this complex. He realized the potential of the new developing medium — television — and coupled Presley with Steve Allen, the Dorsey brothers (still popular from the big-band era), Ed Sullivan, Milton Berle, and others. During a time when the motion picture industry was being hurt by the intrusion of television, Parker created a package for Presley in the movies. His pictures made a lot of money for the movie industry and pointed the way toward the kind of movies that would draw people back to the theaters; ultimately, the same pictures were sold back to the competition — television. The records, which came from the movies, and all the other paraphernalia — T-shirts, pictures, fan clubs — made each part of the package more lucrative. These models were copied in each successive generation and allowed the creation of new stars — the Beatles as an artistic example and the Monkees as a financial one.

It is interesting that the financial empire created around Presley ultimately returned completely to the family, the unit that was so important to him. Vernon Presley became the financial controller of the entire estate, and although he was educated only through the eighth grade, he seemed to do well. Elvis Presley trusted his father more than anyone else, and he gave him power of attorney over everything. It was a great credit to his father that he retained so much of the Presley wealth for his son. If we are to believe the stories, Elvis Presley might have given it all away if his father had not had some control. Of course, the tremendous wealth of this family required the services of financial advisors, which Vernon made use of when necessary.

HIS LEGACY

Elvis Presley influenced a tremendous number of rock musicians, some who had started before him and many who followed him. Bill Haley in later years indicated quite clearly how important Presley was and how much he had influenced the Comets and others. The Beatles acknowledged that Presley was very important to them. Mick Jagger, Pete Townshend, the Beach Boys, Fats Domino, Tom Jones — all of these major performers have acknowledged a debt to Presley. But whether or not performers recognize what he did, virtually every rock and roll musician uses a Presley technique at least once in a while.

His singing style, his stage presence, and the techniques used to build his career were all influential. But the lasting legacy of Elvis Presley is his success. Had it not been for the strength of his personality, he might have been just another good singer with a unique performing style. However, he had that rare quality to generate power over people simply by the way they felt in his presence. That charismatic strength is something all rock and roll musicians either have or rebel against.

Presley must remain a central figure in rock and roll. For all the reasons stated in this chapter, if we had to choose one musician from the 1950s as the most important rock figure, we would have to choose Elvis Presley.

MEMPHIS MAFIA

There were other significant musicians who developed in the same location as Elvis; these musicians were the first wave of Memphis musicians who were important to rock and roll. Sometimes Presley's entourage was called the "Memphis Mafia"; I use that term to describe the rockabilly musicians of the Sun Record Company in the mid-1950s.

The significance of the Memphis crew is that they packaged rockabilly in a new kind of lyric. The lyric content of Bill Haley's music was stereotyped and homogeneous. Ultimately, the Memphis crew, with Elvis as the leader, branched out into other types of music, including novelty tunes and ballads, to produce a more marketable combination of records. The most obvious reaction to rock and roll in country music is the Nashville sound.

Rockabilly, then, is a very important subject in the appreciation of country music. It was pivotal to the economic growth of country music as an industry. It provided country music with a model for future growth and the impetus to create a more dynamic pure country sound. It lent validity to the use of electric instruments (although country musicians had begun that long before rock and roll came around). But most importantly, it showed country musicians and their industry that it was possible to create the ultimate in crossover art. Although rock and roll went through some heavy times because of negative public reaction, it was ultimately accepted (partially as a result of Elvis's going into the army and proving himself a "real" American in the eyes of some of his detractors). Usually one talks about rock and roll as the key story of the 1950s through the 1980s, but the interesting thing is that country music also grew as a result. It was the relationship that developed between rock and roll and country music in rockabilly that created the demand for both forms.

The discussion of the following musicians is in alphabetical order, and the order in no way supposes a rank ordering or order of influence. Some of the examples are more pure country than rockabilly (Johnny Cash, for instance) and some are marginally country (Buddy Holly). However, they were all at least partially influenced by country music.

Johnny Cash

Johnny Cash is not really a rockabilly musician; however, he should be discussed with the other Memphis musicians because that is where he got his start. The kind of sound he used as background instrumental texture was very similar to what the Memphis rockabilly musicians used. Johnny Cash sang in such a way that he could have been a rockabilly musician; however, he developed a unique style that should probably be considered halfway between rockabilly and traditional country.

Johnny Cash was born in Arkansas in 1932. His father was a sharecropper; the family lived in a shack, and John worked in the cotton fields with his family. This dirt-poor existence gave him a perspective on life similar to that of Elvis Presley. They were both poor white boys who would ultimately become successful beyond their wildest dreams. Like many who went from rags to riches, both Elvis Presley and Johnny Cash had difficulties coping with that success.

Cash served in the air force in the early 1950s and after that returned to Memphis, where he was a salesman. He had learned to play the guitar while in Germany and had intentions of becoming a radio announcer upon his return to Memphis. He managed to get an audition with Sam Phillips, the Sun records man who was so important in Memphis, and Sam immediately sensed that Cash had something unusual. He was a songwriter, which ultimately turned out to be very important to his financial success. Cash interestingly enough was somewhat displeased with his first tune, "I Walk the Line," because Phillips had insisted on speeding it up. In this sense, Johnny Cash was initially influenced by the developing concept of rockabilly, that is, the style that Phillips imagined and created. From that point on, Johnny Cash was an enormous success.

Cash's voice, a rich baritone, is very full for a country singer. It was the unique sound of his voice that made Cash, like Presley, so successful. His overall sound is country, but heavily influenced by the powerful background of his band, which was always influenced by rockabilly (sometimes referred to as honky tonk). He used a heavy amplification setup and driving rhythms, with his voice floating over a background with a rock beat.

Cash became more influential in folk music than anywhere else because his lyrics ran to the complex, especially after 1967. He has won numerous awards — Grammys from 1967 to 1970 and the Country Music Association Entertainer of the Year in 1969. He has had minor ups and downs in his career and in his life, but

Buddy Holly *(Photo copyright © William F. Griggs. Used by permission)*

he has been a major performer for almost thirty years. He has performed hits with many other important musicians, one of whom he married in 1967, June Carter of the Carter Family. Johnny Cash was elected to the Country Music Hall of Fame in 1980.

Buddy Holly

If Buddy Holly had only lived longer, he might have been as important to the history of rockabilly as Presley was. Holly's career lasted only from 1956 to 1959. Born in Lubbock, Texas, he was at first a country musician, recording in Nashville for Decca. He switched to rock and roll in the latter part of 1956. Between 1957 and his death in 1959, he recorded a great number of hits, both his own songs and the music of others. Some of his most important tunes were "Peggy Sue," "That'll Be the Day," "Early in the Morning," "Shake, Rattle and Roll," "Blue Suede Shoes," and "Rip It Up."

Jerry Lee Lewis   *(Courtesy of Mr. John Singleton and the Sun International Corporation, Nashville, Tennessee)*

Holly, who could also be considered an early crooner, was similar to Elvis Presley in some ways, although Holly's country roots, and therefore his vocal inflections, were southwestern, or *Tex-Mex*. He was capable of using extreme contrast in his voice in order to create different moods, and although he did not have Presley's range or perhaps his innate talent, his performances took advantage of all of his technique. Holly looked like a person in pain while performing, and the main center of attention was his bobbing Adam's apple. His backup group, the Crickets, was pretty good, and at least one of them, Waylon Jennings, went on to great fame.

What was significant about Holly was his image as a performer and the way he elicited sympathy from the crowd. He seemed to be going through real pain while he was performing, which those present also felt and were affected by. Audience identification was high, not because Holly performed to entertain but because of the image he carried through his performances. At the time of his death he was second in popularity to Presley. For some people Buddy Holly was and still is a cult figure; some even feel he was the real central figure of rock and roll in the 1950s.

Jerry Lee Lewis

Jerry Lee Lewis was born in Louisiana in 1935. In many ways an Elvis imitator, he was originally a country western musician, and he returned to country western in the 1960s. He was probably the first important rock and roll piano player, which associated him with honky tonk country music because that was the only form that used a piano. He recorded for Sun Records and had his first success in 1956 with "End of the Road." His most popular song was "Great Balls of Fire" in 1957. He toured England in the late 1950s and failed miserably, primarily because of public scandal over his thirteen-year-old wife. He made a comeback in the 1960s as a country singer.

Lewis's style was straight shouting. He pounded the keyboard, used his fists and arms, and screamed at the audience. He sang a number of the same tunes that Presley did, but he usually recorded only the fast ones. Most of the songs were fast blues progressions (jump blues), which best fit his technique. Although successful as a rock and roll shouter, he did not show Presley's versatility, nor was he managed as well. His image was certainly right for a rock and roll star, but within a relatively limited spectrum. He has continued to be in the news and has had eight wives at last count.

Carl Perkins

Carl Perkins, a singer, guitarist, and songwriter, was born near Jackson, Tennessee, in 1932. He was poor as a child and his family were sharecroppers. In

Carl Perkins   *(Courtesy of Mr. John Singleton and the Sun International Corporation, Nashville, Tennessee)*

his teenage years he formed a band with his two brothers called the Perkins Brothers. He developed as a traditional style country singer and obtained a position in 1951 on the Big D Jamboree in Dallas, Texas. Better than average on the guitar, he quickly gained recognition as a country singer. As rock and roll increased in importance he quickly moved toward that kind of sound.

Moving back to Memphis, he started recording for Sun Records in 1955. He really hit it big in 1956 with his own composition, "Blue Suede Shoes." This particular song was a top-10 hit on country, pop, and rhythm and blues charts in 1956 and has been covered a number of times by other musicians. Carl continued

Charlie Rich *(Courtesy of Mr. John Singleton and the Sun International Corporation, Nashville, Tennessee)*

to have some success in the 1950s and 1960s with hit records, but he slowly moved into the position of songwriter and backup musician. He toured with Johnny Cash for years and is especially known for his fine guitar playing. His career suffered a setback when he was in a car accident on the way to perform on the "Ed Sullivan Show"; it was reported that he was going to do "Blue Suede Shoes."

Like Roy Orbison, Carl Perkins was a good example of a mainstream rockabilly musician who shows his country roots every time he plays or sings. The lyrics fit the rockabilly style and were very marketable at the time, but he eventually returned to country music. Carl Perkins took advantage of the popularity of rock and roll for a time and then returned to his first love.

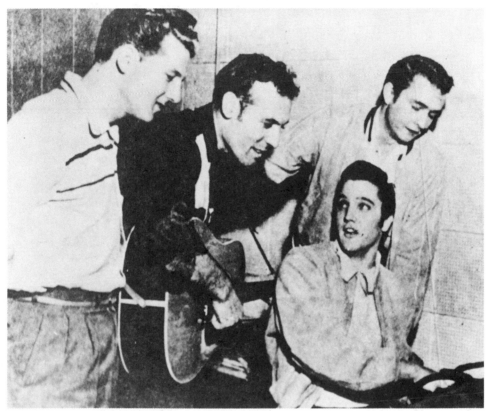

The Million Dollar Quartet: Jerry Lee Lewis, Carl Perkins, Elvis Presley, and Johnny Cash　*(Courtesy of Mr. John Singleton and the Sun International Corporation, Nashville, Tennessee)*

LISTENING

Elvis Presley, *Worldwide Gold Records,* Vol. 1

Elvis Presley, *Elvis in Concert* (1977)

Jerry Lee Lewis, *Original Golden Hits — Sun*

Roy Orbison, *Original Sound*

Johnny Cash, *Original Golden Hits*

Carl Perkins, *Original Golden Hits*

Buddy Holly, *20 Greatest Hits*

CHAPTER 7

BROADENING
OF THE STYLE

THE END OF THE FIRST ERA

This chapter discusses the late 1950s and the mature style of rock and roll. Some of the music mentioned will in fact be from the very early 1960s, as the beginning of the next era does not really start until the Beatles. As usual, in any transition period there are continuations of the basic style into the next era.

Rock and roll is the term we used to describe music from the 1950s; in later chapters we will begin to use the term *rock,* for reasons which will be discussed later. Rock and roll began to encompass more music in the late 1950s than it did within the early period. That is, although the style was still fairly homogeneous, late rock and roll included several types of music that would not have been considered rock and roll earlier. It is important to realize that rock and roll was not really legitimized until the late 1950s and that it took the developments discussed in the first six chapters to create the basis for mass popularization. The distinction between pop and rock and roll was real until the late 1950s. By 1958 there was less of a distinction. An examination of the songs at the top of the *Cashbox* and *Billboard* ratings will illustrate this point. Therefore, we will expand our categories of tunes to define four basic types rather than the three described in chapter four.

This particular period at the end of the 1950s is sometimes called the "decadent" period in rock and roll because of its commercialization. There was clearly an attempt on the part of the artists to communicate on a broad spectrum, and it sometimes led to songs that had little vitality because they were further watered down from their original black or country roots. Although this description is fairly accurate, it should not be seen as a condemnation of this period. It should be viewed as a codification of the style rather than a selling-out. It would take the Beatles to revitalize the progressiveness of rock and roll, but it should be remembered that the Beatles performed in the style described in this chapter until at least 1964.

Four Types

By the late 1950s we can see four specific types of rock and roll: rhythm and blues/shouting, crooning, specialty songs, and novelty/monster songs. Of course, these are extensions of the three types discussed earlier.

There continued to be a vibrant group of performers in the rhythm and blues tradition. Many of them were considered to be simply rockers, but musicians like Chuck Berry and Fats Domino still remained in the rhythm and blues style. Although it may be hard to distinguish their music from 1950s rock and roll, it must be remembered that their rock and roll was rhythm and blues–oriented. Crossover (appealing to more than one audience) was essential to the success of a 1950s musician, even though he or she might retain the roots of one particular style. In fact, the concept of crossover is essential in explaining the phenomenal success of Bill Haley and Elvis Presley.

Rhythm and blues as a separate form began to fade in the late 1950s, and by 1963 it was removed from the *Billboard* ratings. However, there was a continuing interest in rhythm and blues–oriented tunes, although they were then called pop tunes. The Motown complex in Detroit, which began in the early 1960s, was aimed at the mainstream pop market, although clearly the emergence of soul did rely heavily on black listeners.

Shouters continued to perform during this period, although in some senses they were a continuation of the earlier style. One of the best shouters of the late 1950s was Little Richard, who really took over from where Bill Haley left off. Elvis Presley was an influence in the shouting style, and of course, this was one of his most effective techniques. This style did not change substantially in the late 1950s, but it did become more sophisticated and also more effective.

Crooning was probably the most important style of this period, and rock and roll ballads were extremely important in the rapid commercialization of the art form. By the late 1950s rock and roll was the principal medium for youth dances, and ballads provided necessary relief from the style of dancing to fast songs. (We will discuss this topic at some length shortly.)

Specialty songs are those that are associated with some dance step or some special attitude. Although they could be labeled novelty tunes, they are usually somewhat broader in communication. Some of the most important dance steps (often fads) had songs written specifically for them, for example, the twist or the fly.

It would be easy to dismiss novelty songs as cheap commercialization were it not for the fact that they have remained popular over the years. Some of the best examples are "monster" songs and tunes by groups like the Chipmunks (David Seville). Although these songs are perhaps shorter lived than any of the other types, they are prototypical examples of the commercialization of the form during this period. They usually have some rock and roll characteristics, but they are sold to the general public as either pop or rock and roll.

Free Acculturation

In chapter three we discussed the forced acculturation of blacks within a white society. We also set up the expectation that at some point it would become a free one. By the late 1950s there was free interchange among the various types of music and the market was not necessarily segregated. As long as songs fit into certain models they were accepted with relative indifference concerning the racial origin of the musicians.

Later in this chapter we will take the position that it was Ray Charles who finally legitimized this compromise position, but it should be understood that the market already freely accepted it. It had been established by Bill Haley and also by Elvis Presley. Rock and roll was a combination of black and white models; therefore, rock and roll became the focal point for what we refer to as free acculturation.

This is not to suggest that there did not continue to be music for black audiences and for middle-class white America. But anything designated or thought of as pop or rock and roll usually was accepted by both white and black audiences, that is, those black and white audiences who liked that kind of music.

Opportunities for black musicians were still fewer than for white ones, and there were white musicians who essentially made cover recordings (and we might add, made a lot of money) of songs originally sung by blacks. However, as both white and black musicians discovered the lucrative opportunity in songs that were compromises, they began to overcome racial differences. Although we stated earlier that Elvis Presley was the most important musician of the 1950s, other significant musicians of that time were Chuck Berry, Little Richard, and Ray Charles — all three of them black.

Urban to Commercial

The first step in the path toward rock and roll was the change from rural to urban blues, which occurred before the name was formally coined. Urban music, of course, is city-oriented and carries with it a certain number of parameters and expectations. It must speak to the needs of city people rather than the rural farmer or craftsperson. However, being oriented toward city life does not mean being commercial and/or financially successful. All too often people assume that urban means commercial.

Urbanization led to the circumstances in which rock and roll could be marketed, and certainly most of the marketing techniques already discussed were centered in large cities. However, the commercialization of rock and roll transcended urban and rural distinctions once it got started. The marketing techniques were aimed at people in small towns as well as in large ones. Marketing frequently began as a grass-roots movement, although often in a large town; records by new musicians would be sold in one record store that serviced a small area. The best example is the sale of Elvis Presley's first record in the area near where he went to high school.

Therefore, rock and roll surfaced after the shift from rural to urban blues, which served as its basis, and then went through its own form of change from rural to urban, regional to national. Before it became a major force in music, it had to move from the rural-urban pattern to a local-regional-national pattern, centered around commercialization and marketing.

In other words, rock and roll began as a rough form of music (somewhat like the rural blues of the late nineteenth century), became an urban blues form, and then eventually embraced other forms in order to expand the market. Commercialization led to the free acculturation discussed previously, and consequently the significance of the shift from rural to urban became somewhat less important. It is an explanation rather than a complete description of what actually happened.

Ballads

The actual style of ballads will be discussed in the section on crooners, but we must first take up the issue of why ballads were significant in the late 1950s. The way the ballad expanded the listening audience was extremely important in broadening the form and gaining general acceptance by the public.

The first rock and roll ballads predate the invention of the term *rock and roll.* "Ol' Man River" by the Ravens in 1947 is usually considered part of the history of rhythm and blues, but this tune is essentially a ballad — a slow song with a structure based on two themes (theme 1, theme 1, theme 2, theme 1). The AABA form, as it can also be represented, is a basic ballad form. Many of the "bird" groups (groups named after birds) and later imitators sang slow songs in the ballad tradition (sometimes copying Frank Sinatra). These ballads, done in what was considered to be a black style, were very slick compositions. They usually featured a lead singer with a backup vocal group, sometimes with relatively complex harmonies.

By 1956 or 1957 there was a return to dancing in the United States, which had become somewhat of a lost art after the demise of the big bands. However, this time dancing was for the young, probably as a result of their leisure time and relative affluence. Rock and roll was the kind of music they wanted at dances, and the four types of songs discussed earlier were the ones played.

A party lasting even an hour has some logical prerequisites concerning what music is played. Contrast is the key word in the successful selection of music; with even the most homogeneous of groups, it is necessary to provide different kinds of music.

The most diverse crowd of people to choose music for is probably one attending a large reception. In the 1980s people asked for everything from the Average White Band to Flatt and Scruggs. People at large receptions range in age from two to ninety, and this makes music selection challenging. There has to be a little something for everyone, and it is necessary to have contrast, like a fast song followed by a slow one. If only fast rock and roll or only slow ballads from the 1940s were played, the people would get bored.

The same was true in the 1950s, when dancing became so popular. Although the crowds were more homogeneous (especially at school dances), their needs for changes in tempo and mood were just as precise. The market required different types of songs, which is one of the reasons why four different types emerged, all equally important.

Ballads were significant as elements of contrast, for relaxing the tension of rock and roll shouters. They also spoke to a larger audience because they were based on an earlier tradition. Although they often had quite uninspiring lyrics, as did many of the popular ballads of the 1940s, they were relaxing and pretty.

Also, ballads were used for a particular kind of dancing that was very popular in the 1950s. Some of the dance styles associated with faster music were fairly complicated and frankly acrobatic, but slow dancing was something anyone could do. The bop, the twist, and even the hokey-pokey required some expertise. Slow dancing was often called the "hug-and-squeeze" approach. The male and the female simply held on to each other, moving their feet back and forth or not at all.

The significance of the ballad in the years 1956 to 1959 was major. It expanded the range of music for rock and roll musicians and the size of their audience.

ANALYSIS OF TOP SONGS

In this section we will use information from *Billboard's* "Number One Hit" to trace the emergence of rock and roll as a pop phenomenon. Of course, this is not the only method we could use to determine the effect of rock and roll, but it will give some indications of patterns of popularity.

In 1950 the top single on January 7 was Gene Autry's "Rudolph the Red-Nosed Reindeer." In February the Andrews Sisters had the top spot. In July Nat King Cole took over with "Mona Lisa," which was straight crooning. In 1951 Patti

Page had the top song, "Tennessee Waltz," in January and February, followed by Perry Como, Les Paul and Mary Ford, Nat King Cole again, Tony Bennett, and Rosemary Clooney; the year ended with Johnny Ray's "Cry."

In 1952 and 1953 the trend continued, with Patti Page coming out on top. Most of the songs popular in the early 1950s were either ballads (sung by crooners) or novelty tunes. They were aimed strictly at older white audiences.

Eddie Fisher, Doris Day, and Perry Como started in 1954, consistent with previous trends. However, in the first week of August, "Sh-Boom" by the Crewcuts was number one. This particular tune was probably the first rock and roll–oriented tune to become number one, although a careful listening will reveal virtually no rock and roll characteristics, at least none that would have been so defined at that time. However, this was the kind of lyric that would become the staple of rock and roll ballads in the late 1950s. "Mr. Sandman" by the Chordettes held the top position in December 1954.

In July 1955 Bill Haley made it to the top with "Rock Around the Clock," remaining there for eight weeks. Mitch Miller (who still professes a dislike for rock and roll) took over from the Comets with the "Yellow Rose of Texas." "Love is a Many-Splendored Thing" by the Four Aces followed; and at the end of the year Tennessee Ernie Ford made it to the top with "Sixteen Tons," interestingly the kind of lyric that could work in rock and roll.

"Memories Are Made of This" put Dean Martin on top for the first time in 1956; Martin was one of the great crooners of the 1950s, although he was never involved with rock and roll. Kay Starr was number one on February 18 with "Rock and Roll Waltz," which is a rather strange hybrid. Elvis Presley was first with "Heartbreak Hotel" in April, and he dominated the top spot for the next two years. Guy Mitchell made it briefly with "Singing the Blues" at the end of 1956; Tab Hunter, Pat Boone, Perry Como, and Paul Anka all held the top spot briefly in 1957 with ballads.

Novelty tunes had a banner year in 1958 with "Witch Doctor," "Purple People Eater," "Hang Down Your Head, Tom Dooley," and "The Chipmunk Song." One of the great ballads of the 1950s, "Venus" by Frankie Avalon, was number one in 1959, as well as "Lonely Boy" by Paul Anka. The year 1960 saw the reemergence of Presley and continued success of such novelty tunes as "Alley-Oop" and "Itsy Bitsy Teenie Weenie Yellow Polka-Dot Bikini."

The dance phenomenon of Chubby Checker was introduced in 1961, first with "Pony Time" on February 27, but 1962 was really the big year for twist tunes. On October 20, the last great monster song made the top — "Monster Mash" by Boris Pickett and the Crypt Kickers. This song was reintroduced in the 1970s and was again successful. In 1961 and 1962 Ray Charles was on top several times, but never for what I consider to be the best tune in the 1950s, "What'd I Say?"

The Beatles dominated from the year 1964, but the charts took on a different character. The kinds of songs seen by looking at the entire list from 1950 to 1962 give one view of rock and roll. What happened after that is quite different.

MAJOR PERFORMERS

In this section we will consider eighteen different performers, grouped under the different types of songs previously discussed. Some of the musicians will receive more coverage than others, mainly because they produced more music or were more important. It should be remembered that these are only examples, and there are other musicians who are undoubtedly as important.

Rhythm and Blues

In this section we will discuss Chuck Berry, Sam Cooke, King Curtis, Bo Diddley, Little Richard, Fats Domino, and Ray Charles. Berry and Diddley were great guitar players, at least by the standards of the 1950s; Cooke and Domino were powerful singers and bluesmen; King Curtis was an influential saxophone player (who will also be mentioned as a pivotal figure in the soul chapter); Little Richard was the greatest screamer, and Ray Charles was a significant piano player and singer. These men were known mainly for their contributions to rhythm and blues as it was associated with rock and roll.

Chuck Berry was the most influential of the seven in that many other musicians copied his style; he continued to have influence in the 1960s — on the Beatles and the Rolling Stones among others — and 1970s. He was a seasoned veteran by the mid-1950s, which placed him in a somewhat enviable position. Like Bill Haley, he combined country and western and rhythm and blues. However, as a black musician he had perhaps a better feel for the rhythm and blues part and was a substantially better guitar player. Many people also believe that he was a better performer.

Careful listening to some of his songs from different eras will illustrate that his lyrics were aimed at youth, although they were somewhat more sophisticated than those of other musicians of the time. Many of his songs were not accepted as real classics until years after he had first performed them. "Surfin' U.S.A." had a different title originally; Brian Wilson added the words and turned this song into a model for surfing music. Both the Beatles and the Rolling Stones successfully sang Berry tunes.

More important is the fact that Berry was an excellent technician, that is, a technically good guitar player, which was unusual in the 1950s. Of the big stars, Bill Haley was a competent country and western guitarist, but mainly in the chordal style. Elvis Presley could strum chords on the guitar but was lost when it came to playing melodic lines. Berry could play melodically and quite quickly. He was also a capable improvisor and was definitely the model for the guitar soloists of the 1960s, even the acid rock musicians.

Berry used a riff orientation in his improvisations that came directly from the rhythm and blues tradition. He used the guitar as a complement to his voice, filling in passages at the end of a phrase. But more important, he used the guitar as a solo instrument to break up the vocal domination, as well as expressively to communi-

Chuck Berry   *(Used by permission of Fred Reif, Black Kettle Records, Saginaw, Michigan)*

cate the strength of the song. Although other musicians may have used the guitar visually, Berry combined visual uses of the instrument (stage presence) with playing well.

Berry has changed some over the years, although he retains his rocker roots, going back to the song "I'm a Rocker." His playing has gotten more technical; he uses more electronic devices; and the language of his songs updates the slang usages and subjects. His playing and singing are a constant source of energy, and he continues to play what most musicians feel is very solid, or "good," rock and roll.

Sam Cooke was a tremendously important singer, although he died at a young age in 1964 (he was shot). His style is difficult to pin down because many of his important hits were in fact not backed up by traditional rhythm and blues or rock and roll ensembles. His first release in 1957 was called "You Send Me." His records (over seven years) were mainly of pop tunes, many of them slow songs in a

Sam Cooke *(Photo by RCA Records; used by permission of Ginny Cartmell and Creem Magazine Archives)*

crooning style. In the fast tunes (most of which were released in the 1960s) he revealed rhythm and blues roots, especially in vocal inflection.

However, in public performances Cooke revealed completely his ties to the blues. He had a relatively "clean" voice, in the sense that he was a pure singer. He had an excellent range, very good control, and a fine rhythmic feel. He did not shout at his audience, although he was a good interpreter of the style. Had his career lasted longer or had it been at a different time, he undoubtedly would have recorded fewer pop tunes. In some sense, Cooke was an important figure in the soul movement, although he did not live long enough to grow with it.

King Curtis was mentioned in chapter four as one of the most significant saxophonists in the shouting classification. In fact, he was probably the best saxophonist in that tradition because of pure technical virtuosity; he had a full tone, played a lot of notes, and had a very melodic style. Most saxophonists of the 1950s played stereotyped solos, which were basically the same thing over and over. Curtis came from the jazz tradition and riff orientation of rhythm and blues. Thus, he was able to string together long melodic phrases within the rhythm and blues style. Had he chosen the way of John Coltrane he might have become one of the jazz greats. However, his significance is in rhythm and blues and in his playing strength.

Curtis played tenor saxophone and guitar, wrote music, and sang. Many of his tunes were blues numbers, and he had influence in the soul movement. He had a

King Curtis   *(Courtesy of Prestige Records)*

number of pop crossover tunes and was a continuous example for other saxophone players, many of whom copied his big sound. His technical virtuosity was significant, and although rock and roll did not demand it, other musicians envied his flexibility. In the 1960s he played a great deal of jazz, often with a small jazz quartet. Until his death in 1971 he was known primarily as a tenor player, although he also played soprano saxophone.

Bo Diddley (Elias McDaniel) was a rhythm and blues musician of stature in the early 1950s, and in fact he was one of the major performers in Alan Freed's Rhythm and Blues Extravaganzas. As a guitar player he ranked in importance with Chuck Berry, although his playing was quite different. Whereas Berry had tremendous ability at melodic improvisation, Diddley played with a rhythmic vitality that was unparalleled. In fact, he had what was called the "Bo Diddley Beat." He pioneered the intelligent use of the electric guitar, in his case a solid-body electric guitar (not the acoustic construction). He set the controls on his guitar and amplifier (more on this topic in the appendices) to achieve a deep, guttural sound. The tone, full of distortion and sounding almost dirty, had great influence on guitar players throughout the 1970s. This was really a rather remarkable innovation at a time when technology did not provide many sonic alternatives. An especially good recording to listen to is *Two Great Guitars,* featuring both Berry and Diddley. Diddley's improvisation tends to be more chordal in orientation than Berry's, but he plays with a very solid feel. He had widespread influence in the 1950s and 1960s.

Little Richard (Richard Penniman) was and still is the king of the screamers. He was born in Macon, Georgia, in 1935, and unlike some of the other musicians mentioned, grew up totally within the rhythm and blues context. He had a heavy dose of gospel singing in his youth, and as a young teenager he turned to blues shouting, ultimately hitting it big with "Tutti, Frutti" in 1955 (a million-record seller). From 1955 to 1957 he was constantly on top, running a close second to Presley. In 1957 he quit singing and performing completely for religious reasons, but in the early 1960s he returned to the music scene, first through gospel and then back to rock and roll. In performance he never failed to show that in the shouting style, he was the best. He probably outdid Presley in this style and certainly led to the early demise of Bill Haley's popularity.

Little Richard was a piano player, although probably not a great one. He had no inhibitions at all, either in singing or playing. He wore baggy suits and outlandish clothes, but his main claim to fame was his hair, styled in a high pompadour. Some people have claimed that he was the Muhammad Ali of the 1950s, which is an apt comparison. His image was that of an antihero. He gave off great electricity in performances, and he was a constant bundle of energy. His songs were fast blues progressions, in which the lyrics were relatively meaningless. His stage presence was all-consuming, and he used whoops, slides, dropoffs, and screams. Little Richard belongs on any list of classic rock screamers.

Fats Domino, born in 1929 in New Orleans, was an extremely important musician in the continuing tradition of New Orleans jazz/rhythm and blues. A piano player and singer, he was technically quite good by the time he made his first record in 1949, called "The Fat Man." He played in old barrelhouse piano style, which fit nicely into the rock sound. Probably his biggest hits from a rhythm and blues perspective were "Ain't That a Shame" (1955), "Blueberry Hill" (1956), "I'm Walkin'" (1957), "Whole Lotta Loving" (1958), and "Walkin' to New Orleans" (1960). He literally made the Imperial Record Company until he left for ABC in 1963.

His music was covered by virtually everyone in this chapter, for instance Chuck Berry, Jerry Lee Lewis, and Little Richard (as well as Pat Boone). The Beatles were quoted several times in tributes to Fats Domino. Perhaps not as magnetic in performance style as others, Fats Domino was a solid professional musician who played rhythm and blues in a solid New Orleans style. His vocal style was very relaxed.

Ray Charles   *(Used by permission of Michael Ochs Archives, Venice, California)*

Ray Charles was born in Albany, Georgia, on September 23, 1930. His youth was spent in a small town near the Florida border, Greenville, Georgia. The story of his youth is extremely interesting, and anyone who wants to know more should definitely read his autobiography. To make a long and intriguing story fairly short, his early life was hard: When he was five he saw his brother drown, and he lost his vision when he was seven. His family was poor, uneducated, and downtrodden. Consequently, his development follows the pattern of the black blues singer, as discussed in chapter four. Charles was first in the blues tradition, and he came to rock and roll rather late, that is, in the late 1950s. He developed first as a rhythm and blues musician and gospel singer. By the early 1950s he was a significant jazz musician. When he started doing rock and roll tunes at the end of the 1950s, he brought with him his professionalism and experience in the recording industry. Many record producers, and musicians as well, have talked about how much Charles taught them, rather than the other way around.

Charles is an excellent pianist, a competent saxophone player, and a superb singer. As a blind musician, he evokes feelings that sighted musicians do not. Obviously he served as a model for little Stevie Wonder and for virtually every important black musician from the 1960s on. He was the first soul singer, and any discussion of Motown should start with him, even though he is a Southerner.

The style of Ray Charles is a combination of gospel and rhythm and blues, with some jazz elements mixed in. It is not basically rock and roll, but the resultant sound has been embraced as that of the late 1950s. As well as combining all these elements, he predates many pop and soul musicians in the use of larger instrumental ensembles. During the 1950s he worked the rhythm and blues circuit with a distinctive style of singing.

He has a large vocal range and uses call and response extensively, both between his voice and the backup musicians and between himself and the audience. He uses a shouting style reminiscent of strong gospel singers, and the players extensively imitate rhythmic riffs. He clearly combines elements of the profane (rhythm and blues) with the sacred (gospel).

By the end of the 1950s Charles began working with a larger group of musicians, many of whom have gone on to become leaders in the jazz movement, particularly in Detroit. He used the larger ensemble as a responding unit to his singing, not wanting to be the whole production by himself. His piano playing served both as accompaniment to himself and as part of the ensemble, which was somewhat unique. Many of his recordings from the late 1950s and early 1960s were technically superior to other recordings of black musicians, partly because of the superiority of his band and also because of his knowledge of recording techniques. He was demanding in his standards, although reports of that time indicate that he was a very easy person to work with because he was so professional.

He had difficulties with drugs in the 1960s but managed to surmount them; he also had difficulties with the law. He continued to perform and record in the 1960s and 1970s and is still quite active today. He is a consummate performer in many different styles and is a great credit to the profession.

Charles developed in a somewhat more complete way than any other musician considered in this book. At the school for the blind he attended, he was given formal musical instruction, and by virtue of the time period of his formative years (early 1940s), he was schooled in the outside world in every kind of music. By the time he moved to Jacksonville, Florida, at the age of fifteen, he was already aiming for a career in music; however, unlike many other musicians in this book he did not catapult to fame overnight. He worked hard as a union musician, learning from the best and the worst, playing every kind of job imaginable. He copied other people's playing and learned to play whatever would get him work. As a result, he is able to move freely among blues, jazz, and any other kind of music imaginable. In this sense, Ray Charles is a complete musician.

A description of his entire recording and playing career would take at least one hundred pages because he has done so much. In his performing career he has played with some of the best, starting as a young teenager with Cannonball Adderly. He played with other musicians who were already great, and he also allowed new musicians to play with him before their rise to stardom. Stevie Wonder performed with Charles as a sit-in musician when Wonder was ten years old. As an arranger, Charles made himself important to many of the ensembles he played in; later he was the leader of his own band. His arranging technique was different from most because it was oral. He heard everything in his head and called out the right notes to be written down by the musician in charge of each part. In this sense, Ray Charles is unique. No one else in the history of rock has quite his musical command.

His recording career is equally impressive; regardless of the period in his career, he was always in complete control of the musical forces. In the early 1950s he was called on to produce the right sound for a specific need, both in his playing and singing, and also for the other musicians involved. He has always been the consummate studio musician because of his ability to adapt himself and to understand the roles of the other musicians. His early career provided the necessary tools; he was always interested in the imitative process and being able to do everything. Most rock musicians tend to have a relatively narrow approach to their role in the performing ensemble; Charles adapts himself to whatever is being done at the moment. He is equally at home in a jazz setting, in a rhythm and blues ensemble, or in classical music.

Each of his major hits (and sometimes tunes that did not become popular) illustrates mastery of style, flexibility, and technical precision. Charles was always ahead of the competition in the sense that each of his recorded performances was years ahead of the level of technology and complexity of the time in which it was actually produced. Even when he was producing race records, their technical level far surpassed that of other black artists. In this sense alone, Charles was a leader in his field.

The first tune we will consider is from 1955 — "I've Got a Woman." Although the lyrics seem to fit the model of a shouter, the instrumental backing does not. The ensemble is a straightforward jazz or rhythm and blues group: piano, bass, drums, and saxophone. The song has a number of short verses, although it is not a blues progression — it just sounds like it. His singing style is blues-oriented and features quite a bit of shouting. However, there is a tenderness about the way he sings, and he uses dynamic contrast to make the lyrics more effective. He employs call and response and also what we call *stop-time,* where he sings a short phrase by himself (without accompaniment) and the instruments respond; then he returns to the standard format. This particular device derives from gospel music and is a trademark of Charles's style. Probably the most significant contribution of this technique is audience involvement, which the trait will eventually evoke.

"Hallelujah, I Love Her So," which came out in 1956, is truly unique in the history of rock and roll and pop music of the 1950s. It uses a small big band as an extension of the instrumental ensemble in the earlier recording. The band is riff-oriented, which probably goes back to some of Charles's playing experiences and most certainly to his listening ones (Count Basie, Louis Jordan, and others). The lyrics, a combination of gospel and rhythm and blues, have religious as well as sexual overtones. Charles certainly loves women (many of them) and the lyrics of this particular song illustrate some of his feelings. There is a particularly attractive place where he sings about a woman knocking on the door; the drummer plays several repeated rim shots to suggest the knocking. We should always look for examples of this "word painting" in music.

A pivotal song in the history of rock and roll is "What'd I Say?," recorded in 1959. This song became almost a union card of sorts in the early 1960s. In order to get into any rock and roll band a musician had to be able to play the tune and to sing at least six verses of it. Much in the way that Charles had to be competent in a certain number of musical styles and songs in order to get work as a struggling musician, musicians now had to master his tune in order to get a job. This is a fitting tribute to Charles's struggle for success.

A fact we have not mentioned yet is that most rock and roll tunes from the 1950s were fairly short, only two to three minutes in length. Most versions of "What'd I Say?" run about eight to ten minutes. This song is made up of very short lyric phrases (of eight measures); it is not a blues structure per se, although it is blues-like. It is really drawn from the old rural blues or primitive blues tradition. There is a refrain and there are many verses. The verses in the version on record are pretty clean, although they are obviously sexual in orientation. The verses in live performance are a bit more earthy.

The song begins and ends with audience participation. After singing many verses of the song, Charles stops. The audience starts responding, in a similar manner to gospel songs. He begins to respond to them and then finally breaks into a vocal utterance that is repeated by the audience. This continues, builds, and then he breaks back into the song. He stops and starts it again. In this sense, he uses the audience like a rhythmic riff, building tension through repetition. This technique is based on rhythm and blues concepts, but in this piece, Charles uses all his talent — big-band backing, virtuoso piano playing, grunting, groaning, and audience participation. The sound of the song is simple but its overall structure is captivating.

Crooners

The crooners came mainly from the North, or more properly, from the white tradition. We have stated that crooning was essentially started by white singers, going back as far as Rudy Vallee, and that black musicians adapted the style to their own form of pop music in the late 1940s. The crooners of the late 1950s were white performers, and this particular style of singing was clearly aimed at a white audience.

In the 1950s it was easy to call the shouters rock and roll musicians, but the crooners were hard to classify. We consider them to be part of rock and roll, but that belief is at least debatable. However, these songs were performed partially for the rock and roll audience, at least insofar as that means young people. Crooning songs, or ballads, relied on the following basic characteristics:

1. A clearly recognizable singer who had charismatic attraction
2. A slow and dreamy lyric, which was often about a simple emotion
3. A slow, continuous background of instruments and/or vocal group

4. A rhythmic feel, which often broke up the measure into twelve beats (four groups of three)

5. An attempt to characterize life as happy.

Whereas many of the rhythm and blues and shouting tunes were critical and/or pessimistic, ballads were almost always optimistic. In some ways, the history of the ballad is a more precise social indicator than other types of rock and roll.

A few of the crooners mentioned started their careers before what we will call the "golden age of slow songs" (roughly 1957 to 1960), but these tunes were sung more extensively at this time. That is, although previously musicians could get by singing just fast tunes, by 1957 they had to have contrast ballads in order to survive. Again, the movement toward dancing (culminating in the cultivation of particular dance steps) probably had more to do with this development than any other single factor.

As the movie industry capitalized on the romantic view of life with Elvis Presley, the recording and performing industries capitalized on the pretty faces of white northern crooners in their attempt to capture large markets, including middle-class America. Marketing and commercialization undoubtedly had a great deal to do with the rise of slow songs, but so did the attitudes of society. American life in the late 1950s can be seen cynically as the lull before the storm of the 1960s, but it could also be viewed as a relaxed and comfortable era.

In this section we will consider Paul Anka, Frankie Avalon, Pat Boone, Dion and the Belmonts, Fabian, Ricky Nelson, and Tommy Sands. There are of course many others who could be considered, but these performers are a good cross-section of this type.

Paul Anka, originally from Canada, achieved tremendous success. In 1958 he had his first hit tune, "Diana," which sold nine million copies; he was fifteen at the time. A prolific composer, he wrote well over two hundred songs in the next five years and was a self-made millionaire by the time he was twenty-one. From the very beginning he had a natural ability to meet people and to act appropriately in front of audiences. He became a leading power in the music industry because of his shrewd business sense.

Anka, who had an extremely beautiful voice, was a classic crooner. As a teenage idol, he was cute, smiled a lot, and was the darling of women, especially women who were older than he was. His songs spoke of love, embracing, and other images that fit well with dancing. He was definitely a pop musician in that he spoke to a wider audience than that solely associated with rock and roll and/or rhythm and blues. His performances in public, for instance, Las Vegas, were packed, and he appealed to a wide spectrum of society. Anka was a perfect model for the kind of phenomenon described in the ballad era, and he was one of the leaders; he also continued to be popular over time.

Frankie Avalon is another good example of the young musician who has a big success with one song and then continues to be popular, although he did not

Paul Anka in 1981   *(Photo by Barry Rankin, Saginaw, Michigan)*

continue to be a major force like Paul Anka. However, he did have nostalgia value, even after the Beatles became popular. Avalon was originally a trumpet player, and his first big hit was "Venus" in 1959. He was in the movies in the beach-party format and continued to produce hit tunes until roughly 1964. He had a beautiful voice and was quite attractive.

The most important thing about Avalon was probably the lyrics of his songs and the way he sang them. As a singer, he was a romantic crooner without any awesome stage technique; he just presented beautiful songs. His lyrics were packed with images of love (mostly love at a distance), and he was a symbol of man reaching out to woman (or vice versa). "Venus" was a verse and refrain song, with contrast between the musical presentations of the two parts; the verse had a light-textured rock beat, and the refrain had more of a swing beat. It was efficient music without too much complexity; but it was technically well done and was quite successful.

Pat Boone had an enormously successful career, which he passed on to one of his children, Debby Boone. Although some people may question his inclusion in a book on rock and roll, his popularizations of rock and roll hits were significant. Boone performed other people's music, not his own, and changed it so it would be palatable to a large audience. He was known for religious songs, renditions of old standards, and cover versions of rhythm and blues tunes. In this last context he was quite important, although he must always be considered a crooner.

Although Boone was criticized by people on both sides of the issue, he legitimized rock and roll by making it popular with nonrock audiences. He stood for strong Christian values, was a representative of white middle-class America, and presented a clean-cut image. To those who supported that position, his singing of rock and roll was questionable. To those who supported other values, he was an inappropriate spokesman; they would have preferred someone more within the tradition singing their songs. When he did "Ain't That a Shame," originally by Fats Domino, and other songs from the rhythm and blues repertoire, he offended the purists who would have wanted the original artist to get the credit and the money. However, for the audience that liked the song no matter what its source, Boone presented a version of a song that might not have been acceptable had it been sung by the original black artist.

The important point is how Boone changed these original tunes and what the resultant sound was. He sang in a pure voice without any of the blues inflections of rhythm and blues singers. The background sound was more swing beat or big band in orientation than rock and roll. He sang fast tunes in medium speed with a smooth and mellow voice. He took the hardness out of fast songs, and he took the mushy emotionalism out of slow songs. In essence, he watered down the sound as well as the lyrics. Although white proponents of the rhythm and blues tradition before Boone (Haley and Presley) had watered down the lyrics slightly, they still retained the rhythmic and emotional intensity of the originals. Boone watered down those elements as well. In this sense, he was a crooner even when he sang rhythm and blues tunes.

Dion and the Belmonts, with Dion DiMucci as the leader, represented a particular tradition within this era. In 1960 this group emerged with "teenage" songs, that is, songs specifically aimed at a teenage audience, and often with the word *teenager* (or *teen*) in the title. In 1961 the group made the top of the charts with "Runaround Sue." Some of their other important songs were "Teenager in Love," "Teen Angel," and "Lonely Teenager." They were one of the first groups to perform what would later be called "bubble gum music."

The Belmonts were all of Italian descent—DiMucci, D'Aleo, Milano, and Mastrangelo—and the vocal sound was high pitched and very emotional. It was plaintive, reminding some people of a weak version of Italian opera. There was a definite rock and roll feel to the music, but it was light rock. The instrumental backing was generally simple, and the focal point was the lyric and the sound of the voices. The lyrics were clearly aimed at teenagers, in particular, young teenagers. The tunes tended to be sung at medium speed and had little improvisation or technical virtuosity. Although their audience was quite specific, it was also quite lucrative. We might be tempted to dismiss this group as not very interesting, but "teen rock" is a big business, and at least one example should be mentioned.

Fabian (Fabiano Forte), also of Italian descent, was essentially groomed as a

Presley look-alike. When a major artist was successful, there were always attempts to capitalize on this success by patterning other people after the same model. This had happened with the "bird" groups in the late 1940s, and it happened again with Elvis Presley. Fabian was signed by a record company when he was thirteen years old and was literally made into a rock and roll star. His one hit song, "Tiger," in 1959 seemed to have justified this experiment. However, he was to have little impact in future years.

Fabian was and still is an extremely good-looking man. His long hair, dark skin, and strong body made him a natural sex symbol. Ultimately getting into pictures, with John Wayne in "North to Alaska" and in other less notable, beach-party films, he was successful in the image he was presenting. However, his style only worked at that time and did not endure the changes of the 1960s. Fabian is occasionally mentioned on television record ads, but his career is now obscure.

Although Fabian at times tried to emulate the great shouters, he was primarily a crooner in the softer rock and roll tradition. He was most at home in the emotional kind of song performed for the beach-party set. He was not endowed with a tremendous voice, but as Stan Freeberg pointed out in his parody on rock musicians, that was really not necessary. What he exuded was good looks, and during his period of success, that sufficed.

Ricky Nelson is an interesting example because he was popular before he became a singer. As the younger son on the famous "Ozzie and Harriet" television show, he was simply the cute kid who did normal boyish things. However, as the show got older, and the characters along with it, Ricky Nelson began to emerge as a symbol for preteens and then ultimately teenagers. His singing career began on the television show and was then marketed in the Presley tradition. Fan clubs were formed all over the world, and by 1959 Nelson was an important entertainer. His greatest successes occurred between 1959 and 1964, before the Beatles became popular. One record, "Travelin' Man," hit the top in 1961.

Although he consciously patterned himself after Presley, particularly in his body motions and sneer, Nelson was really much more of a crooner or soft rock performer. He appealed to a wide audience, but most of his records were sold to young teenagers. He was a good singer and made a serious comeback in 1969; as a seasoned performer he was very good with audiences. The television show and his recording career went together, sort of like that of the Partridge Family. It was a neat package, and it fit the marketing techniques of that period. Ricky Nelson died on December 31, 1985, in a plane crash; he was on his way to a New Year's Eve performance.

Tommy Sands is another Presley imitator who was fairly popular in the late 1950s. Although best known as the person who married Nancy Sinatra, he was important as a singer of young teenage songs, definitely in the crooning tradition. Examples of his songs are "Teenage Crush" and "Cutie Wootie." In some ways, his career and characteristics were interchangeable with some of the other musicians mentioned here. He was in the films of the time, he was good-looking, and he sang moderately well within the style.

Ricky Nelson   *(Courtesy of Capitol Records)*

Specialty Songs

Many of the "bird" groups mentioned previously used a low bass voice as an element of contrast, which would make them singers of specialty songs. One particular example is the line, "Why is everybody always picking on me?" from the Coasters' "Charlie Brown." These phrases often take on some narrating quality in the sense that they express the real emotional and lyrical content of the whole song.

When a performer reveals him- or herself or something about a character, it is unique and often occurs through these special devices.

J. P. Richardson (known as the Big Bopper) used one line consistently in his performances and recordings. It was, simply, "this is the Big Bopper speaking." His only major hit was "Chantilly Lace" in 1958, an uptempo song about a particular girl. Very popular at the time, but different from other tunes, it communicated through the medium of the Big Bopper. Although it was undoubtedly a clever piece, what was important was the autobiographical nature of the narrating function. Had Big Bopper not been killed in the same plane crash with Buddy Holly and Richie Valens, he might have continued this concept over the years. As rock musicians began to see themselves as communicators of significant and major ideas, the predilection to communication in the first person would happen more and more often.

Chubby Checker was a specialty song performer, and it is easy to explain why. He was a rhythm and blues piano player and, frankly, an excellent musician. His roots go back to the stride pianists previously mentioned. However, his career would have been insignificant had it not been for the twist. In 1960 he recorded the "Twist," a composition by Hank Ballard, and the dance craze took off. The twist was popular with different kinds of people, and it even enjoyed great success in Europe. Although the music was good, the only important thing about it was the dance step associated with it — which is why it was a specialty song.

Monster Songs

Monster songs are really a subclass of novelty tunes, of which there were many in the period under consideration. Novelty songs are present in every era of music. One of the best examples of one from the big-band era is the arrangement of the "Woody Woodpecker Song" in which the instruments imitate the sound of a woodpecker, or the train effect at the beginning of Glenn Miller's "Chattanooga Choo-Choo." Novelty songs are catchy and they rely on some special image to attract attention. We mention monster songs here because they seem to be a rather nice model, especially for musicians who would have been otherwise unknown.

The idea of monsters is, interestingly enough, attractive to rock musicians. Certainly the *Yellow Submarine* of the Beatles incorporates the idea of monsters, in this case, evil monsters who set out to keep the world from having music. The monster image in the Who's *Tommy* and the blatant monsters of Kiss or heavy metal groups are quite apparent. However, the monsters in the 1950s were somewhat less evil; they were benevolent monsters who were not to be taken seriously. As such, they were slightly more redeeming characters, ludicrous at times, but always entertaining.

Two rather attractive monsters from the era were "Purple People Eater" by Sheb Wooley in 1958 and "Monster Mash" by Boris Pickett and the Crypt Kickers in 1962. The first monster was a happy little fellow who came to visit and wanted to stay. He flew but was not really dangerous; he was cute. The "Monster Mash" was a dance step, and again the monster image was benevolent. These tunes were up-tempo pop songs designed to hit the charts quickly. They both did so and then became collector's items. Monster records are still occasionally produced, bringing together fifteen or twenty of the most successful songs of the genre.

SUMMARY

Rock and roll in the 1950s was honest music that communicated in simple terms. Because this is a chronological study we have the opportunity to sharpen our listening skills when the demands are not too great. As we progress through the history of this art form, listening will become difficult, especially in the more complicated styles.

The period of the late 1950s is often thought to be the dead time in rock and roll because there was some fairly undignified pop music in that era. We had lost the hard edge in rock and roll (or the way it was in the beginning). However, we should be able to see this period as part of the acculturation of the form. It was becoming the communication medium of the general population, and it was also becoming big business.

The style in the last part of the 1950s capsulized everything that had happened in rock and roll. Although it may have lacked in creativity in some ways, and some of the energy of the shouters had begun to wane, rock and roll made up for these losses by reaching out to many people. The marketing techniques and the sociological implications continued to be influential in the 1960s. Of course, we will see great changes in that decade, but this late period of rock and roll provides the basis for them. Later musicians return to the style of the late 1950s when they attempt to recapture the essence of rock and roll.

LISTENING

Paul Anka, *Lonely Boy*

Chuck Berry, *Greatest Hits*

Bo Diddley, *Two Great Guitars*

Buddy Holly, *20 Golden Greats*

Buddy Holly, *At the Hop*

Little Richard, *Biggest Hits*

Ray Charles, *Best*

CHAPTER **8**

SOUL/MOTOWN

This chapter begins a discussion of music that was important primarily in the 1960s, although some of the musicians to be discussed began performing in the 1950s and continued to perform into the 1970s and 1980s. However, the significant part of their careers for the study of this art form occurred in the 1960s. The next two chapters on the Beatles and California — North and South also look at this decade.

The title of this chapter explains its focus, even though some of the discussion will not deal specifically with soul music or with Detroit. For instance, Phil Spector is mentioned here because some of his innovations had enormous impact on the development of rock as a popular medium in the 1960s. As it turns out, he has had a lasting impact on the entire form although his personal career essentially came to a close in 1966. We have also included a short section at the beginning of the chapter that describes basic attitudes of the 1960s.

One of the underlying issues in the following discussions is the rather incredible sophistication and substantial changes in technology that came about in the 1960s. Primarily as a result of inventions of the previous decade, general improvements in recording technology, market concerns, and media expansion, we see in the music represented here and in future chapters a substantial improvement in quality and cleverness. Even when the lyric is simple in character the musical presentation is fairly sophisticated. And much of the story of the development of soul and especially Motown has to do with the quality of its presentation.

ATTITUDES OF THE 1960s

The 1960s reflected more intense change in the United States than any other time since the Revolutionary War. It is important to understand that many people were committed to the sense of change, committed in a way that perhaps they had never been before. Comprehending the depth of that commitment is imperative for a proper understanding of the art forms that sprang from it.

In the cycle of political change, the 1960s were Democratic years; that is, the Democratic party was in power. Like all cycles, it was probably a reaction to the Republican administration that had preceded it. The beauty of the American system is that it almost guarantees a slow shifting of power back and forth between progressive and conservative attitudes. The 1950s were basically conservative, and the 1960s were basically liberal. Political rhetoric always stresses the importance of moral and ethical philosophies, but in the 1960s the political ethic was based on philosophical values more than in other politically liberal times, for instance, in Franklin Roosevelt's administration.

The 1960s began with a new political image, that of John F. Kennedy, whose significance as a charismatic figure must not be understated. Kennedy represented a new dream for young Americans for many reasons. He was young; he had a beautiful wife; and he had young children. He was an Irish Catholic, and although he came from a powerful and rich family, he represented oppressed minorities. The Kennedy mystique was important, although we can objectively question how much substance it contained. Kennedy was handsome; he held crowds spellbound with his looks and with his speech. He was the first media politician in the sense that he won a close race with Richard Nixon, many people believe, mainly on the basis of their famous television debates. The reason he won, say most analysts, is that he simply looked better and more statesmanlike. It is interesting that Nixon in his triumphant return to politics in 1968 probably used television even better than Kennedy had. However, Kennedy used the media and some marketing techniques much as rock musicians would.

More than anything else, Kennedy gave faith to the American public, but a very different kind of faith from that of the 1950s. Let us remember that the 1950s were secure and prosperous for middle- and upper-class America. However, Kennedy suggested that it was time to spread that wealth to the rest of America and to other parts of the world. He proposed a New Frontier, developments in outer space, the Peace Corps, and nuclear limitations. After becoming president, he did do quite a bit to promote international relations and he became a world symbol for the oppressed. He was especially popular in Latin America (probably, in part, because he was Catholic).

In his inaugural address he spoke of "passing the torch to a new generation of Americans"; although it may not have happened during his brief presidency, it was at least a good symbol for the younger generation. When Kennedy was shot in 1963, the entire world went into mourning. No matter how history will judge Kennedy as a president, his image will remain a symbol of the 1960s.

There can be little doubt that the president responsible for real change in America was Kennedy's successor, Lyndon Johnson. Johnson was in effect the person to whom the mantle was passed. Kennedy's thoughts were to be translated into legislative action by Johnson, who really was more capable of controlling the politics of Congress. Johnson was personally responsible for most of the civil rights legislation and a score of governmental actions (social programs) that serve as the legacy of the 1960s. Unfortunately, Johnson lost his credibility over Vietnam, but most historians will give him tremendous credit for his role in domestic changes.

Although Richard Nixon was elected president in the 1960s, he must be seen as a symbol for the end of that decade and the predictable swing to conservatism. The 1960s were energetic for a number of reasons, but by the end of the decade the movement was falling apart; the conservatives quickly took over.

One of the strong movements was the ecology movement, which began with Rachel Carson's book *The Silent Spring*. The book was an argument against the proliferation of chemicals, which were destroying the delicate balance of nature. The ecology movement would become especially important by the mid-1960s. Natural foods became the rage, a belief that carried over into the 1970s. Attitudes were progressive, and there was a curious trend toward simplifying life, which was basically what the ecology movement was all about.

Some of the interesting developments of the 1960s led to inventions; a good example is Buckminster Fuller's geodesic dome (an energy-efficient style of architecture). Ralph Nader's book *Unsafe at Any Speed* was a condemnation of American technology, although it was specifically aimed at the automobile industry. It was believed that technology must be controlled, or at least, must consider human needs.

Integration was a fundamental issue. Although theoretically integration began in the mid–nineteenth century, it was not until the 1960s that political action on a widespread basis had any effect. The black Muslim movement, riots over racial issues, and civil rights legislation (the Act of 1965) all pointed to the need for change within society. Although the black movement was first, it was quickly followed by other minority movements and ultimately by that for the Equal Rights Amendment.

Student demonstrations were focal points for change, first against the system and then against the Vietnam War. Students gained power within the system, and although there was ugliness, which led ultimately to the massacre at Kent State

University, there were some significant changes in students' rights. The importance of the student movement was that youth were demanding and getting responsibility. This demand ultimately would have an effect on rock, as a topic for lyrics and as a vehicle for changing its message.

The drug movement and the sexual revolution were important in the 1960s. The antiwar movement was also powerful and ultimately led to the end of President Johnson's administration. Some would argue that it significantly lowered the prestige of the United States. Even the image of professional athletes was affected, and for the first time our heroes became antiheroes—Joe Namath and Muhammad Ali, for example. Such figures garnered admiration because of their antisocial views rather than their all-American image.

In conclusion, the 1960s were times of tumult and confusion. Establishment ethics were questioned, and people were committed to new ideas. The only value that seemed to be paramount was that of change. In my opinion, the 1960s represented the most compact historical change in the evolution of America. Even the Constitution was being questioned, that is, seriously questioned as opposed to reinterpreted. Rock music clearly had new messages, and fortunately the musicians popular during that time came up with new means to communicate the new values. The state of the art expanded, and the difference between rock and roll in the 1950s and rock in the 1960s is like night and day.

PHIL SPECTOR

Phil Spector was born in New York in 1940; he moved to Los Angeles when he was twelve. An active and gifted musician, as a teenager he produced his first hit in 1958 with a composition based on his father's death, "To Know Him Is to Love Him," with the Teddy Bears. This tune, in the tradition of the Golden Age of Ballads, was a slow sentimental song designed for dancing. It was also a national hit and suggested the sound that would eventually be characterized as the Spector Wall of Sound.

Subsequently he moved to Philadelphia and then to New York. In 1960 Atlantic Records took him on as a producer, musician, and writer. He began to run up a string of teen hits that would make him one of the most successful producers at that time. His first major hit was with Ben E. King's "Spanish Harlem" in 1960. After his success in New York he moved back to Los Angeles, where he worked on "He's a Rebel" by the Crystals and "Zip-A-Dee Doo-Dah" by Bob B. Soxx and the Blue Jeans. By this time he had established his own record company, Philes (with Les Sill, one of the independent producers who took Spector seriously in Los Angeles when he was eighteen).

As a result of the last two songs mentioned, he returned to New York and went into serious production work. His efforts over the next few years would create twenty major hits—all teenage love songs. While the list of these songs might not seem impressive, the sophistication with which the songs were made is quite important. In retrospect, the message of these tunes was consistent with the times and was of course commercially viable. The significance of Spector's work is that it was appreciated as the state of the art in recording technique. Some of those hits were "Da Doo Ron Ron" (Crystals), "Be My Baby" and "Baby I Love You" (Ronettes), and "You've Lost That Lovin' Feeling" (Righteous Brothers). Most of the recording sessions were done on the West Coast, using the best studio musicians available (including Glen Campbell and Sonny Bono).

However, Phil Spector's true impact was not in the particular songs he did, nor in the fact that he wrote or co-wrote many of the lyrics and melodies. What was significant was the way he produced the recordings. He was a recording studio genius. He used sound-on-sound recording technique before anyone else had heard of overdubbing. Through very experimental techniques he developed the sound of a multitrack recording studio before it was invented. Therefore, many Spector-produced songs sounded as if they had massive instrumental forces behind them, when in fact the effect was produced by overdubbing. Also, he tended to accentuate the high and low spectrums of musical sound, making the music sound bigger or more dense. All of these qualities were coupled with a mania for working out everything down to the smallest detail, especially the enunciation of words and the accent of lyrical phrases.

In short, Phil Spector's career did not last very long, although he has continued to return to production work occasionally. His important impact was from 1960 to 1963, and his musical output is probably appreciated more for the technique and quality of production than for the lasting social impact of the compositions themselves. However, with the possible exception of Motown, Phil Spector was the consummate artist of rock creators of the early 1960s. His impact continues to be felt today. He also helped to establish the significance of "girl groups," and the technical style of a great deal of popular rock.

INSTRUMENTAL GROUPS

Prior to the early 1960s, very few rock and roll tunes relied heavily on the rhythm section because the style was so vocally dominated. However, the emergence of totally instrumental tunes started in 1956 with Bill Doggett's "Honky Tonk." Although still in the minority of tunes produced in this era, we do have examples such as Bill Justis's "Raunchy," Duane Eddy's twangy guitar tunes, and Johnny and the Hurricanes. The Ventures, from Seattle, Washington, had a number two hit in August 1960 with "Walk, Don't Run," and there were numerous successful surfing instrumentals — for instance, the immortal "Wipe Out" by the Surfaris. However, most of the tunes and musicians mentioned failed to bring the technical expertise to instrumental rock and roll that was generated by the continuing tradition in Memphis at Atlantic Records, and by the lone instrumental group represented by Motown, Jr. Walker and the All Stars.

Memphis, Tennessee, was always a hotbed for the production of rockabilly and traditional blues. A number of major artists would continue recording in Memphis during the 1960s — Otis Redding, King Curtis, Wilson Pickett, Sam and Dave, the Staple Singers, and Isaac Hayes. As a result of the rockabilly craze, Memphis became a center for musical activities, but most important for this chapter it became a center for studio recording. In particular, the Stax Recording Studio (associated with Atlantic Records) became a center for fine instrumental studio musicians.

Typically these studio musicians served only as background for vocal artists, including those previously mentioned. However, due to their fine technical ability it was only natural that they would eventually make instrumental recordings, because there was a market for these types of recordings. The two classic examples of this phenomenon were the Mar-Keys and Booker T. and the MGs.

The Mar-Keys was formed in Memphis in 1957 as a quartet but the ensemble that had a hit with "Last Night" in 1961 included guitar, bass, drums, piano, two saxophones, and a trumpet. Basically, this was the group of musicians responsible for the Memphis instrumental sound, and they served as the house band for Satellite Records (later Stax-Volt). Their hard-edged style of playing, which had a great influence on backup bands like James Brown's Flames, evolved directly from the blues style (riff-oriented), but they played with a technical ability that approached perfection within that style. The Mar-Keys later merged with the next group mentioned, Booker T. and the MGs.

Booker T. Jones was an organist with the Stax Label starting in 1960. He worked with members of the Mar-Keys in the studio and eventually he and Steve Cropper, house guitarist and member of the Mar-Keys, formed a group they called the MGs (short for Memphis Group). They had several major hits in the 1960s, such as "Green Onions" in 1962, "Boot-Leg" in 1965, "My Sweet Potato" in 1966, "Hip Hug-Her" in 1967, and "Soul Limbo" in 1968. They also did two film soundtracks in 1969; one hit from those soundtracks was for "Hang 'Em High."

The band toured with the Stax/Volt Revue, analogous to the Motown Revue discussed later, although the MGs was a group with floating personnel. They performed whenever they could, although most of the members were primarily studio musicians. Their importance of course was for their contribution to a definitive Memphis instrumental sound. Individual members continued to have influential and productive careers. Steve Cropper (guitar) and Donald "Duck" Dunn (bass) joined the Blues Brothers in 1978, and Booker T. Jones (organ) had a disco hit in 1982 with "Don't Stop Your Love."

A number of other musicians came to record at Stax in the 1960s because it had developed a reputation for fine technical recordings, and for having good studio musicians in either a traditional blues or rockabilly vein. Such notables as Dusty Springfield and King Curtis regularly went to Memphis for recording. Curtis (who was discussed in chapter seven) especially fit the style of the Memphis sound.

This particular recording center became known for its dynamic instrumental sound, technical quality, and expert production. Some have claimed that the reason the technical quality was so high was because the Memphis establishment was attempting to compete with the Nashville sound, only they would produce gospel/ blues/soul instead of mainstream country music. However, I prefer to view the quality of instrumental performance simply as an outgrowth of backing up so many fine artists. It was only natural that expert musicianship would spring from constant activity. Although perhaps not as dominant as Motown would be in the creation of a black pop music, Memphis certainly created its share of commercial recordings and did set a high standard for recordings of relatively pure soul/gospel music. One might add in conclusion that Atlantic Records had developed a good "track record" for technical recordings in previous work with King Curtis, and especially the 1950s recordings of Ray Charles. Certainly, Jerry Wexler, vice-president of Atlantic Records, had a great deal to do with the development of this market, and the subsequent support of Atlantic's Memphis subsidiaries.

One other instrumental group that certainly deserves mention is Jr. Walker and the All Stars, who recorded for Motown (their only instrumental group). An excellent performer on piano and saxophone, Jr. Walker started performing purely instrumental hits with his bluesy tenor sax style (actually very progressive at the time), but toward the end of the 1960s he began doing more singing. However, the All Stars were billed by Motown as an instrumental group and they were certainly a good one. Jr. Walker and the All Stars influenced other groups, especially fusion and jazz/rock ensembles from the upper Midwest. Although the primary period of the band's success was the 1960s, Walker played on a 1981 hit called "Urgent" by Foreigner.

Also worthy of mention is the backup band for Motown Records. Most notable were James Jamerson, bass; Robert White, guitar; Earl Van Dyke, keyboards; and William "Benny" Benjamin, drums. Clearly, there were many more musicians who were employed on Motown recordings, but these were the four central figures who made up the rhythm section, the heart of funk. Interestingly, they called themselves the Funk Brothers. Of course, these are the men behind the recordings, but their presence is a very real part of the Motown sound. They were the ones who trained the other musicians, and often the singers—Van Dyke even gave free keyboard lessons to Little Stevie Wonder. They were also the people responsible for creating the musical end of the road shows.

GOSPEL AND SOUL

Although many important musicians within this genre did record in Memphis for Atlantic during the 1960s, there was of course a continuing tradition of gospel, traditional blues, and soul (after 1964 on *Billboard*) throughout the United States. Memphis was to continue its influence as a center of activity in the South with people like James Brown ("Papa's Got a Brand New Bag"), Sam and Dave ("Hold On I'm Coming"), Percy Sledge ("When a Man Loves a Woman"), Wilson Pickett

("Mustang Sally"), Aretha Franklin ("Respect"), and Otis Redding ("I Can't Turn You Loose" and "Merry Christmas Baby").

A rather interesting change occurred in 1963, the last year that *Billboard* used rhythm and blues as a description for black music. In 1964 they replaced it with soul. At first the term meant little more than rhythm and blues; however, it soon incorporated gospel music and blues. The resultant style was a blues/shouting style exemplified by the musicians discussed within this section. Some have argued that this particular style was southern, and even though Wilson Pickett (formerly of the Falcons) came to Memphis from Detroit, clearly the suggestion that this music had to happen in the South makes sense.

The basis of the blues/shouting style is traditional Afro-American blues style with a great deal of influence coming from older blues musicians such as Muddy Waters, Bessie Smith, Ethel Waters, and B. B. King. However, the difference is in aggressive and shouting emotional exuberance. Also, the backup instrumentals are solid renditions, often employing expanded musical ensembles. Most of the significant compositions from this group of musicians came in the mid- to late 1960s, but it was a very hot style for the time. The styles of many of these musicians have continued to influence others in the 1970s and 1980s.

Of course, the major influences on these particular singers were blues and gospel. All of them were trained in the church, as illustrated by their singing styles. The gospel tradition is fundamentally a preaching style and therefore the singing technique is both emotional and physical in flavor. Words are often pushed out of the throat and extramusical utterances such as "Amen" are frequently a part of the informal lyrics. There is also a good deal of call and response in the music.

Also, many of the singers being discussed were influenced by Ray Charles and Little Richard. (Otis Redding was a Little Richard imitator, a shouter, at the beginning of his career.) The call-and-response pattern set up by Ray Charles in "What'd I Say?" was often imitated in Atlantic sound music (it was originally recorded by Atlantic, but the influence of Jerry Wexler caused some people to call it the Wexler sound). Obviously, it would later be called the Memphis sound. Interestingly, Wexler was one of Phil Spector's supporters in New York City. Atlantic Records also quite often chose to record in the South rather than bringing people up north, for a more hometown type of production. Although the Memphis studios were very important to the production of these artists, Muscle Shoals, Alabama, was also important.

The Muscle Shoals area was also a part of Atlantic's southern operation and the Muscle Shoals Sound Rhythm Section served as the backup band for a variety of performers, including Aretha Franklin, Wilson Pickett, Percy Sledge, Paul Simon, the Staple Singers, Sam and Dave, Cher, King Curtis, Bob Seger, and Eddie Rabbit. Rod Stewart and the Rolling Stones have recorded at the Muscle Shoals Sound Studios. Individuals from that illustrious group of studio musicians have even produced such artists as Lynyrd Skynyrd, Canned Heat, Bob Dylan, Joan Baez, and Dire Straits.

Aretha Franklin   *(Photo by Arista Records; used by permission of Ginny Cartmell and Creem Magazine Archives)*

Although it is debatable, some have suggested that soul music really died at the end of the 1960s, analogous to what happened to the hippie movement. Even though there is no question that the soul/blues/shouting/gospel tradition continued in the funk, rap, and fusion music of the 1970s and the 1980s, the pure style of soul as performed by these musicians undoubtedly did weaken toward the end of the 1960s. One significant reason for the change in attitude was the death of Martin Luther King, Jr., in 1968.

Martin Luther King, Jr., was an extremely important symbol and source of inspiration for the civil rights movement, a fairly optimistic and nonviolent phenomenon up until the 1967 Watts riots. Although debatable, it is a valid generalization that King's death changed the feeling of the civil rights workers.

The process of change continued, but it became bureaucratized. The particular kind of black music that represented the civil rights movement probably changed with it. As a stylized form of communication concerning itself with some relevant issues, the pure form of its expression was probably over by the 1970s.

Representative Musicians

Samuel Moore (from Miami) and David Prater (from Ocilla, Georgia) made up an extremely popular black vocal duo. In terms of major success their banner years were from 1966 to 1968; their biggest hit was "Soul Man" in 1967 (number one R & B and number two pop). They moved to Stax in Memphis in 1965 and were effectively billed as a soul duo.

In the center of this particular category—gospel and soul—is Percy Sledge (born in 1941 in Leighton, Alabama). Another Atlantic/Stax singer, he had his greatest success with "When a Man Loves a Woman" in 1966. His warm and emotive style was slightly gospel-oriented, especially in the plaintive quality of the singing. His career tapered off in the mid-1970s.

Wilson Pickett was born in 1941 in Alabama, but as a teenager, moved to Detroit. His first musical experiences were with a gospel group called the Violinaires, with whom he performed in churches. In 1959 he joined the Falcons, a rhythm and blues group with whom he had some success; "I Found a Love" was a hit record in 1962. He had two solo hits in 1963 and signed with Atlantic Records in 1964. In 1965, after some unsuccessful work in New York, Jerry Wexler took him to Memphis where he recorded "In the Midnight Hour" (co-written by Pickett and Steve Cropper). The recording was done with Booker T. and the MGs (the Stax house band). Pickett then had a succession of hits through the early 1970s, recording in both Memphis and Muscle Shoals. His singing style is very strong and somewhat rough in texture.

Aretha Franklin is the most "gospel" of the musicians mentioned in this chapter and is certainly the best female performer from a technical point of view. One is tempted to speculate what she would have sounded like had she recorded for Motown, but appropriately for her style she recorded for the Atlantic complex, both in Muscle Shoals and in New York, with a band led by King Curtis. By 1968 Aretha Franklin was known as "Lady Soul" and her connection to the civil rights and Black Power movements was important.

Aretha was born in 1942 in Memphis, where her father, Rev. C. L. Franklin, was a nationally known gospel singer. Aretha grew up in the gospel circuit, both traveling and at her father's church in Detroit. As a teenager she knew many gospel singers, including Mahalia Jackson and Sam Cooke. In 1959 she moved to New York to sing for Columbia Records, where she had only minor success in the rhythm and blues market. Her only real hit was in 1961 with "Rock-A-Bye Your Baby with a Dixie Melody," an old Al Jolson tune. In 1966 she signed with Atlantic and the ever-present Jerry Wexler took her back to the South. Her first session, in 1967, produced "I Never Loved a Man (The Way I Love You)," a phenomenal

James Brown   *(Photo by Polydor Records; used by permission of Ginny Cartmell and Creem Magazine Archives)*

success. In 1967 "Respect" was number one on both charts and earned her a place as a spokesperson for the Black Power movement. She had numerous successful records through the mid-1970s with a clearly gospel-oriented style, and she moved in the direction of pop music in the 1970s and 1980s, for instance from late 1985, "Who's Zooming Who?"

Aretha did both R & B and pop material. She also co-wrote a number of her songs and was one of the more often imitated black female singers. Although her career has not been remarkably successful in recent years, she still commands instant respect. She was a definite asset to the Atlantic group and is the best example of female gospel/soul of the late 1960s.

Otis Redding was born in 1941 in Dawson, Georgia. He began his career as a

Little Richard imitator and had undistinguished success with a few small recordings such as "Shout Bamalama," which was released by a Los Angeles independent label in 1960. He was a chauffeur for Johnny Jenkins and the Pinetoppers on the southern circuit, starting in 1962. It was with Jenkins that he went for an audition at Stax, which ultimately put out one of his two songs, "These Arms of Mine." He went on to have numerous hits between 1965 and 1967, many of which he wrote. With his strong, impassioned performance style he became one of the most popular musicians of his time; he and James Brown were two of the most popular black entertainers of the mid-1960s.

Redding appeared at the Monterey Pop Festival in 1967 and was introduced to white audiences; he certainly would have had great success as a result of the blues revival, which was beginning at that time. However, in 1967 Otis Redding and his band, the Bar-Kays (from the Memphis studios), were killed in a plane crash in Wisconsin. The last recording they did, "The Dock of the Bay," went to number one on both charts after they died.

Many have considered his album *Dictionary of Soul* to be the finest example of Memphis sound music of that era. His performance style was reminiscent of older blues musicians, but it had the vibrancy of 1960s gospel/soul. Like James Brown, Otis Redding was a very physical and moving performer and his lyrics spoke directly to the issues of that type of music. Sometimes his style was reflective, and sometimes it was powerhouse gospel, preaching and screaming, yet mellow at the same time. Otis Redding was probably one of the finest singers of all time, and it is a great tragedy that he did not live long enough to enjoy that deserved success, and to evolve naturally.

James Brown claims he was born in Georgia in 1933. He was involved in gospel singing early and had his first professional experiences with gospel groups — first the Swanees, then the Famous Flames. With the Flames he made a record called "Please, Please, Please" in 1956, for Federal Records, a subsidiary of King. In 1958 they had a national hit with "Try Me." In the last part of the 1950s, James Brown put together, with help, the James Brown Revue, which included a large stage band (the JBs), the Flames, and opening acts. The entire show was dynamic, and at the center was James Brown, gyrating and doing splits. As a result, James Brown became known as the hardest working performer in the music business.

By 1965 he had obtained complete control over his productions because of his notoriety and success, now with King Records (the parent company). "Papa's Got a Brand New Bag" was released in 1965 and completely substantiated his claim to fame. The gospel/call-and-response/riff-oriented use of a full horn section created a thoroughly polished, yet powerful sound. From 1965 to 1968 James Brown had phenomenal success and impact, ultimately being called the Godfather of Superheavy Funk, among other things. His harsh voice, guttural screaming, and emotive style created a sound that was absolutely distinctive. He had plenty of imitators. The instrumental quality of his music featured a tightly choked guitar style, in which the guitar is used as a rhythmic instrument; a very staccato bass line (early funk); horns used to play riffs (usually slightly behind the beat or offbeat in a backbeat fashion); and a generally percussive ensemble. African roots are very clear in James Brown's music, especially in the polyrhythmic character of the entire texture. His R & B (called soul) album, *The James Brown Show Live at the Apollo*, stayed on *Billboard's* charts for 66 weeks, climbing as high as number two.

In the late 1960s Brown became an informal spokesman for the Black Power movement, especially with his 1968 song "Say It Loud—I'm Black and I'm Proud." He is still on the scene today and is one of the few rock musicians who can return periodically with massive impact. As a clear example of gospel/soul he is also interesting because he was connected with neither Motown nor Atlantic.

MOTOWN

As a prelude to this next section, we should define *doo-wop*. Although the style of doo-wop is part of the evolution of Motown, the examples we will give are from a diversity of groups. Doo-wop describes the background vocal groups that traditionally accompanied lead singers. The name comes from two nonsense words that might have been sung by these backing groups of the 1950s and 1960s. Examples of doo-wop groups are the Platters ("Only You" and "My Prayer"), Frankie Lymon ("Why Do Fools Fall in Love"), the Five Satins ("In the Still of the Night"), the Penguins ("Earth Angel"), and the Monotones ("The Book of Love").

The Motown (short for Motor Town) sound is to rock what the Nashville sound is to country music, in the sense that a very specific set of characteristics makes up each type of music. Also, it is technically so well done that its success ratio is unparalleled in pop music statistics. Of the 535 singles put out by the Motown complex between 1960 and 1970, 357 made the charts—a success rate of 67 percent. (The average record company charts 10 percent of its releases.) One of the reasons for this success ratio was painstaking work and selective releases; another major reason was Berry Gordy, Jr.

Berry Gordy, Jr., was born in Detroit in 1929. In his late teenage years he was a professional boxer; he joined the army in 1951. In 1953 he returned to Detroit to open a record store called the 3-D Record Mart, which closed in 1955. Gordy then went to work on the Ford assembly line, but he quit in 1957 to work on writing songs. In 1957 he co-produced and co-wrote a song for Jackie Wilson, an important singer of the time, called "Reet Petite." Although this song was basically a parody of the Elvis style, it caused enough sales that he was able to do further production work. Later the same year he did "Lonely Teardrops," which was number one on the R & B charts and on the top ten pop chart.

It is important to understand the Motown sound as the creation and product of the maniacal drive of Berry Gordy, Jr.—that is not meant as a criticism. Berry Gordy had a vision to create a particular type of music. He also had a thorough understanding of what would sell and went to meticulous pains to obtain the precise results he wanted. In 1958 he established a publishing company, Jobete, using the first two letters of his three children's names. Of course, this was substantially before he had anything to publish; but this publishing company is obviously quite significant now for its holdings. He started his first record company, Tamla, in 1959, and Motown in 1960. By 1962 he had purchased many of the smaller subsidiaries in Detroit, and his business holdings represented a monopoly called the Motown complex.

An important hit for Gordy was "You Got What It Takes" (1960), by Mary Johnson for United Artists. On this particular tune, he illustrated excellent production sense in the solid instrumental work and crystal clear recording. Probably the trademark of the Motown sound was its slick production work and music that appealed to a crossover market influenced quite heavily by white pop music.

Gordy started discovering groups quite early in his career — groups he would mold to fit the type of sound he wanted. He discovered the Miracles (with Smokey Robinson) in 1958, followed by the Satintones (1960), Marvellettes (1960), Supremes (1961), Marvin Gaye (1961), Temptations (1961), Contours (1961), Martha and the Vandellas (1962), Spinners (1963), and Four Tops (1963). These were the vintage acts of Motown, although there were many more, including Little Stevie Wonder, Gladys Knight and the Pips, Jimmy Ruffin, Jr. Walker, Originals, Jackson 5, Commodores, Lionel Richie, Grover Washington, and the Fifth Dimension. Pat Boone, Sammy Davis, Jr., Jose Feliciano, and Bobby Darin recorded for Berry Gordy–owned companies in the 1970s. When one simply looks at the star list that has grown through Motown, one realizes that a good bit of rock history is contained within it.

Up until the early 1960s, there were several locations in the United States where recordings of the types of songs that would ultimately become the Motown trademark — crossover hits with black artists doing white-influenced music — were made. However, by the early 1960s the only real black-owned competitor to the growing monopoly in Detroit was Vee-Jay Records in Chicago. Established in 1953, this record company was responsible for gospel recordings, blues, and doo-wop (El Dorados, and the Dells, for instance). As a black-owned company, it had some ideas similar to Motown; however, Vee-Jay Records closed in bankruptcy in 1965.

There were several other important record companies in Chicago, and were it not for the career of Berry Gordy, Jr., they might very well have been the big story told here. However, the efforts of ABC with the Impressions ("For Your Precious Love," 1958); Columbia (Okeh) with Curtis Mayfield, Billy Butler, Major Lance, and others; and Chess, first with blues artists, and then in the mid-1960s with a Motown-influenced concept were important to Chicago, but not as significant as Motown. Mary Wells, who recorded first in Chicago, and many others, including some Vee-Jay Records artists, moved to Motown because that was where it was happening in black music in the mid-1960s.

There are several distinctive qualities to Motown sound music. First, it does not have the hard edge of Aretha Franklin or James Brown; it is clearly different from Memphis music. The rhythm section, the Funk Brothers, provide a rhythmic background that is full and less clipped than other styles; the sound is relatively smooth and light in texture. However, the overdubbing and harmonic mix are full in texture. The beat is always slightly behind, which creates an incipient funk sound that is, relatively speaking, quite relaxed. There is a clear desire to communicate the words of the song in such a way that they are easily understandable, with a lyrical or melodic quality that is pop in orientation. Lastly, fewer blues tunes are used, and many songs use chord progressions based on white forms (see analysis of "Baby Love" in the appendix).

Motown music was technically precise and followed a reasonably homogeneous pattern. By 1962 Berry Gordy had put together the writing team of Lamont Dozier and Eddie and Brian Holland (known as H-D-H), probably one of the most important teams of writers in popular music history. They developed a very close relationship and a clear understanding of what types of lyrics would work for the stable of musicians available, and for the Motown philosophy.

The Motortown Revue, a traveling group of Motown stars, started in 1962. Like the Grand Ole Opry, they presented long evenings of entertainment with as many as forty-five performers. The most obvious indication of the importance of this concept at the time was the number of companies that started similar groups. During the 1960s the Motown Revue became the meeting place for black people, and in the late 1960s an extension of the Black Power movement. Interestingly, by the late 1960s, non-Motown black artists, like the Ronettes (of Phil Spector fame), and Cassius Clay, would also be associated with the Revue.

However, the single most important characteristic of Motown music was its technical perfection. Gordy established a policy of always listening to recordings on records rather than just on studio tapes. He was also personally involved in experimenting with the mix of a recording, the combination of the individual instrumental and vocal parts, and the adjustment of the sound quality of each. He would often make as many as twelve different recorded versions (all of them in record form), before making a decision. Out of all the songs recorded, very few would be released, and then only those that fit his perfectionist model of what would sell. He also used the sound quality of a car radio to determine at which points harmonic adjustments would be made. In other words, he matched his product to the consumer device over which it would most likely be heard, the car radio. All of these ideas became standard business practices by 1963.

As a part of the Motown Revue, Gordy trained all of his musicians in showmanship, musicianship, behavior, elocution, and etiquette. He taught them how to do everything as if they were a part of white society, because he fundamentally believed in integration for business reasons. Motown is a black-owned company, but it does have white employees in key leadership roles. One must remember that Berry Gordy, Jr., created a model for popular music production, but that the fundamental reason for his business was free enterprise. If there was any point at which black artists began to recoup some of the losses they sustained in the early history of rock and roll, it was certainly with the Motown complex.

Ultimately, many of the important artists, such as the Jackson 5, would leave Motown for artistic and financial autonomy. Berry Gordy sometimes got what he

Diana Ross   *(Photo by Barry Rankin, Saginaw, Michigan)*

wanted through authoritarian means, and the Motown model at times left little room for experimentation. However, the initial purpose of its creation was to develop a business, and for that Berry Gordy is one of the most important men in rock history. He also set a standard for the creation of a black popular music (especially for crossover success), and the level of technical recording quality of all pop music was substantially raised as a result of his efforts.

The Temptations *(Photo by Gordy Records; used by permission of Ginny Cartmell and Creem Magazine Archives)*

Representative Musicians

Lloyd Price was not a Motown artist but is discussed here because of his influence on the style. He was born in 1934 in New Orleans and first came to prominence in 1952 with an R & B hit, "Lawdy Miss Clawdy." In 1957 he returned from the Korean War to begin recording mainstream pop tunes in a much smoother singing style. The song "Personality" exemplifies this combination of R & B, the use of a riff horn section, and a smooth singing style. Similarly, Sam Cooke (discussed in chapter seven) had an influence on the Motown sound—especially his recorded material. Sam's live performances tended to be R & B–oriented, but most of his recorded works feature a very smooth vocal style (white pop). For instance, his "Twistin' the Night Away" uses a Ray Charles–type horn introduction and a full textured harmonic mix. His style in general resembles early Motown.

The Four Tops   *(Photo by ABC Records; used by permission of Ginny Cartmell and Creem Magazine Archives)*

The Satintones was Berry Gordy's first group. They released the first Tamla Record with "Motor City" on one side and "Going to the Hop" on the other. They also did the first records for Motown. Essentially a doo-wop band with accompaniment, their music is characterized by an extremely smooth sound (hence the name), and a relatively polished production style for the time.

The Miracles were discovered by Berry Gordy in 1958 at an audition. Their 1960 recording "Shop Around" established the group and Motown Records at the same time (number one R & B, number two pop). Smokey Robinson, a key member of the group until 1972, wrote many of their songs, as well as songs for other important Motown groups. His material continues to be covered today. The Miracles were probably the first significant group in the Motown complex, and their music completely represents the stylistic characteristics of the company.

Mary Wells, born in Detroit in 1943, was one of Motown's first stars. Her debut single, "Bye Bye Baby," was successful on the R & B charts in 1960. In 1962 she began singing Smokey Robinson's material and her style became more pop-oriented. Her biggest hit was in 1964 with "My Guy" (number one pop).

The Marvelettes actually resembled the traditional girl group sound because there was no obvious leader; it was a vocal ensemble. They enjoyed a successful career starting with their first record in 1960, "Please, Mr. Postman," which

Stevie Wonder   *(Used by permission of Ginny Cartmell and Creem Magazine Archives)*

stayed on the charts for six months. Although their career essentially ended in 1968, the pattern of their hit songs followed the evolution of the company. They did primarily R & B tunes until 1966, when Smokey Robinson started writing for them. The biggest mistake of their career is that they turned down "Baby Love."

The Supremes may well be the big story of Motown, at least in the 1960s. From 1964 to 1970, they had ten number one singles. They were fully trained and produced by the entire Motown establishment, and their songs are perfect exam-

Lionel Richie   *(Used by permission of Ginny Cartmell and Creem Magazine Archives)*

ples of the Motown style. Several of their more important compositions are "Stop! In the Name of Love" (1965), with its huge texture, overdubbed vocal sound, echo effects, and subdued instrumental texture; "You Can't Hurry Love" from 1966, also illustrates the style well, as does "Baby Love" from 1964, a pure pop single (see appendix for analysis).

Marvin Gaye had a long and illustrious career until his death in 1984. An organist and church singer, he joined doo-wop organizations in Washington, DC, in the mid-1950s. He was part of a backup band called the Moonglows. In the course of his travels, he was signed by Gordy in 1961 and became a session drummer for the Miracles. Starting in 1962 and continuing through 1968, he had a string of hits. His style was quite similar to Sam Cooke's. For instance, "How Sweet It Is" (1964) was a swing tune, but smooth and sensual in style. His style changed quite demonstrably in 1971, when he gained artistic control in making his records. He and Stevie Wonder started the exodus from Motown's control, although Marvin Gaye remained with Motown Records until 1982, when he changed to Columbia. He also did some controversial songs, such as "Sexual Healing."

The Temptations signed with Motown in 1960 (or at least some of the members did); although at that time they were known as the Primes. Interestingly, they were an important influence on the Supremes, who had originally called themselves the Primettes. The members of the Temptations actually came from a variety of other vocal groups in Detroit. Starting in 1964, they hit the charts with single after single produced with the Motown group. For instance, "The Way You Do" in 1964, although really R & B–oriented with a strong backbeat, was a popular success (number eleven pop). Their basic sound is fairly strong, but it was with softer tunes like "My Girl" that they had the most success. Although not the original group, the Temptations still toured regularly in the mid-1980s.

The Contours was a significant Motown group from 1962 to 1965. They did primarily dance tunes, for instance, "Can You Jerk Like Me?" in 1965. Their last hit, a ballad, was in 1967—"It's So Hard Being a Loser."

Martha and the Vandellas developed around Martha Reeves, who was hired by Motown in 1960 as a secretary to A & R executive Mickey Stevenson. In typical Motown fashion, Martha and her singing group did backup vocal work for other musicians. In 1962 they cut a single, but it was "Heat Wave" in 1963 that set them up for a career. Unfortunately, they were only significant until 1967; their last two singles that year were "Honey Chile" and "Jimmy Mack." "Jimmy Mack" was really a gospel/shouting style and quite far from the original "Heat Wave," which was prototypical early Motown sound.

The Spinners was an interesting group in the Motown stable. Although they had some successes, things did not happen for them as much in the 1960s as in the 1970s. The Spinners was a male vocal ensemble put together by Harvey Fuqua of Tri-Phi Records. When Tri-Phi was swallowed up by Motown, the Spinners and the Four Tops came with the deal. It is questionable why they were not more successful, but most sources indicate that they were not considered a major act at Motown. Their success in the 1970s would suggest that this was a bad decision.

The Four Tops was a vintage Motown act, with the company from 1963 to 1972, after which they recorded for ABC/Dunhill. They had numerous hits during their time at Motown, including "Baby I Need Your Loving" (1963), "I Can't Help Myself" (1965), "Reach Out, I'll Be There" (1966), and "Standing in the Shadows of Love" (1967). Basically a smooth vocal group, they could occasionally sound like the Atlantic groups, for instance, on "I Can't Help Myself." Levi Stubbs has had massive impact on other singers, and the Four Tops is still made up of the original members.

Little Stevie Wonder was born in 1950 in Saginaw, Michigan, and introduced to Berry Gordy in 1960. The multi-instrumentalist and singer ultimately had a phenomenal teenage career, which continues unabated today. He started as a Ray Charles imitator, and in many ways he never really fit the mold of a Motown artist, except for the part about making money. From his first major hit, "Fingertips (Part 2)," through the mid-1960s, he did mostly upbeat R & B songs. However, from 1966 on, with Bob Dylan's "Blowin' in the Wind," he created a different type of song. As he matured to adulthood, he began to do more tunes of an experimental nature. The most interesting thing about the development of Wonder's career is that it seems to move in several directions at once. He is both experimental and commercial at the same time. For instance, his 1972 hit "You Are the Sunshine of My Life" was a number one pop hit, number three R & B, and yet contains some very experimental instrumental work. The best way to describe Stevie Wonder, who in 1971 was the first Motown artist to gain autonomy over his work, is that he is a multitalented individual who represented his recording company very well, but did it in a diversified manner.

Gladys Knight and the Pips, originally from Atlanta, Georgia, is a family act. They signed with Motown in the mid-1960s after being a guest act in the Motown Revue. They had several major hits in the late 1960s and early 1970s, but they have had much greater success since leaving Motown. Their recordings from 1973 to 1974 represent their best work.

The list of Motown artists could go on forever, but we will mention just a few more. The Jackson 5 recorded for Motown starting in 1969 and left in 1975, although Jermaine Jackson remained with the Motown label. The Isley Brothers recorded for Tamla from 1965 to 1967. The Commodores signed with Motown in 1971, and Lionel Richie, whose career in the 1980s was phenomenal, stayed with Motown. A last interesting case in point is Rick James. He originally signed with Motown in the late 1960s with a band named Mynah Birds; the band consisted of Rick James, Neil Young and Bruce Palmer of Buffalo Springfield, and Goldy McJohn of Steppenwolf. That band did not make it, so Rick James went out on the road. In 1978, as the king of punk/funk, he started putting out hit records — with Motown.

SUMMARY

In this brief exposition we have examined the impact of Phil Spector, discussed some significant instrumental groups, illustrated the importance of Memphis, Muscle Shoals, and gospel/soul singers, and shown conclusively that the Motown recording monopoly deserves credit for being the capital of black music. We have also tried to stimulate the reader into listening more intently to music of this era in order to discover its diversity. There is a substantial difference between the sound of Motown and that of, say, James Brown. While we may rudely lump all soul music together, there is a wide variety to it, and the most fundamental way to determine that is to examine the musical characteristics on a song-by-song basis, and then make our comparisons.

Of course, all of the music covered in this chapter ultimately has influence. The later chapter on jazz/rock, funk, and disco develops directly out of the discussions of this chapter. Although the clarity of the Motown style and 1960s James Brown are now history, there can be little doubt about their impact. And even though rock purists may lament the loss of these styles so unfettered with complete crassness, it was precisely the technique and care used to create these earlier styles that allowed for the technical mastery of today's music.

LISTENING

Kennedy's inaugural address and speeches by Martin Luther King, Jr., and Muhammad Ali.

———— , *The Motown Story: Anthology*

James Brown, *The James Brown Story*

Booker T. and the MGs, *The Best of Booker T. and the MGs*

Wilson Pickett, *Wilson Pickett's Greatest Hits*

Smokey Robinson, *Smokey Robinson*

Diana Ross, *Diana Ross and the Supremes*

Temptations, *Temptations*

Stevie Wonder, *Stevie Wonder's Greatest Hits*

Rick James, *Glow*

Lionel Richie, *Can't Slow Down*

Otis Redding, *Best*

CHAPTER 9

THE BEATLES

No book on rock and roll would be complete without a major discussion of the Beatles, for a number of reasons, although it is confusing that the most significant rock influence from the 1960s would be from England. Those tumultuous times had little effect on the Beatles themselves; in fact, they helped to produce some of the changes in the musical world of the 1960s. The Beatles is perhaps the only significant rock group whose entire history falls within that decade, even though, of course, it began in the late 1950s.

Our discussion of the Beatles will have two parts: biography and musical analysis. For the sake of brevity we will not repeat our previous analyses of stage techniques, marketing, and media expansion. For most of the groups from the 1960s on, such information is readily available either in books or magazines or as common knowledge.

BIOGRAPHY

John Lennon (1940–1980) was born in Liverpool, England. His father, Fred, was employed on ships and had very little to do with his wife and son. John's mother, Julia, did not in fact raise him; it was his Aunt Mimi who was given that task. His mother came into his life at various points; according to Hunter Davies[1] she was a bad influence.

Lennon was not good at school, although he clearly had intelligence. He was a rebel and a tough kid, and he dressed and acted like a Teddy boy, a British hoodlum. He was a juvenile delinquent, to put it in American terms. When he attended Quarry Bank High School in 1952, he quickly developed an unfavorable reputation.

It is important to realize that Lennon's life was a sad one. His father was nonexistent; his mother gave him up; and his Aunt Mimi's husband, George, died when Lennon was thirteen. He was in trouble at school, and although he was good at art, his artistic endeavors were not establishment-oriented. Although he ultimately went to art school, even that was not very satisfying. The only thing that ever led to anything concrete came out of a student gang he formed at Quarry High.

This group became musical only incidentally. Although it eventually included Paul McCartney and George Harrison, the initial group was simply a bunch of tough kids who hung around together. The interesting point, of course, is how they became musical, an event that occurred in the first part of 1956. The musicality of the Quarrymen could be summed up in one word: primitive. Most of their music was imitative and of low quality. The musical style they imitated was called *skiffle.*

Skiffle has a fairly interesting history (see *Skiffle* by Brian Bird). The form derived from the United States as a combination of early rent-party music (described in chapter three), country rhythm bands, Dixieland, and dance bands. Skiffle was "discovered" in England in the late 1940s and still thrives as a country kind of sound. It requires guitars, a bass instrument, miscellaneous percussion — for instance (a washboard), and singing. The best analogy in the United States would be a jug band, which is normally associated with country and/or folk music. At best, skiffle is simple music; at worst, it is just noise. What the Quarrymen produced would probably be classified near the bottom end of the spectrum.

The significance of skiffle can be traced through the early hits of the Beatles, although it can be heard primarily in the instrumental background. It has a continuous beat and is related only slightly to rock and roll. However, even a skiffle background can be used in back of a rock lyric. Many of the original Beatle tunes of the early era are in fact skiffle songs, and even the cover records of American rock

---

[1] This biography relies rather heavily on information from the Hunter Davies biography. One might wish to consult Brian Epstein's *A Cellarful of Noise* or John Lennon's *Lennon Remembers*. For useful information on analysis of their music, one could use Wilfred Meller's *Twilight of the Gods: The Beatles in Retrospect* (New York: Viking Press, 1974).

and roll classics have a very different instrumental backing. Although this point is seldom made about English rock, there can be little doubt that skiffle was important, and its influence is one of the typically English characteristics — as opposed to the American ones — of rock.

The Quarrymen were of course inconsequential. While Elvis Presley was a star, the Beatles were still school kids (in 1956 John Lennon was sixteen and Paul McCartney was fourteen), and their music was no more than beating on garbage can lids.

James Paul McCartney was born in Liverpool in 1942, the first son of Jim and Mary McCartney. Their second son, Michael, was born in 1944. McCartney had a relatively sanguine childhood and seems to have had a close relationship with both his father and mother. As his parents were both musical, he learned some of his musicality at home. In particular, his father was in a dance band and at several times did actually assist Paul and John. Paul's mother died when he was fourteen, and this most certainly had an effect on him.

McCartney was good at school, achieving higher academic success than the other Beatles. He was a prolific writer, and at the age of eleven he won an essay contest. He always had an interest in art and certainly could have become a professional artist. However, his mother's death seemed to turn him away from normal existence. His family continued to take care of the boys, but clearly things were rougher for them after the loss of their mother. His father bought him a guitar, and he spent much of his time learning to play it and experimenting. It was at this time that he became interested in American pop music, particularly in Elvis Presley. In the next two years music became a dominant force in McCartney's life.

The Beatles rose to musical fame from relatively austere beginnings. None of them was a child genius, nor did they have formal training. Of all of them, McCartney probably had the most help in music, primarily through his father. But to say he was a phenomenal musician technically would be to overstate the issue. He experimented with very simple chord changes (progressions). It took him months to figure out the chord progressions of tunes that other musicians would grasp in fifteen minutes. His eventual fame probably came from his lyrics, his singing style, and his energy.

George Harrison, born in 1943 to Harold and Louise Harrison, was the youngest of four children. His family situation was happy and normal, and he grew to be an independent child. Davies's *The Beatles* points out that Harrison's mother was very important in his life because she was so supportive of whatever her children wanted to do. However, it was not until Harrison was fourteen that he showed any real interest in music.

In 1956 or 1957 he became interested in skiffle as an activity; the most important artist to him was Lonnie Donegan, who led a skiffle band. Again, the importance of skiffle was paramount as it led Harrison to develop some real talent in picking out tunes and in playing relatively complicated figures on the guitar. He started playing guitar at the same time as his older brother, Peter, and by the time he met Paul McCartney at the Liverpool Institute, he was an accomplished player, at least by comparison to McCartney. He eventually joined the Quarrymen in 1958, primarily because he was a better instrumentalist than either McCartney or Lennon. Over the years, Harrison made a lasting contribution to the Beatles from a technical perspective. Although he did not have the impact or visibility of McCartney and Lennon, many of the songs were in fact written around some chord change or melody he initially inspired.

The development of the Beatles from 1958 to 1962 is fascinating because we would be hard pressed to predict their achievement of any kind of success. They were basically a guitar group, and they remained skiffle-oriented. They added a drummer, Pete Best, who was important in establishing the group as a Liverpool institution. Best's mother ran a club called the Casbah, and this location became their home base.

They also went through a number of different musicians and different names for the group. Johnny and the Moondogs and the Silver Beatles were the most lasting, but there were many others. They were in the process of evolving from a skiffle band to a rock and roll band (English style). A concert tour of Scotland was frankly a failure, but they did several stints in Hamburg, Germany, in the early 1960s.

The year 1962 was important for the Beatles, as they had finally come to call themselves. Although they were still not the most important group in England, they had become quite competitive. They met their Colonel Tom Parker, Brian Epstein, during the last part of 1961; in 1962 they became associated with George Martin, who became their producer. In the late summer of 1962 they replaced Best with Ringo Starr, who at that time was more popular than the other three put together.

Ringo Starr was born in 1940 as Richard Starkey. His parents were divorced when he was three years old, and his mother remarried in 1953. His early life was rather tragic in that he had two major illnesses, both of which put him in the hospital for long periods. By his own admission he was very slow in school and in fact, could not read or write until he was eight or nine. To this day he has trouble with communication. He supposedly learned to play percussion instruments during his second hospital stay as a teenager. He rose to musical prominence by the time he was twenty-one, first through skiffle and then through pop music. Although he had no association with the Beatles, he was very popular by the time he finally joined them in 1962. In fact, some chroniclers have indicated that Starr was much more significant than the Beatles until 1962. His drumming style, although it was not flashy, was apparently right for the Beatles at that time.

By the fall of 1962 the Beatles were the center of British rock and had firmly established their particular style. They did a concert with Little Richard in October 1962, produced by Brian Epstein. Beatle mania was about to occur, if for a time only in England.

The years from 1962 to 1969 are probably best covered by the development of their music. However, it is important to realize that the Beatles were in their early twenties (George was nineteen) when they became successful. They were far from being mature individuals, psychologically or musically, and their career growth coincided with their personal growth. In some senses, their careers hindered their growth as people and in some ways it forced them to mature. Ultimately, the breakup in 1969 undoubtedly had something to do with their development as individuals.

Their personal relationships with one another are interesting. Any musical group develops a group identification. The Beatles, like other groups in the making, literally lived with each other, even when they were still living at home. From 1956 until the mid-1960s Lennon and McCartney were inseparable, joined by Harrison in 1958. They spent a great deal of time with each other, even when they were not working on their music. However, they generated their musical identities by living them out with each other, long before the time when these identities would be successful performing techniques.

When they began playing engagements they did so as a group, traveling to and from the job together. They knew everything about each other, and as a result, they developed a sense of family. Even as the four of them began to marry and have separate family lives, they still remained the closest of friends. In fact, they were so close that their wives had difficulty breaking through to their husbands. Lennon's first marriage broke up, partially because of his inability to separate himself from the Beatles.

The Beatles began to develop an international reputation with "She Loves You." Before coming to the United States, they also put out songs like "I Want to Hold Your Hand" and "Please, Please Me." The first album released in the United States was *Meet the Beatles,* and by the end of 1963 they were quite successful here. (The style of these early tunes will be discussed later.) As a social phenomenon they were perhaps more interesting. They were foreigners, but it was precisely their foreignness that made them so captivating. They spoke with an obvious accent and their music was very different, even if it had certain structural similarities to American pop music. The lyrics of their songs fit the lyrical messages of the time. The songs were about girls, and in some ways, were really preteen songs in an English style. By this time they had perfected their stage routine, but they had yet to be very innovative.

In February 1964 they came to the United States for a brief and successful maiden voyage. They were on the "Ed Sullivan Show" and played at Carnegie Hall and in Washington, DC. They were an instantaneous national success. Some critics have said that the timing was just right and that musically they really were not much good. However, the combination of the clothes, the Beatle "mop," and the foreign image was extremely successful because it was so well done. The marketing techniques were sophisticated, but even in their early era, they were good at what they did. We can always take cheap shots at performers in earlier stages, criticizing their technique or the simplicity of their songs. However, we should remember that the Beatles were in their early twenties, they were trying to establish themselves, and they came from humble backgrounds. Had they not gone on to make such sweeping changes in the form, these criticisms might be valid. In view of the result, they are not. Even in "Twist and Shout" the Beatles proved themselves showmen, and their basic energy in performance was significant even at the beginning.

They quickly followed this success with the production of their first film, *A Hard Day's Night,* which kept their popularity high (along with many hit releases). The fact that the Beatles remained a British phenomenon was probably important in their tremendous popularity. Like Presley's stay in the army, it exuded a mystical quality for Americans. We could not touch the Beatles because they did not live here. Also important was the relative dearth of significant rock groups at that time. Although the Rolling Stones started in 1964, they were not to have a real impact until later (see chapter twelve).

During the summer of 1965 the Beatles returned to the United States for a second tour and were even more successful. The middle era of the Beatles really started after that tour, in which most of the concerts featured early tunes and a traditional Beatles look. Although they consciously avoided the comparison, they were certainly influenced by the rougher image of the Stones and Mick Jagger. *Help* was released in August, *Rubber Soul* in December, and *Revolver* in August 1966. These three albums are the most important releases of the middle era (1965–1966) and represent a slow change toward more complicated material. By this time the Beatles were maturing as a musical group, and clearly their interests and their message were becoming more profound.

They stopped touring in 1966, for several reasons. They were financially successful and did not need additional exposure. From this point on, they were strictly a studio and film group. The albums of the late period (*Sgt. Pepper's Lonely Hearts Club Band* in June 1967 through *Abbey Road* in October 1969) are true masterpieces in the history of rock. They illustrate a complexity of message and a profundity seldom found. The Beatles had gone full cycle by 1969, and their split was inevitable.

The breakup of the Beatles was undoubtedly caused by some of the following: (1) the end of group creativity, (2) a need for individual creativity, (3) a personality conflict, (4) family pressures, (5) legal complications, and (6) financial necessity. We can argue for any or all of these causes. The group had accomplished so much in the evolution of its style (perhaps more than any other rock group), it is conceivable that there was nothing left. Also, both Lennon and McCartney had individual creative needs, which were not necessarily compatible. They had produced most of the songs together as a team. Obviously, as they began to grow they also began to diverge. Their music during the 1970s illustrates a real difference, which probably existed before they split up.

Much has been made of the personality conflicts, and comments made after Lennon's death magnify the influence of Yoko Ono. However, this particular allegation seems less convincing. It is obvious that the Beatles would begin to develop individual differences. After all, they were thirty years old. Although

The Beatles *(Photo by Guy Greve. Used courtesy of Guy Greve, Bay City, Michigan)*

there was a need to establish independence, this in itself would not have been sufficient to dissolve the group.

Family pressures were very real. The fact that the Beatles developed different lifestyles is well documented. Certainly the pressures of their wives and growing families must have had something to do with breaking out on their own. Legal complications led to infighting, although we contend that this was incidental in comparison to the other factors.

Finances probably had more to do with it than anything else. As a result of their phenomenal seven-year career as a group, they were all rich. The tax structure in England was such that intelligent financial planning was necessary in order to cope with this new-found wealth. Both the implications of having so much money individually and some fighting over the proper share of royalties were significant factors in creating a split. Each Beatle related to his new stature in life differently, and money was certainly at the bottom of it. Success was sweet for these poor lads from Liverpool, but when they achieved great wealth, they each had a different way of handling it.

Life for the Beatles after 1969 has been diverse. McCartney has been very active, although at first he retired to the country. His group, Wings, was quite excellent in its own right, and although he has settled into a middle-of-the-road kind of rock, he continues to have many admirers. Lennon was most productive lyrically, in conjunction with his wife, Yoko Ono. He became the most progressive of the Beatles, and although at times reclusive, he remained creative until his death. The other two Beatles have been less active musically, although Harrison had a new album that was successful in 1981, *Somewhere in England.*

The life stories of the Beatles are fascinating, but even more fascinating is the fact that from these rather simple people came something terribly complex. None of them was a superb technician, although Harrison was probably the best player. McCartney has a beautiful voice; Starr seldom sang at all, for perhaps good reasons. They developed interesting lyrics and much has been said about the deep significance of the words in their music. However, for sheer technical reasons, there is little to suggest such phenomenal success. Certainly the presence of George Martin as producer and orchestrator was important, as they came up with one technical innovation after another. The marketing techniques were abundantly successful and the timing was right.

All the standard reasons are appropriate for explaining their success at the beginning. They were an unusual group at that time. However, like all great artists, they had to have something substantive for their success to continue. They were the first to be internationally famous *as a musical group,* as opposed to having one big star. The Beach Boys was another group famous in that era, but even it was identified with Brian Wilson in the early years. The Beatles had no sure-fire leader; they were all important.

MUSICAL STYLE

For our purposes, all the music before 1962 should be considered pre-Beatles. Although we will discuss that music it is really not terribly important, nor frankly was it very good. The Beatles can be defined musically in three fairly distinct periods: early Beatles, 1962 to 1964; middle Beatles, 1965 to 1966; and late Beatles, 1967 to 1969. There are not many rock groups that can be so easily classified. This developmental quality makes the Beatles slightly more interesting than other groups. Also, their stylistic periods reflect changes in the times; and although they were a British group, they do reflect changes in American attitudes.

Pre-Beatles

This period begins in 1956 with Lennon and the Quarrymen and extends through the first part of 1962, by which time the Beatles had achieved national prominence in England. This period can be defined as experimental, which is why we will not consider it part of their true musical style.

In 1956 they were little more than a teenage gang which occasionally beat on musical instruments instead of old ladies. They were heavily influenced by skiffle and were not capable of playing any different kinds of music. By the time Harrison joined the group in 1958, they probably had not progressed much and were essentially three guitarists who had fun making music. They were influenced by a number of musicians, but they were doing very poor imitations. By 1959 they began to pick up momentum, especially with Pete Best as their drummer in 1960 and the Casbah as a place to play. However, they were still just another group trying to establish a style.

From a musical perspective, the most important event for the Beatles was their experience in Hamburg, Germany, where they were put into competition with other European pop bands. The pop circuit in Europe is somewhat different from that in the United States. The demands on musical groups are more diverse, in that they need to play different styles in order to succeed. Also, Hamburg was different from Liverpool, if for no other reason than having a multilingual audience that was used to very loud, almost decadent types of music; the Beatles had to become stronger stage personalities in order to compete. Although there had been some demand for shouting songs in their formative years, by the time they reached Hamburg they had to develop a style that included loud rock and roll.

When they returned to England in 1962, after several trips to Germany, they were seasoned veterans (if not by age, by experience) and had developed a style. With the help of their manager and public relations, they came back to England as successes, and musically they were prepared to deliver.

Early Beatles

Early Beatles music had the following basic stylistic traits:

1. Simple lyrics
2. Simple background accompaniment
3. Rock sound from the 1950s
4. Simple drumbeat and rhythmic patterns
5. Simple bass lines
6. Domination by lead singer or unison singing.

The lyrics were basically rock lyrics from the 1950s with relatively little creativity.[2] The songs were primarily about boy-girl relationships on a platonic or nonphysical level. There were a few hard rock tunes, such as "A Hard Day's Night," but most of them were soft rock in medium tempo. Typical of rock music in the 1950s, the songs were fairly short, roughly the two- to three-minute attention span of young teenagers at that time.

The background accompaniment was well done but simple. However, because it was a little different from that heard in the United States, many people thought the Beatles were strange. The background had a continuous quality with even accents on all four beats. It was skiffle, basically just rhythmic changes with a few chord changes. Interestingly, most of the Beatles' hits were not rhythm and blues; at least they did not use the blues progression. In all the music in the early period there were continuous guitar chords, a simple bass line (McCartney was really learning to play the bass, and left-handed at that), and continuous four-beat drumming. Ringo's drumming style was pop and did not have the heaviness of rock drummers in the United States.

The Beatles, influenced by Presley, Little Richard, and many others, consciously copied particular traits and songs of other musicians, although they played these tunes with their own style. They used background vocals, mainly screams and woos, and they extensively sang in unison. When there was a lead singer, the other singers provided backgrounds and unison singing for support of the main line.

The rhythmic patterns were also fairly simple, with relatively little riff orientation. The Beatles did not use rhythmic figures to hold a song together but rather relied on the melody. In the early era, at least, they did not develop internal energy through musical devices but rather through stage presence and the "Beatles look."

The bass patterns were pop-oriented and rather simple. Although McCartney would eventually become a competent bass player, his orientation was really toward singing and melody. This interest did not seem to transfer to his bass playing, where he relied mainly on the primary or tonic note of the chord. However, there probably was a lack of models at that time, as the bass line concept had not been developed in rock and roll in the late 1950s.

The lead singer was all-important in early Beatles music, and the two main lead singers, McCartney and Lennon, developed different singing personalities. McCartney was the lyrical and beautiful singer; Lennon was more of a shouter and a strong singer.

One last important thing about the early music is that the Beatles played songs that had little relationship to each other, except that many of them said the same thing. In their albums of this period the songs were each separate and there was no

---

[2] We are overgeneralizing in this section on the Beatles, implying that their early music was simple. In comparison to the times, they did quite a number of things that were highly experimental — they used blues variants and blues singing style in songs that did not use the blues progression; they included unusual instruments; and they used changing accent patterns. However, by comparison to their later music, the music of the pre-Beatles and early Beatles periods was simple.

real logic to the combinations. In later eras they would begin to make statements with their selections; in the early era they just sang songs. Fortunately, they were successful and pleasant songs.

Middle Beatles

The basic stylistic characteristics of the middle Beatles period included the following:

1. Poetically more complex lyrics
2. Symbolic lyrics
3. More creative music
4. Universal point of view
5. Sometimes critical words
6. Growing dissension among group members
7. More guitar-oriented and less percussive
8. Folklike
9. More complicated guitar sounds and electronics
10. More subjects in musical lyrics
11. Better background accompaniment.

The Beatles really came into their own during the middle period, which began after their fame in the United States. It is hard to imagine that a group could come so far in two or three years, but it must be understood that it was a world-famous group just three years after it had reached some prominence in its own city. By 1965 the Beatles were already wealthy and had at their disposal a number of support mechanisms not previously used by rock groups. Electronics, technology, and studio techniques were advancing at a very rapid rate in the mid-1960s, and the Beatles had the resources to tap into them. Thus they could make rapid changes, and they did so. This was a period of experimentation for them, but they were experimenting from the top and that makes a difference.

The first three style characteristics can be illustrated by any song from this era, for example, "Help," "Day Tripper," or "Nowhere Man." The poetry was more complex, the specific words acted as symbols for larger ideas—which is a basic definition of good poetry. The music was more creative in this period because it did not rely on proven models but rather used new textures. Also, it was aimed at an older audience; it was no longer preteen music.

The music began to take on a universal perspective; that is, it aimed at the world rather than just England or America. Most important was the tendency for the lyrics to be occasionally critical of some institution or segment of society.

"Taxman" by George Harrison is a good example of that development. From careful listening we could discover many nasty slurs about various topics, which illustrate the point that the Beatles saw themselves as commentators on the human condition and that their music began to contain true messages.

Their last English tour was in December 1965, and their last concert was in May 1966. Their last tour in America was in August 1966, which turned out to be their last public concert. The reasons for the cessation of public activity are analogous to their reasons for breaking up the group three years later: (1) They were doing the same act over and over, which became boring; (2) they were incapable of using as many effects and extra instruments as they wanted; (3) performing was becoming dangerous; (4) generally, touring was unpleasant; (5) although touring was financially lucrative, it was not as lucrative as other activities; and (6) they were beginning to have personality conflicts (although they had not admitted it).

Right after they stopped touring, the group began to splinter. Harrison went with his wife to India. He studied the sitar, a north Indian string instrument, which he ultimately used in subsequent Beatles records. John Lennon took a part in the film *How I Won the War.* Paul McCartney went to Africa, and Ringo Starr stayed home. Harrison and Lennon were most dedicated to their individual roles, and McCartney was probably the most discontented with the idea of individual Beatles. However, their different activities in the last part of 1966 led to one of their greatest times of creativity, in which drugs, mysticism, and great messages would become most significant.

The music was more guitar-oriented and less percussive, primarily because the songs were more complex and the words more important. The music was folk-like, often with three-quarter meters and very pretty melodies. We do not often associate rock with beautiful folk melodies. Because the message of the song was often associated with the emotions of the words, the Beatles were much more interested in the overall texture of the sound. This development called for less continuous background and a change from the earlier sound of skiffle.

Generally the technical level of the music in the middle era was substantially more complex. Although the Beatles were satisfied with very simple chord constructions in the early style, by the middle period they were successful in the use of rather complex chord progressions. Both Harrison and McCartney had become accomplished on their instruments, especially Harrison, and as a result, both the lead guitar and the bass lines improved. With the technical advances available, they became important parts of the texture. Previously the background sound was continuous, without contrast and significance.

That the Beatles considered more subjects in their songs can be confirmed by simply looking at some of the titles. Also, the albums of this era began to show some continuity. There was a logic, albeit a loose one, in the way the songs were placed on the albums, and there was consistency in the kinds of sounds. The continuous influence of Brian Epstein and George Martin could be heard in the use of larger musical forces in the background.

Late Beatles

The characteristics of the late music were:

1. Electronic music
2. Studio music
3. Technically precise music
4. Mystical allusions
5. Total communication.

The music of the Beatles from 1967 to 1969 was, paradoxically, both diverse and homogeneous. There were traits of the two earlier periods in the music, but the new characteristics made the music more convincing than in any other period. The albums were technical masterpieces, and they may have been artistic masterpieces as well. During this time there was always an aura of mystery surrounding the Beatles, and this may have been the most important quality of the music of their most mature period.

The four main albums of this era were *Sgt. Pepper's, Magical Mystery Tour, The Beatles* (White), and *Abbey Road.*[3] Of course there were others, and perhaps they were more important, but these four albums sum up the group's musical message. Each album was based on the idea of traveling through the world, as a group, on a ship, or simply walking down the street. The Beatles were world travelers, commenting on the world as they journeyed. This image of the traveling musicians is an old one and is important in understanding music; in some senses, musicians travel through life and occasionally make valid statements about it.

The Beatles used the most sophisticated studio techniques available to produce their albums. They used many electronic devices to amplify and modify their own sound, and they employed many extra musicians (even the London Symphony Orchestra) to expand the musical texture when it was appropriate. The music could not have been produced in a live performance because of the forces and electronic taping devices required. No matter how far technology goes, especially in microcircuits and miniaturization, rock groups will never be able to perform all their music live; some groups will have to rely on studio performances in order to achieve certain effects.

The Beatles had control of every parameter of music. Whereas they may have been able to crank out an album in a short time during the first part of their career, albums on the scale of the late period took countless hours in performance and then an equal amount of time in redubbing and editing. These were large-scale efforts in comparison to earlier records.

The message of each album was a mystical one, a message given by a group of

---

[3] We did not include *Yellow Submarine* as a major album because it was not exclusively a Beatles' creation.

A Beatles collage *(Courtesy of Capitol Records)*

people who saw themselves as significant commentators on the world, and who felt they were in a position to have influence. "Yellow Submarine," the song and the symbol, can be viewed in many different ways, which is, of course, the mark of truly great poetry or literature. It can be seen as a simple story without much meaning, or as the story of four people who are out to save the world, protecting it from the loss of true values (that is, music). The albums were commenting on various topics, criticizing, suggesting changes, and pointing out things that might not be obvious but should have been. Allusions to drugs were overt, but they were also part of the message. Although the Beatles did not communicate in the same way as the San Francisco groups (see chapter ten), their message was the same. And even though many critics condemned them for it, they were successful in this communication.

However, the most significant part of the late music is that each album and perhaps the whole period were organically tied together by a thematic logic. On a particular album, the songs lead one to another, rather than being separate entities. The Beatles finally achieved total communication, in that we must listen to the whole album in order to understand the message. This is a level of sophistication seldom reached by rock groups, or for that matter, by any artist.

Whereas the musical style of the early period was just background sound for the singing, in the late period the musical style was interwoven with the message of the singing. As the orchestra increased in size, so did its complexity and internal integrity.

SUMMARY

Much could be said of the Beatles' marketing techniques and influence, but these topics are common knowledge. Moreover, the marketing of the Beatles is still going on, as we could confirm in any record store. Presley was the most imitated musician of the 1950s, the Beatles of the 1960s. We must wonder why an English group could so accurately reflect that tumultuous time, but the chaos in the United States was reflected all over the world. This particular English group just happened to achieve stardom and wealth at a time when its members could take advantage of their achievements and become the minstrels of the world. It is particularly fitting that they retired at the end of the decade rather than trying to continue, as so many American groups did. Obviously, the Beatles did not quit solely for idealistic reasons, but for those of us who were children of the 1960s, it is a comforting thought.

LISTENING

Early Beatles
Revolver
Yellow Submarine
Abbey Road

CHAPTER **10**

CALIFORNIA—
NORTH AND SOUTH

In this chapter we will discuss the difference between music from the southern part of California (that is, Los Angeles) and that from the northern part (that is, San Francisco). We see the musical situation in California as a reflection of what happened in other parts of the United States, just as we saw the Beatles as representing British rock. California is a model for the rest of America, a fact particularly true in the 1960s. It is relatively isolated from the rest of the United States, and there is still a sense of separation from the East.

SOUTHERN CALIFORNIA

In the 1960s California still represented for many Americans a kind of perfection —in the weather, the beach, and the sunshine. In many ways, southern California lived up to its utopian image. Life was relaxed, the weather was beautiful, and money did not seem to be a problem. There were movie stars, Disneyland, and fast-food stands. Social change could be ignored because life already seemed perfect.

California was being populated by people from other parts of America because they wanted to share the dream, and southern California was where they wanted to live. Once people became southern Californians, they wanted desperately to keep it to themselves. Even though it was hard to find people who were born there, no one wanted to change the social order. Therefore, it was reasonable that it would be politically conservative. Southern Californians were restrained, although they were outwardly very friendly. The "laid-back" approach is a southern California trait, but it is a relaxed conservative approach rather than the liberal "hang-loose" approach of northern California.

Materialism was very important to people in that area. Cars were necessary both for transportation and for status. In the 1960s the lifestyle in California was hedonistic, and the economic situation supported that philosophy. Success stories were all around, and everyone naturally gravitated toward those patterns of existence.

The lives of youths, at least in the coastal areas, were dominated by visions of the beach or of "hanging out." They could participate in any activity they wanted by driving to it. They could ski in the mountains without having to live with snow, and they could surf in the ocean without having to live with sand. Because they were used to driving short distances (sixty to one hundred miles is considered a short trip in California), they were able to take advantage of the natural resources. And because they were not too concerned with the future, they did not seem to care if those natural resources might not be there in twenty years.

Surfing Music

Pop music in California was really quite diverse. Many people of the older generation liked big-band music, which was sometimes associated with the film industry, and there were also many country and western fans. The rock and roll that was popular in the 1950s was the ballad or novelty styles. California really did not have its own kind of music until surfing music came along. Until that time, the people enjoyed a mixture of pop styles from other parts of the United States.

People normally assume that the kinds of cultural forms that came from California before the 1960s were in fact California-based, but nothing could be further from the truth. The film industry was important to the California lifestyle, as was the entertainment circuit, and there was clearly some association with California tastes. However, entertainers moved to California because the lifestyle was enjoyable and they could get work in a rich industry. But that industry was based on making films and entertainment packages for the rest of the United States. Although they naturally capitalized on the natural resources of California (and those images came through the products), these packages were designed with the viewer in Des Moines or upstate New York in mind.

Surfing music was a result of a growing population of young people in southern California, a population that had significant wealth. At first, the music was primarily designed for large dances held in public places on the ocean. Then it became packaged and sold much as Presley had been sold. There were more surfing bands than could be imagined, and they had a proven model. The originator of the form was Brian Wilson, who founded the Beach Boys. The model he generated was truly unique, and in the intense desire to share in that success, most of the other surf bands turned out song after song that sounded exactly like the original. In short, surfing music was unique, but once we had heard one surfing song we knew all the musical characteristics of the style. Everything else sounded the same.

The story of the Beach Boys would not be so interesting if they had not eventually progressed beyond that original model, which of course they did. But the point is that they invented something pretty clever, and the basic model worked very well, was extremely popular, and still has validity today. Surfing music reflects attitudes in southern California and thus is a perfect model for art reflecting life.

The Beach Boys represented the image of the southern Californian. They all lived in Hawthorne, were clean cut, went to school, and surfed after school (well, maybe not Wilson). Wilson was musically creative and formed a group with his two brothers — Carl on guitar and Dennis on drums. The original group also had as members Mike Love and Al Jardine. By 1962 Wilson had formed the group around the idea that it would sing surfing songs in a mostly vocal style, with a background that was smooth and continuous. The music was different from that of the Beatles in their formative years, maybe not much better but much smoother. The vocal patterns were mostly sung in unison, but they did contain some harmony. Wilson sang in a falsetto voice, and the group in harmony sometimes sounded like the Hi-Lo's or the Four Freshmen. The combination of surfing songs and the sound of the Beach Boys was unique at the time, and Wilson had the energy to keep doing it the same way until he got it right.

In 1963 he adapted "Sweet Little Sixteen" by Chuck Berry and turned it into "Surfin' U.S.A.," which helped the group achieve national fame. Surfing music was really designed for southern California, but it also worked in places where surf had never been seen. The Beach Boys were popular in California, but eventually they became even more popular in the Midwest and in other places in America. Wilson wrote a number of surfing songs during the first few years of the group's existence, and he also wrote for Jan and Dean, who rode the model to success.

The music of the Beach Boys can be conveniently broken up into two stylistic periods, although some critics may be tempted to add a third period for material from the late 1970s. We will consider two periods — one before and one after 1966. The first period can be defined in terms of the kinds of topics they sang about — girls, cars, surf, sun, and beach, and devotion.

The "girl" songs are brilliantly uncluttered with real emotion, in that they exist on a platonic level. They depict removed love and are simple in context. The

The Beach Boys *(Courtesy of Capitol Records)*

lyrics express ideas of protectiveness ("Don't Hurt My Little Sister") and puppy love. They are simple, but very touching.

Some of the best songs from the first period are the "car" songs. These are simple models for materialism and identification with the power technology of southern California. Many teenagers spent hours after school riding around in "cool" cars and these songs pay homage to that. "Little Deuce Coupe" or "409" arc great songs, if only for the simplicity of the message. "Little Old Lady from

Pasadena" is probably one of the cleverest novelty tunes from the history of the art form. The car became a person in these songs, a person with whom we could entrust major parts of our ego. To think that these songs do not invoke valid nostalgic emotion today is to ignore a part of our reality.

The "surf" songs are classics and pivotal to the image of the Beach Boys. Songs like "Warmth of the Sun" reflect the ideal life in southern California and can be especially pleasing to someone in the upper Midwest during the last part of winter. These songs evoke feelings of a simple life in which we need not worry about double-digit inflation or war. Part of the appeal of this first period is that the types of songs allowed us to forget about reality.

"Devotion" songs usually had something to do with a particular institution and the good things in it. For example, in "Be True to Your School," the Beach Boys invoke the all-American image that our school is the best around. That value is sadly gone today, but the songs of the early Beach Boys can bring it back, if only for a minute.

Musically, the first period is fairly easy to define: continuous singing with uncomplicated harmony, rhythm, and backgrounds. If we listen carefully, we can hear cheerleading sounds in the background figures, like rahrahrah, sis-boom-bah or other nonsense words. The Beatles also used simple phrases like these; simplicity often works best.

In the second half of 1966 Brian Wilson stopped touring with the group and was replaced by Bruce Johnston (his song "Disney Girls" was on the *Surf's Up* album of 1971). Wilson had a good marketing technique for the Beach Boys and was brilliant in creating a model. However, for a variety of personal reasons, he stopped having a direct impact on the group in terms of growth, and Carl Wilson, who had been the silent partner up to this point, took over. The Beach Boys began to lose their clean-cut image, growing longer hair and beards, and they began to experiment (especially with electronics) and to make social comment.

Brian Wilson went into collaboration with Van Dyke Parks, a poet and lyricist, with whom he created songs in a new image. This association was to continue for years, although Wilson returned to the Beach Boys on a sporadic basis. His songs created with Parks have been poetically more complex and socially significant and a great deal more contemporary. Probably the most significant album in the collaboration is *Pet Sounds*, made in 1967. It contains experimentation equal to that of the Beatles, especially in its complex melodies and dense harmonies. The poetry is quite complicated in comparison to early Beach Boys material. Several songs in collaboration with Parks appear on the *Surf's Up* album.

The process of change to this 1971 album was slow. The Beach Boys continued to tour between 1966 and 1971 and to sing songs of the first era. But by 1971, when they produced *Surf's Up*, they had changed almost completely. They began to reflect social views, and they were judgmental in songs like "Student Demonstration Time." This album, which also contains songs about the ecology, has more complicated lyrics, at least in comparison to earlier material. Their sound was

The Beach Boys *(Photo by Caribou Records; used by permission of Ginny Cartmell and Creem Magazine Archives)*

different, and although they still could sing and play in a smooth style, they often did not. "Student Demonstration Time" sounds a lot like Bob Dylan, someone whom they certainly would not have imitated in a song about cars or surfing. Even the title does not sound at all like an early tune. In this album the Beach Boys are asking serious questions, something a southern Californian simply did not do in the early 1960s. In essence, the influences of San Francisco had been felt, even on the Beach Boys.

Nonsurfing Music

There was an underground movement in southern California that eventually produced some significant musicians. Probably the most significant group in Los Angeles that was not surf-oriented was Jim Morrison and the Doors. Morrison was an extremely high-energy rock singer who teamed up with Ray Manzarek, a rhythm and blues piano player originally from Chicago. Although a blues-based band (somewhat like the Rolling Stones), it established itself as a national success in 1967 with its first album, *The Doors*. These musicians were ahead of their time in Los Angeles but not in the rest of America. Their main lyrical themes were sex and death in a very blatant style. In their theatricality, they were almost pre-punk. They were very important until Morrison's death in 1971.

NORTHERN CALIFORNIA

The difference in attitudes between Los Angeles and San Francisco is striking. First, the climates are totally different. San Francisco is another waterfront town, but it has a grand harbor with hills and fog. It rains a lot and the weather is colder, not like the Midwest, but damp cold. It is, relatively speaking, a much more sophisticated town. Whereas Los Angeles is a relaxed community of sun worshippers, San Francisco is artistic, cultured, and just a bit snobbish. It is historically significant, being associated with the gold rush and migration from the East. It was the port for immigrants from the Orient and was involved in the building of the railroad. Its history is no longer than that of Los Angeles but it is substantially more cosmopolitan. Although both towns have Spanish names, La Ciudad de Los Angeles is much more Spanish-American in culture.

While southern California had quick increases in population, San Francisco stayed basically the same. The people there did not take to the surfing tradition at all, and it was not until the mid-1960s that the city began to develop its own musical tradition. But the San Francisco sound was to become more important to the history of rock than surfing music, not in record sales or money, but in influence.

As the bastion of liberalism, specifically at the University of California, Berkeley, San Francisco became a hotbed for new and radical ideas. The first significant movement was the free-speech movement, which probably started as early as 1963. The first music associated with it was folk music, which became the focus for the rock music that eventually sprang from it. The folk music of San Francisco was radical; that is, it carried an intrinsic message that parts of society had to change — "The Times They Are a-Changin'."

The student movement carried with it a number of ideas that brought youth and oppressed people together. From it evolved the hippie movement, with its central concepts of love and freedom, the vehicle to those goals being drugs. Sexual freedom and freedom of lifestyle created communal living in places such as Haight-Ashbury, a section of San Francisco. Although there were communities of hippies living elsewhere in the United States (for example, in Venice, near Los Angeles), the hippie community in San Francisco was stronger because of its association with Berkeley. For many reasons (its liberalness being the major one),

San Francisco developed itself as the center of movement, and musically, folk music turned into a particular kind of rock.

Acid Rock

The San Francisco sound can be defined as *acid rock* or *psychedelic rock,* which means that it is associated with LSD, or acid. San Francisco rock became associated with very loud music and a deafening use of electronic amplification. It has had an influence on many other rock musicians and led to increased use of electronics and multiple banks of speakers. In the late 1960s it was responsible for more than one complete electrical failure in theaters where these kinds of bands were booked. The function of acid rock is to provide a stimulus for the total experience of the people involved, musicians and audience alike. It is not like a concert in which people sit in straight rows, separate from the performers. The entire crowd and the band become part of the musical and physical experience. The music is meant to be felt rather than just heard, and anyone who has ever attended a performance of an acid group knows that it can be felt. Amplifiers are turned up to the breaking point, and there is a great deal of created distortion.

Although acid rock could be understood as an extension of the shouting tradition from the 1950s, it is really much more intense. The emphasis is on loud sounds from the lead guitar and the singer, although the words themselves are not very significant. The singer functions as another part of the musical texture, and it is very hard to distinguish the words. Acid rock could not succeed on the power of the words (that is, their meaning) alone. It is the total art work that is important, not any one constituent part.

The subject matter for acid rock is normally antiestablishment and/or drug-oriented. San Francisco rock was designed for a particular audience in a particular state of mind; it was not designed for mass consumption, which it seldom achieved. It was quite clearly a cult type of music, although it would eventually have somewhat wider implications. Other than folk rock it was the message of the 1960s, much more so than the music of the Beach Boys.

To understand its musical and technical characteristics, it is probably necessary to listen to acid rock under certain controlled situations. *(We are not recommending drugs.)* We need powerful amplifiers and speakers so the volume can be turned up. Acid rock is not successful at low volumes because the experience was not meant to be soft. Therefore, if we want to experience the music as it was intended, we have to turn up the volume. The same thing can be said about some groups from the 1970s, the Who, for example.

In the following section we will discuss four groups from San Francisco who exemplified this kind of music: Moby Grape, Jefferson Airplane, Big Brother and the Holding Company, and the Grateful Dead. All these groups were most significant in the 1960s, even though some of their musicians are still around; the Grateful Dead still performs together, although its musicians seem a little older and

Jefferson Airplane *(Courtesy of RCA Records)*

a little tamer. As usual, there are other groups we could have chosen, but these are good representatives.

Acid Groups

Moby Grape lasted for about two years, after which the members broke up and joined other groups or worked as singles. However, from May 1967 to 1969, Moby Grape was a fairly important group, combining country, folk, pop, and rock with psychedelic elements. Its music was quite strong and its act was definitely psychedelic. Probably its most interesting album was released in April 1968, *Grape Jams. Grape Jams* featured spontaneous improvisation by several guest artists — Al Kooper, the organist from Blood, Sweat and Tears, and Mike Bloomfield, guitarist with Electric Flag. These jams, or free improvisations, illustrate the basic style of acid rock in the spontaneous energy of the melodic runs. It is very powerful music and is done rather cleverly. In some sense, Moby Grape was a fairly soft version of acid rock, but it had all the elements of a psychedelic band.

Jefferson Airplane was an important and lasting group. It began in 1966 and was the most influential of the San Francisco bands, probably because of Grace Slick, who was a powerful and attractive singer. The message of the Airplane was drugs, and many of the songs were strictly about drugs. The band used a psychedelic advertising package and was the first San Francisco group to be successful in New York. It had an amazing potpourri of musical styles—blues, folk, jazz, rock—and in San Francisco–type crowds was very free in performances. The members exhibited that quality of "hanging loose," but they were very controlled within their freedom. They made extensive use of light shows and were the first to work out the light show so that it completely supported the music.

The Airplane was of course analogous to the Beatles in *Yellow Submarine*. Its members were traveling in this symbolic manner to bring their message to the world, and their theme song, "Fly Jefferson Airplane," became the chief message. In songs like "White Rabbit" they told us what life was about and incidentally reminded us of what *Alice in Wonderland* was really implying. Other people had known about the drug allusion in Lewis Carroll's tale, but the Jefferson Airplane advertised the idea. Besides the packaging, Jefferson Airplane was a competent group of musicians, and Grace Slick's voice was significant in terms of its impact. In the mid-1970s it changed its name to Jefferson Starship and continued to enjoy some success into the 1980s.

Big Brother and the Holding Company was a group of the late 1960s, the peak of their popularity being in 1968. The strength of this group was in its musicality as it supported the enormous talent of Janis Joplin. Although Grace Slick was the first female singer to be highly successful with a rock band (at least in the white tradition), Joplin was probably more important. At the Monterey Festival in 1967 she brought the house down because she was so strong, sexual, and different. Her singing style was straight from the rhythm and blues tradition, and in fact, before joining Big Brother, she was a powerhouse blues singer (even though she was quite young). Her singing style was gutsy. She used groans and all the old blues tricks, and her voice was raspy and almost masculine.

Although not an extremely beautiful woman, Joplin had an erotic way about her and absolutely captivated audiences. She exhibited the same power that Jimi Hendrix did with his guitar. Like Buddy Holly a decade earlier, Joplin made you feel the pain she was going through, and she used every part of her body to communicate it. She was undoubtedly the most powerful female performer of the rock era and has continued to serve as a model for other women in rock and roll.

The Grateful Dead is the supreme acid band, and it functioned as the leader of the cult. It was idealized in Tom Wolfe's *The Electric Kool-Aid Acid Test* as the group that traveled around and spread the message, that is, LSD. The image in that book was that of a bus painted with psychedelic messages and a huge stereo system traveling around America, giving away acid and putting it into water reservoirs. The statement is constantly made, "You're either on the bus or you're off the bus.

The lead guitar player, Jerry Garcia, has been the molding force of the Dead, which originally began as a country and blues band. It started in 1966 and was most popular between 1967 and 1969. However, unlike some of the bands in this era, it is still performing in basically the same style today. Surprisingly, the Grateful Dead is not loud or shocking. It became the center of attention because of its commit-

The Grateful Dead   *(Photo by Arista Records; used by permission of Ginny Cartmell and Creem Magazine Archives)*

ment to the San Francisco movement and only incidentally because of its music. The members lived in Haight-Ashbury and were a part of the "love-in" and "flower child" attitude. They lived as members of the commune and played for countless hippie parties. They have given more free concerts than any other big-name band and have endeared themselves to the community that immortalized them. Therefore, the Grateful Dead became the symbol for the San Francisco sound and for its music because its members were truly part of the movement.

Their music is psychedelic, but in a relaxed kind of way. Although they may have seemed shocking at the time, there were other bands that took what they did much further, Black Sabbath, for instance, or later, Kiss. But the Grateful Dead were and still are solid rock and blues musicians, and their songs were powerful within the context of the times. The fact that they are still around speaks to the universality and competency of their music.

SUMMARY

The psychedelic bands were important to the development of rock for several reasons. Rock had after all lost its identification as a movement, and the acid bands united that identification with rebellion. The San Francisco sound, which combined folk music with rock, became the central symbol for the student rights movement, the sexual revolution, the drug revolution, and ultimately the antiwar movement. It was a way by which youth could stand apart from the older generation, and the history of rock gains momentum every time some way is found to rebel against the establishment.

Acid rock was significant in that it represented a time of great freedom for youth, and, at first, a significant change in philosophy. Young people wanted to be free of the restrictions of contemporary society. They sought a release and an escape. Unfortunately, the flower child society began to break down; acid rock started to lose its significance, even though its influence would continue into the 1970s. This was not an affluent movement, and it did not make a lot of money. However, that is precisely what the San Francisco scene was all about, that is, rejecting the materialism of the 1950s. In some ways acid rock was a reaction against what was successful in southern California in the early and mid-1960s; it was San Francisco's response to Los Angeles. The interesting thing is that the San Francisco sound was eventually influential on the leader of southern California music, the Beach Boys.

LISTENING

Beach Boys, *Little Deuce Coupe* and *Surf's Up*
Moby Grape, *Wow/Grape Jams*
Jefferson Airplane, *Surrealistic Pillow* and *Bless Its Pointed Little Head*
Big Brother, *Cheap Thrills*
Grateful Dead, *The Grateful Dead*

CHAPTER 11

FOLK-ROCK

FOLK-ROCK

Folk music is usually defined as the music of the people, the folk's music. It is normally regionalistic in that it expresses the feelings of one particular area or group. It is usually simple music, and except for styles like bluegrass, it is vocal in orientation. The words are more significant than the music, although they are normally set to beautiful melodies. The music is repetitious, allowing many verses to be sung to the same tune. Although it has quite often been adapted to other styles, such as the blue or Dixieland, folk music is usually thought of as a separate art, and its practitioners see themselves as folk musicians. The music in its pure form is generally not commercial.

Whenever folk music takes on popular dimensions, that is, commercial value, it is usually because the particular themes being expressed have meaning for the society at that time. And whenever folk music becomes mixed with other forms, it is usually because the individual musician wants to speak to a larger audience. Folk-rock represents the attempt by folk musicians to raise the consciousness of the rock audience. Only later in the development of this particular marriage of rock and folk do rock musicians use folk techniques.

Folk music has enjoyed a relatively separate audience through the ages, and the times had to be just right in order to mix that audience with the one for rock — which was not to occur until the mid-1960s. Folk music could be traced back to the settlement of the United States. Much of what we said about slave music could be applied to folk music. There was black folk music, and there were white forms of folk music. For our purposes, the folk music before the eighteenth century was not too interesting because it was a derivative of European styles. However, beginning in the late eighteenth century, there were waves of migration to the United States by different cultural groups, all developing and enjoying their own folk styles. Although we will not seek to trace each different form, we could illustrate the folk music roots of Irish, German, Italian, and other national groups as they moved to the United States. Each one developed a regional style of folk music and eventually added to the variety of American music.

The most interesting forms of folk music were the Southern style (Appalachian), the Western style (Texas-Mexican and country and western), and a combination of ethnic styles from the north. Of course, each of these various branches of the folk music form has a different audience and different subjects, although musically they are very similar. Broadly speaking, these various styles provided the musical material for folk singers in the twentieth century.

Although there were many significant folk singers from the period before 1960, two of the most important, at least in terms of influence, were Woody Guthrie and Pete Seeger. Although Guthrie was from Oklahoma and clearly reflected Southern styles, he was a spokesman for middle America in general. He sang many songs from the folk-blues tradition, but his most important contribution was as a social commentator. He was one of the first political commentators among musicians, and he became a folk hero in the early 1960s, when he was dying. His son, Arlo, is important in his own right, particularly for "Alice's Restaurant."

Pete Seeger is also significant in any discussion of folk music. His father, Charles Seeger, was an eminent musicologist, and the son developed an interest in collecting folk music very early in life. He traveled with Alan Lomax, also a musicologist and anthropologist, and in these travels he absorbed many of the regional styles of folk music. Perhaps no other folk musician spent as much time in learning the tradition as Seeger did. He is still productive in writing about the American scene and his background (travels and a Harvard degree) has made him singularly capable of articulating American views through words and music. His politics are liberal, and he has given us such tunes as "We Shall Overcome" and "Where Have All the Flowers Gone?"

With these two musicians as important predecessors, we can turn our attention to the folk musicians of the 1960s, who were for the most part protest singers. Although each of their styles was different, they all learned from Guthrie, Seeger, and others. Some critics described the folk music of the 1960s as *new wave,* but it was musically derivative of earlier styles, just as new wave music in the late 1970s was partially derivative. However, the message was a bit more obvious than it was in music before that time.

Folk music in the 1950s was either pure folk music, sung by one person who accompanied him- or herself on guitar, or by folk groups like the Kingston Trio. In other words, it was either folk music or it was pop music. The folk music of the

Joan Baez *(Photo by Willard E. Shattuck)*

Peter, Paul and Mary   *(Photo by Barry Rankin, Saginaw, Michigan)*

1960s combined the two styles in such a way that it had the power of the folk groups with the message of the individual singer.

Bob Dylan was the big story of the 1960s. However, he was a product of a particular time, and without the support of several other musicians, important in their own right, he would not have been as famous as he was. All of the following influenced Dylan and were in turn influenced by him.

Joan Baez preceded Dylan in popularity, becoming famous in 1959. She was a strong singer who identified herself very early with protest. She was against the Vietnam War and was antiwar in general. She was a constant participant in the student movement, especially in Berkeley in the early 1960s. She sang many of Dylan's tunes before Dylan himself had become famous. She and Dylan worked together for years, and they were inseparable at folk extravaganzas. Baez was one of the first really significant female folk singers of the 1960s, predating Janis Joplin and Grace Slick. She did not record with a rock band until the 1970s, but her style of singing led to folk-rock form.

Joni Mitchell was important to the development of folk-rock because of her singing style and the way she used her backup musicians, one of whom was Stephen

Bob Dylan *(Courtesy of Columbia Records)*

Stills. As her career progressed through the late 1960s and 1970s, she constantly expanded the form by adding rock and jazz. She has become quite proficient on several instruments and illustrates well the development of a folk singer into a folk-rock musician.

Peter, Paul, and Mary was an important group for two reasons: It was extremely popular, and it popularized the music of other, less well-known musicians. The three were all good musicians, and of course they were excellent performers. The vocal blend they achieved would later be copied by other musicians, such as Crosby, Stills, Nash and Young, to produce complex textures within a rock sound. The significance of Peter, Paul, and Mary was that they were a symbol for the entertainment of the 1960s. Even when they sang protest songs (Dylan's included), they did it within a context of entertainment. When they sang children's songs, they evoked feelings of childlike behavior. Although they generally conveyed happiness, they were communicating to a generation of Americans who were deeply concerned about social issues.

Judy Collins was a classically trained pianist, but while in college in Colorado she began to perform as a folk singer. The rising political consciousness of the times began to affect her and she soon found herself performing at protest meetings, singing music of other young folk singers. She was much more versatile than other musicians mentioned in this chapter and was involved in acting, films, and musical fusion. She made extensive use of electronic devices in rock and folk, also including classical and jazz influences.

But of course the most important was Bob Dylan. Born Robert Zimmerman in Duluth, Minnesota, he made his singing debut in Minneapolis while a student at the university. He left Minnesota in 1961 and came to New York, where he became famous rather quickly. His first effective recordings were folk songs of the new left, exactly in the mold of Woody Guthrie. His two main themes were antiwar and antibigotry. His style was heavy, almost shouting, but from a folk-singing perspective. He was deeply imbued with blues styles, but not the shouting rhythm and blues style at all; rather, it was pure folk. Dylan's early popularity was completely tied to the 1960s and the protest movement. He was a significant musical phenomenon because he represented commitment to an ideal. His singing style made it impossible to miss the message because it had no pop overtones. In fact, Dylan has seldom reached into the pop bag at all, with the exception of some funk tunes later in his career.

Of major significance is his performance with the Paul Butterfield Blues Band at the 1965 Newport Folk Festival. This marriage of a folk singer with a rock band was probably the major catalyst of the folk-rock tradition. Subsequent performances with the band identified the style of folk-rock, for which Dylan was responsible. At first, people reacted negatively, believing that Dylan had sold out to commercialization. However, in retrospect we can see that this was a perfectly normal kind of evolution. It made the message of the folk style even more powerful. Rock was the perfect backdrop for vocal-oriented music, providing an effective and interesting background.

It should be pointed out that Dylan was responsible for raising the level of sophistication of the lyrics. Some critics have said that Dylan is ultimately not very musical and that most of his significance comes from his lyrics, which are real fine poetry and will have lasting impact. However, the fact that he chose to convey it through musical form makes him a part of minstrel tradition, which conveys messages through words set to music. No serious consideration of the significance of lyrics in rock would be complete without an appreciation of what Dylan did to raise the standards. Although he may have been a product of the 1960s, his influence extended well into the 1970s and beyond. We can hear his influence on many musicians of importance and in the significance of the words in much of the music of the 1970s.

Several bands in the late 1960s used folk music within a light rock style. These groups could be considered commercial responses to the folk-rock tradition, which began in the 1960s.

The Fifth Dimension was a black singing group that began in the early 1960s. It was basically a soul group at first, but it crossed over into the folk-rock market

The Fifth Dimension *(Courtesy of the Sterling/Winters Company)*

without being identified as a strictly black group. It toured with Ray Charles and had a number of hits. Its music was technically well done, which may have resulted from its association with Ray Charles. It used musical contrast well, and the combination of two women and three men was very effective. It has remained active throughout the 1970s and into the 1980s.

The Lovin' Spoonful, a rock band from the 1960s, was folk-oriented. John Sebastian, the leader, was a collector of folk music, and before the Lovin' Spoonful, he was in several blues groups. His band, although short-lived, was extremely interesting if for no other reason than its diversity. The musicians were involved in film scores and recorded music for Frank Zappa's record company. Sebastian as a single continues to have a minor cult following.

The Mamas and the Papas grew out of the same band as the Lovin' Spoonful, but its later identification was different. It was a hippie band and basically a folk-rock group; except for their clothes, the members of the group were really not very psychedelic. Probably the biggest thing about the Mamas and the Papas was Cass Elliot, who died in 1974. The sound of this group was all vocal harmony, and its music was pure folk music with a light rock background.

Seals and Crofts was a vocal duo from Texas that enjoyed success in the early 1970s. At first they had been Tex-Mex rock musicians; however, after some religious changes, they became folk musicians. When they came out with *Seals and Crofts* they quickly achieved some prominence. At first they just sang by themselves, although later they used a light rock sound as a backup. They represent a style that combines acoustic sounds (nonamplified guitars) within a folk-rock context.

One last example from the 1960s should certainly be Simon and Garfunkel, who were both good musicians. Paul Simon, who later performed by himself, is an effective writer and is certainly responsible for some big hits during his career, most notably "Mrs. Robinson." Although they used only light rock backgrounds, if at all, they were important in that they commercialized the art form and discovered many clever ways to make statements about society without offending anyone. Their music is for the most part watered down in its impact, but it is very well done and the total package is compelling.

Most influential in the creation of a true folk-rock form in the 1970s was a 1960s group called the Byrds. The Byrds were formed in Los Angeles in 1964. The leader, Roger McGuinn, had been a part of the backup group for Judy Collins and also for Bobby Darin. David Crosby was one of the original members, joined by Gene Clark, Chris Hillman, and Michael Clarke on drums. The Byrds were an unusual southern California group, at least at the time. They imitated the Beatles although their music was not lyrically like that of the Beatles. They sang material by Dylan and also the Fifth Dimension, and although their music was derivative, they were successful. From 1965 to 1967 they used mostly folk-rock material and after 1967 began to fall apart. What is important about the Byrds is that it was a folk group, especially in the texture of the sound. Some of its members became part of various country-rock bands of the 1970s — the Flying Burrito Brothers and the New Riders of the Purple Sage.

Buffalo Springfield enjoyed some moderate success during its short-lived career (1966 to 1968) and later in re-releases of its albums. However, probably its most important contribution was as a proving ground for what would later become Crosby, Stills, Nash and Young (CSN&Y). The original Buffalo Springfield was made up of Neil Young and Stephen Stills; Richie Furay, who went to Poco; Dewey Martin, who became a soloist; and Bruce Palmer, who was deported to Canada. At one time, Jim Fielder played bass, but he eventually went on to Blood, Sweat and Tears. In short, Buffalo Springfield was not a stable group.

Crosby, Stills and Nash   *(Courtesy of Atlantic Records)*

However, its musical concept was very stable in that it featured an acoustic sound with up to four independent vocal lines. The harmonies formed by the voices were very tight and served as a model for what CSN&Y would do later. The original compositions by Stills and Young, sung first by Buffalo Springfield, would form the stock of songs for CSN&Y — and in this fact lay the significance of Buffalo Springfield. It gave these two musicians a chance to work out their music within the controlled environment of the studio, and being in Los Angeles allowed them to work with the best of the available musicians. Jim Messina put in some time with them as well as other fine musicians from that area. For the development of folk-rock, Los Angeles was the studio location because of the availability of fine quality musicians, similar to what Nashville would do for country music.

Crosby, Stills, Nash and Young was a short-lived group, but it was an important one in the early 1970s. David Crosby was with the Byrds, Stephen Stills and Neil Young were with Buffalo Springfield, and Graham Nash was with the Hollies in England. It is interesting that the original collaboration took place at John Sebastian's house, where Crosby, Stills, and Nash combined to sing vocal trios. They subsequently decided to make albums together, putting out an extremely popular one in 1969. Neil Young joined them to form CSN&Y, after which they recorded *Deja Vu* in 1970.

The addition of Young allowed Stills to double on electric piano and synthesizer, and it also allowed for four independent vocal lines, a musical texture that had been tried in Buffalo Springfield. These four musicians were capable of singing very complex melodic lines, which became the cornerstone of the group's style. In some senses, CSN&Y illustrates the final stage of evolution for folk-rock. In this group, electronic devices were quite important, but only as backing for the vocal texture, the chief characteristic of folk music.

The actual musical sound of CSN&Y was a combination of acoustic guitar with lightly amplified electronic sounds. The chordal framework (that is, the progressions) was fairly complicated, and there was constant motion. The group had a continuous sound (perhaps reminiscent of surfing music), but the fluidity of the musical texture was quite a bit more complicated. It was soft rock in the sense that no one shouted and the words were always presented in a sophisticated texture. It was an organic sound rather than plastic. It grew with the words, that is, supported the words with musical textures appropriate to the text. The music of CSN&Y was very sophisticated, technically excellent, and communicated through a basic simplicity (that is, the complexity was disguised).

In conclusion, folk-rock has many different aspects. It was pure in the beginning, more folk than rock. The folk origins were couched in a political context, and when it was relatively pure, it was generally protest music. However, as the form became more sophisticated, there was the inevitable desire to make it speak to a larger audience. Rock, jazz, country, and other musical textures were added experimentally, ultimately leading to a fusion. Many of the musicians discussed in this chapter have used various musical media to expand their audiences, but most notably they have used rock forms. Therefore, rock combined with folk was a natural occurrence, which could have been predicted. The evolution of the form can be followed logically and explained chronologically. CSN&Y seems to be the logical conclusion. However, the influences of folk music on rock are still present, and for that matter, probably always will be.

ATTITUDES OF THE 1970s

As we get closer to the present time, it becomes harder to generalize about attitudes. Whereas the 1960s are really history, the 1970s are closer to the present. Although it is hard to tell when attitudes shifted and when they ended, it is easy to identify the 1960s at the time of social change and to describe the various movements. Probably the best way to deal with the 1970s is to say that its attitudes were those that ran counter to movements of the previous decade, even though some attitudes of the 1960s may have reemerged during the 1970s and early 1980s.

The election of Richard Nixon in 1968 was certainly a signal for the end of the decade. Of course, his election was partially a result of the typical reaction against the status quo, but in this case it also represented a shift backward in time. People wanted to return to a hardline approach toward communism.

The 1960s reflected constant change, which was confusing to people, even to those who were not changing themselves. The Vietnam War had a devastating effect on America, perhaps more so than realized. It was, after all, a war that was undeclared and which America did not seem to be winning. We entered it as an advisor and found ourselves drawn into the actual fighting. In previous wars we were clearly on one side, a side that was being oppressed according to our point of view. In South Vietnam the enemy was nebulous.

The shift in attitudes was partially caused by the technological explosion, an expansion of technical capability previously unmatched by any other point in history. Communications systems became much more sophisticated, and information was available instantaneously.

The election of Nixon represented frustration with the uncontrollable state of the 1960s, in a sense a desire for solidarity. His election reflected a wish on the part of middle America for a return to the old days, even though that was of course not possible.

Even Nixon must have realized that the attitudes of the 1950s were no longer relevant, but this did not stop him from implying that they were, especially in his second campaign for the presidency in 1968. After being elected, he moved very quickly to establish a position of strength. He offered a real alternative to the confusion of the 1960s and ushered in a new era of conservative control.

The idealism of the 1960s died for two reasons: The movements had been successful insofar as they could have been, and they had begun to breed corruption from within. One example will indicate the general state. At Kent State in 1970 four students were killed when the National Guard was brought in to control a riot. We will not make value judgments about the legality or morality of that particular action, but it does reflect a changing concept toward demonstrations. From that point on, any changes in society would have to be accomplished through regular processes. As the movements died of their own impetus, routine process took over. Therefore, we see the 1970s as the time of the great bureaucrat.

That decade also saw a return to materialism. Without ideals, young people were left with a void, and they placed themselves in that void. The 1970s became a time in which the main concern was protecting ourselves rather than fighting for the protection of others. The political climate was such that Americans began to defend themselves against others.

That there were good reasons for protecting ourselves cannot be doubted. After all, the 1970s saw the beginning of real financial problems, which became a key difficulty throughout the decade. We were being pressed by the government, by the oil industry, and by inflation in general. As we were pushed harder and harder, our reaction against government and other controllers became stronger, ultimately leading to the election of Ronald Reagan, who as the symbol for the 1980s, promised to defeat the bureaucratic dragon.

Another important symbol in the early 1970s was Watergate, whose significance was on the same psychological level as the Vietnam War. The Vietnam conflict had ended, as we lost face as a result of it. However, Watergate was to drop a great blanket on our trust in government. Everything ugly in American society was reflected in Watergate, which was devastating in its impact. Society had changed, and the result was massive depression. The American people had lost faith in their government; it does not seem as if we got it back during the 1970s.

Jimmy Carter was elected in 1976 as an outsider in Washington. His promise was to manage the government and to remove the stigma of power politics. Whether or not he succeeded will be judged by history, but he was not successful in maintaining a positive image over time. It is probably accurate that Carter failed his reelection bid because of the times rather than any innate weakness in himself or his programs.

Ronald Reagan was certainly elected by the same emotions of the people as Carter was, that is, that this man will control the government and make it as it was in the past. The problem is that nothing can be done to reignite the feelings of the 1950s and 1960s. Technology cannot be controlled; we will probably never again have a stable economy (much less an expanding one); and our place in the world is no longer that of the undisputed leader. Whether or not these political and social predictions are true, society in the 1970s and early 1980s reflected a negativism that seemed to have no positive alternatives.

LISTENING

Bob Dylan, "Hey, Mr. Tambourine Man"
Peter, Paul, and Mary, "The Times They Are a-Changin' "
Fifth Dimension, *Up, Up and Away*
CSN&Y, *Deja Vu*

CHAPTER **12**

ENGLISH ROCK

As the next chapters sum up the history of rock in the 1970s and early 1980s, it is appropriate to point out here that the chapters are organized according to topics or styles rather than chronology. For some to the topics the discussion will start with developments in the 1960s and end in the 1970s. The style of music in the former decade sometimes led conclusively to its continuation in the latter, and it is better to consider that overall sweep rather than trying to force the style into two periods. Where there are different styles that correspond to the different decades, we will indicate that fact.

Also, it was our contention that music of the 1950s and its extension into the early 1960s was more appropriately named *rock and roll,* and that the music from the mid-Beatles on should be considered *rock.* Our basic position is that this change resulted from rock becoming a way of life (a philosophy affecting clothing, political views, and all other aspects of existence). It was at this point that we began to use the term *rock.* The chart in this chapter illustrates various movements in rock until 1971, and it should indicate the complexity of the art form.

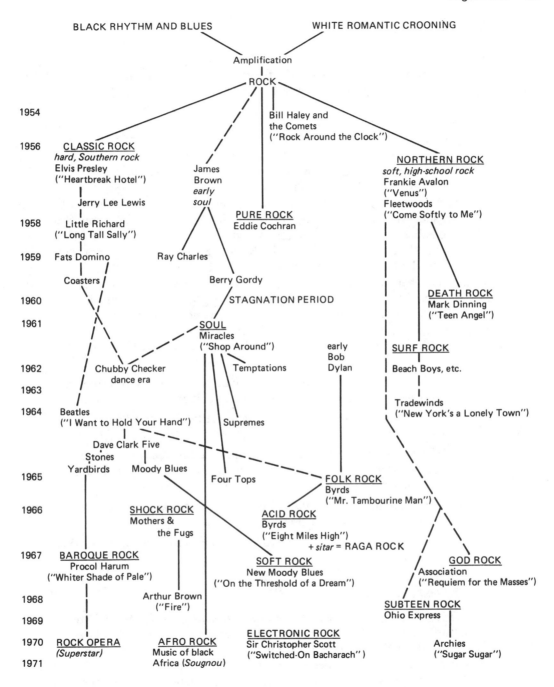

BLACK RHYTHM AND BLUES   WHITE ROMANTIC CROONING

Amplification

ROCK

1954

Bill Haley and
the Comets
("Rock Around the Clock")

1956   **CLASSIC ROCK**
hard, Southern rock
Elvis Presley   James
("Heartbreak Hotel") Brown
                 early
     Jerry Lee Lewis *soul*

NORTHERN ROCK
soft, high-school rock
Frankie Avalon
("Venus")
Fleetwoods
("Come Softly to Me")

1958   Little Richard   **PURE ROCK**
("Long Tall Sally") Eddie Cochran

1959   Fats Domino

        Ray Charles

    Coasters

        Berry Gordy

1960   STAGNATION PERIOD

DEATH ROCK
Mark Dinning
("Teen Angel")

1961   **SOUL**
    Miracles
    ("Shop Around")

              early
              Bob   **SURF ROCK**
              Dylan

1962   Chubby Checker Temptations   Beach Boys, etc.
    dance era

1963

1964   Tradewinds
Beatles   Supremes   ("New York's a Lonely Town")
("I Want to Hold Your Hand")

    Dave Clark Five
    Stones
    Yardbirds Moody Blues

1965   Four Tops **FOLK ROCK**
                       Byrds
                       ("Mr. Tambourine Man")

1966   **SHOCK ROCK**
    Mothers &   **ACID ROCK**
        the Fugs   Byrds
               ("Eight Miles High")
                 + *sitar* = RAGA ROCK

1967   **BAROQUE ROCK**
    Procol Harum   **SOFT ROCK**   **GOD ROCK**
    ("Whiter Shade of Pale") New Moody Blues Association
                ("On the Threshold of a Dream") ("Requiem for the Masses")

1968   Arthur Brown   **SUBTEEN ROCK**
         ("Fire")   Ohio Express

1969

1970   **ROCK OPERA**   **AFRO ROCK**   **ELECTRONIC ROCK**
    (Superstar)   Music of black Sir Christopher Scott   Archies
              Africa *(Sougnou)* ("Switched-On Bacharach") ("Sugar Sugar")
1971

POST-BEATLES BRITISH ROCK

We are of course guilty of seeing rock and roll as a particularly American phenomenon, allowing for the influence of African music through Afro-American tradition. However, it is the purpose of this chapter to outline the significance of British
rock bands through three examples. There are citations in the bibliography for
some encyclopedic materials that could provide more complete coverage.

English rock encompasses a tremendous diversity of styles, and at least in the
post-Beatles stage, it continues to have a viable effect on American rock and pop
music around the world. Rock was a worldwide phenomenon in the 1970s, and the
exclusion of rock groups from non–English-speaking countries in this book does
not imply that such groups did not exist. For example, probably the most significant and successful European rock group in the 1970s was ABBA, but it did not
influence subsequent groups or set new trends.

In this chapter we will discuss the Rolling Stones, who were contemporary
with the Beatles but who remained active up to the 1980s. We will also discuss the
Who, which had major impact in the late 1960s and early 1970s, and we will
comment on Elton John as one of the most significant rock musicians of the
mid-1970s. Later we will discuss several British musicians in the late 1970s because
Britain was the leader in both punk and new wave music.

English rock has a distinctive sound for several reasons:

1. Depending on their upbringing, the musicians speak and sing with a distinctive accent, and of course they use British English.
2. There is a slight influence of skiffle in the beginning stages of music from
   the 1960s.
3. The technology of the amplified sound is different in that the amplifiers
   are set to amplify the harmonic spectrum differently in Britain than in
   America.
4. Musical symbolism tends to be different and at times draws from the
   literary tradition of Europe.
5. The blending of voices tends to be less emotional and at times rougher in
   quality.

The Rolling Stones

This group began in the early 1960s. There is a great deal of debate about its
image and precisely what it represents. Our position is that it ultimately reflects
attitudes of the 1970s. If punk rock is an artistic response to the 1970s, then rock
bands the reflect punk attitudes, even in the 1960s, are in fact ahead of their time.
The Rolling Stones fit any model of punk (as perhaps the Who does also), and
therefore, its philosophical image is one of the 1970s.

Mick Jagger and Keith Richard were the two original Stones. They had actually gone to school with each other when they were six years old, but it was in 1960 that they met as musicians. At the age of seventeen, they were both aspiring musicians in rhythm and blues, which at that time was an expanding entertainment form in England. They joined several other musicians, including Charlie Watts on drums, to form a group called the Blues Boys, not to be confused with the Blues Brothers. They also used the name Blues, Inc.

At this point, they were pretty rough, and their group included several juvenile delinquents. In 1962 they added bass player Bill Wyman, and in 1963 Charlie Watts joined permanently. In 1963 they signed on as one of their managers Andrew Oldham, who was to have significant impact on building their image.

The period of the 1960s was largely spent in competition with the Beatles, although it was a competition of different energies. It must be understood that the Rolling Stones were great admirers of the Beatles and vice versa. However, comparisons were made that in some ways were helpful to the Stones, who after all started a little bit later than the Beatles. The Rolling Stones became a significant group in the mid-1960s, whereas the Beatles had achieved worldwide importance by that time.

The Rolling Stones were highly individualistic. The major difference between them and the Beatles arose from the kinds of music that influenced them. The Stones were most influenced by rhythm and blues (in particular Chuck Berry), although skiffle may have been a minor influence. They took their name from a Muddy Waters song, and during their formative years they played mainly blues. They were probably more technical than the Beatles in the beginning, but they seemed to have little concern for pretty melodies. Throughout their career, they were and still are hard rock musicians, and even when they sang songs originally designed as love songs, they sounded angry. Their roots are more in the shouting tradition than in crooning.

Their early career parallels in some ways the careers of Bill Haley and Elvis Presley, the giants of the 1950s. The Stones' career was shaped around the concept that they were tough guys, primarily as a contrast to the image of the Beatles. Rhythm and blues has an earthy quality, which is what made Presley so fascinating. The Stones also assimilated this quality, singing black music in a black style, even though they were white. They left the sexual meanings in their songs and emphasized them with body language and their general behavior. They purposely manifested the decadent in society and were justly condemned for it. However, nothing did more to build their early career than the condemnation of society.

As the press began to take up arms against the Rolling Stones and their public behavior, they developed a cult following. In 1963 and 1964 they recorded compositions by Chuck Berry, the Beatles, and Buddy Holly. These were successful in England, and in 1964 their first album was produced. In 1964 they had their first tour in America, which was quite successful, if only for the riots it caused. It must be understood that the Rolling Stones had a certain magnetism because they were

English, but they were different from the Beatles in that they were completely unacceptable to the middle class. Although the Beatles were strange, they were at least cute. There has never been anything cute about the Stones.

Until 1965, they recorded material written by other people. However, from 1965 on they produced their own material and established themselves as the bad boys of rock. "Satisfaction" in 1965 was probably their first important song in that it validated their earthy message. This particular song has a blues basis, but it carries the blues style into another sphere. It is sexual but it is also decadent sexuality. It has a riff orientation; we hear the main words until it feels as if they were pounded into our heads. It is negative in context, conveying the futility of trying in an age where nothing is in control. In my estimation, "Satisfaction" was the first punk rock tune.

From 1966 on, the Rolling Stones had legal problems. They were constantly being arrested for possessing drugs, and the press coverage made instantaneous heroes and villains of those involved. Mick Jagger and company became antiheroes for a society that treasured those kinds of things at that time — and their music continued to reflect that mood. They were involved with mysticism and psychedelics and were generally self-destructive. In short, every thing they did was wrong, but it continued to build their image.

Their music in the late 1960s was good loud rock, but it was always combined with some catchy idea, either sexual or antiestablishment. One of their most significant, although less successful, albums of this period came out in 1967 — *At Their Satanic Majesties Request.* It was overshadowed by the Beatles' *Sgt. Pepper's Lonely Heart's Club Band,* but the Stones' album contains some of the best mystical rock ever. The evil side of mysticism is aptly covered. Whereas *Sgt. Pepper's* tends to be optimistic and Messiah-like, the Rolling Stones do the same thing from the devil's point of view. Again, although it was not a blatant competition, the Rolling Stones always managed to force the comparison by doing pretty much the opposite of what the Beatles did.

We should remember that the music of the Rolling Stones was technically quite excellent. In the later 1960s they had psychedelic characteristics, even to a heavy metal or acid sound. It was strong rock with a blues base, which is what caused many people to say with awe that they may not like the people, but they played extremely good rock. The early style of the Rolling Stones certainly reflected vulgarity as a conscious reaction against middle-class values.

In the 1970s they continued to perform some of the same kinds of music, but by this time they had perfected the model. The Stones continued to spit out the words and scream at us as they did in "Satisfaction," but by the 1970s they were doing it with gusto and consistency. Brian Jones, who died in 1969, was replaced by Mick Taylor until 1974, who was replaced by Ron Wood from Faces. The technical expertise of the band got even better. Mick Jagger became the undisputed leader of the group and a cult figure through films and clothing styles. He had a major impact on trends in the 1970s, and it is largely for this reason that we consider him and the Stones to be that decade's image rather than one of the 1960s.

The Rolling Stones on their 1975 tour   *(Used by permission of Ginny Cartmell and Creem Magazine Archives)*

The music of the Stones can be divided into at least three, if not four, distinct stylistic periods. The first period runs from 1963 through 1965 and should be called the "rhythm and blues" period. Their first single was a cover of Chuck Berry's "Come On" in 1963. Albums up to *Out of Our Heads,* which included "Satisfaction," contained primarily covers of American R & B tunes. "Satisfaction" (analyzed in the appendix) was quite different in style and represents what was to come. "Satisfaction" was also their first number one hit in the United States and the first to feature a distorted guitar sound.

The second period runs from *Aftermath* in 1966, which was totally made up of original material, through 1970. One song from that album, a ballad called "Ruby Tuesday," was a number one hit in the United States and was quite unusual. Their basic message during this period concerned mysticism, drugs, and sex. They also had massive legal difficulties during this period, and Brian Jones (guitar) died in 1969. Certainly *At Their Satanic Majesties Request* (1967) was one of their more important albums, although it was slightly overshadowed by the Beatles' *Sgt. Pepper's.*

The third period clearly begins with *Sticky Fingers* in 1971, the first album put out by their own record company, Rolling Stones Records, a subsidiary of Atlantic Records. This period is less blues-based, more esoteric, and the music is generally a bit more complicated. By this time, the Rolling Stones were no longer the bad boys of rock and roll, but rather the decadent stars. By 1972 they had established a policy of only touring the United States every three years. Thus, their tours of 1972, 1975, 1978, and the last one in 1981 were phenomenally successful. By holding themselves back from the world market in Europe, the United States, and other countries, they increased their mystical attraction and allowed time for more artistic studio productions. Their records in this era continued to be interesting, such as *Goat's Head Soup* (1973), an artistic success which was panned by critics; *It's Only Rock'n' Roll* (1974), which contained a cover of the Temptations "Ain't Too Proud to Beg"; *Black and Blue* (1976); and *Some Girls* (1978), which was their biggest selling album to that point.

The fourth period began in 1980 or 1981. It was certainly in effect by the time of the *Tattoo You* album of 1981, the biggest seller to date. The film of their 1981 tour, *Let's Spend the Night Together,* was not overly successful, but it chronicles the final years of a group of great interest. This last period certainly reflects a growing commercialism, and a growing influence of funk/commercial black music. The Rolling Stones have always been influenced by black music, but in each of their periods the influence has been different. They were perhaps less influenced by black music in an overt sense during the late 1960s.

First Period: 1963–1965

1. Skiffle- and riff-oriented
2. Rhythm and blues covers
3. Bad recording quality
4. Simple beat patterns, guitar, and bass
5. Short songs
6. Loud vocals and lead singer dominant
7. Sexual lyrics

Second Period: 1966–1970

1. More use of electronics and special effects
2. Guitar solos more important
3. Sexual and mystical
4. Original material

5. Stronger beat

6. Drugs

Third Period: 1971–1980

1. Technically clear recordings

2. More complicated guitar sounds

3. Extensive use of electronics

4. Studio recordings different from live performance

5. Toured less

6. More diversified

7. Rhythm and blues

Fourth Period: 1981–

1. Commercial

2. Funk-oriented

3. Variety of instruments used

4. Bigger sound

5. Complicated use of guitar and percussion

6. More use of instrumental solos

The Who

This group was originally made up of Roger Daltrey, Pete Townshend, and John Entwistle. They were later joined by drummer Keith Moon, who died in 1978; Moon was replaced by Kenny Jones of Faces. The band's original name was the Detours, which was changed to the Who by one of their early managers. The original concept of the Who in the mid-1960s was to be a mod band, which was quite different from other rock bands in London at that time. The mods were a subculture of people who dressed in outlandish and avant-garde ways. Although the music that seemed to thrive in a mod environment was rhythm and blues, there were many contradictions in its use. The mods were contemporary people who in some sense were part of high society, analogous to the people who followed be-bop jazz in the late 1940s and 1950s.

The term *mod* comes from clothing styles and is of course derived from the word *modern*. But more than simply reflecting a style of dress, mods were people who wanted to be ahead of their society. By definition, it is an urban movement, and in the case of England, it was found primarily in the high society of London. Most mods were fairly young or at least young at heart, and those who assimilated this style tried to set themselves apart from the rockers, that is, people who liked rock and roll. The distinction may have been artificial but it was viable. The Who began as a mod band the played in the pubs in London.

The Who *(Used by permission of Michael Ochs Archives, Venice, California)*

One of the Who's trademarks has always been a purposeful chaos. Even in the beginning of their career, the members were a disparate group, playing in an abnormal way; each musician's function within the ensemble was not clearly defined because the basic concept of mod was a form of anarchy. The drummer played in a sporadic manner, beating his drums as if he were rebelling against society. The guitarist, Pete Townshend, was a power player, using the instrument like a battering ram. Although we are tempted to make the obvious comparison with acid or metal rock, Townshend's form of power was really quite different. It was not used to set up a psychedelic or other-world trip but rather to make a strong statement about the world as it really was.

The Who established itself as a band dedicated to the ridiculous, or perhaps even absurd. The musicians did many things that would become trademarks of punk bands later in the 1970s, such as marching in place, jumping up and down, twirling the mike on its cord, turning the guitar against the amplifier for purposeful feedback, even smashing instruments. They were destructive first for attention and then finally as a statement in itself.

We have always taken seriously the image of a rock group or an individual musician. However, most of the musicians we have discussed were really rather flexible in the kind of music they performed. Seldom did they set themselves against the mainstream in quite the way that the Who did in the first part of their career. Whereas most musicians would play ballads or freely adapt their style to whatever would work at the time, the Who did not. They stuck to the style of being outlandish, before it was chic to do so.

Much of the Who's early music could be dismissed as that of four musicians who were covering for their inability to play. However, they were all accomplished musicians by the time they got together. Interestingly, they had little in common with each other, and this became their trademark: people playing together who had different ideas and at times did not even like each other. Their controlled chaos was a rallying point, and like the Rolling Stones, they established a cult following.

Some of the early music important in establishing the Who's style is found in the albums *I Can't Explain* (1965), *My Generation* (1966), *A Quick One* (1966), *The Who Sell Out* (1967), and on numerous singles. The style of the early period was strong and destructive, with the guitar playing of Townshend pervading the musical texture. Some of the songs began to evolve into rather complicated structures and were strong in composition. Even if the lyrics were confusing, the underlying music was creative. It was natural that the Who would go on to lengthier statements, and the ultimate result was *Tommy,* made in 1969, a giant among rock compositions.

After *Tommy,* the Who continued with major contributions: *Quadrophenia,* with its heavy orchestration and lengthy pieces; *Meaty, Beaty, Big and Bouncy* in 1972; *The Who by Numbers* in 1975; and *The Story of the Who* in 1976. They also recorded solo albums, which was reasonable since they were considered to be separate performers. All in all, the Who continued to be successful, even with the loss of Keith Moon. It was a 1970s band in attitude, even when it started in the 1960s.

The concept of a rock opera is intriguing because it melds a very traditional form with rock, which is a nontraditional form. By definition, the creation of a rock opera implies that the Who took themselves seriously, even while they were poking fun at themselves by their attitudes and stage antics. *Tommy* is an extended piece of some ninety minutes and contains most of the traditional elements of an opera: prelude songs, reciting sections, instrumental interludes, and concluding piece.

An opera is basically a play or a story totally set to music, either played or sung. The prelude, or instrumental piece at the beginning normally contains the themes of the opera, both symbolically and melodically. The story is then told chronologically through songs and reciting sections and is separated by instrumental pieces. There is usually some kind of moral or character evolution during the entire composition. *Tommy* is a traditional opera in its structure because it has all these elements.

Tommy is an unusual musical project; it contains some musical elements characteristic of the Who and some that seem to be too melodic for them. Most of the main melodies fit the lyrics to which they are attached, which is a sign of good writing. There are occasional bits of music that support specific words, which is called *word painting* in music. Word painting is seldom found in rock, and it is fascinating when it does occur.

The story of *Tommy* can be explained on various levels. The simple story is about a child, Tommy, who because of a bad experience becomes deaf, dumb, and blind. As he grows up, he has some normal and some abnormal experiences. At the peak of his power, he becomes a pinball wizard and influences other people in this way. He becomes a cult leader, who by virtue of his charisma can get other people to follow him. His power finally breaks down completely, and we can see that he will eventually become a failure. It is a simple story, and we cannot help following Tommy through his adventures feeling both joy and sorrow for him as things happen.

On a deeper level, the development of Tommy can be seen as an autobiographical sketch of the Who, or of any child growing up in the late 1960s. We can also view *Tommy* as a religious work, defining the way inspiration can emanate from a gifted individual. From a literary perspective, Tommy can be seen as the blind prophet, the one who can see more clearly because he is blind to traditional reality. This image goes back to the golden age of Greece and the blind Tiresias. The beauty of the story of *Tommy* is precisely that it can be taken on many levels and appreciated by different people in many ways.

The music supports the story and the evolution of the main character. It is carnival-like when it needs to be; it is sad when the story is sad; and it fills space when that is needed. Some critics have argued that it is not great music, but of course the point is that the music works. After all, Mozart wrote some music in his operas which if isolated from the context might not be considered great either. The significance of *Tommy* is that it fits together as an organic whole, which is the best definition of art.

In conclusion, other rock groups have taken on a messiah-like role, such as the Beatles in *Sgt. Pepper's* and *Yellow Submarine*. *Tommy* is probably the best example, but careful listening to other music of the Who will reveal the same wisdom, even if it occasionally becomes clouded by chaos, ridiculousness, and confusion. In the rock opera, the Who succeeds in putting together two disparate forms of music. The 1970s became the time for fusion in many art forms, but the Who started the process in the late 1960s. The Who remained energetic, and although some will maintain that it never matched the strength of *Tommy,* it was still a viable group in the 1980s.

Elton John

The third representative of the 1970s in England, Reginald Kenneth Dwight was born in Pinner, Middlesex, on March 25, 1947. He grew up as a relatively uninteresting person, even by his own admission. He was chubby and, except for his interest in playing the piano, rather bland. During his teenage years he showed little interest in anything other than the piano, and his mother and stepfather encouraged him to become a musician. He began playing engagements with a rhythm and blues band named Bluesology when he was sixteen. At this time he was strictly a piano player and really never dreamed that he would be a singer, much less a rock star. It was not until 1969 that he began to be successful.

Through an audition for new talent, Elton John met Bernie Taupin, who was a lyricist. After John had composed music to Taupin's lyrics for some time, he and Taupin began to search for a producer. The first album produced in England, *Empty Sky* (June 1969), was not tremendously successful. However, their second album, entitled *Elton John* (April 1970), was, and one cut from that album, "Border Song," was especially successful. Although the song was not a record breaker, it has been sung by a number of other musicians, including Aretha Franklin. *Tumbleweed Connection* (October 1970) was also quite successful, both in England and in America, and by this time John had established himself as a major artist.

His dominance as a star occurred between 1970 and 1975. The following albums were significant during this time: *Friends* (1971), *Madman Across the Water* (October 1971), *Honky Chateau* (May 1972), *Don't Shoot Me, I'm Only the Piano Player* (January 1973), *Goodbye Yellow Brick Road* (October 1973), and *Captain Fantastic and the Brown Dirt Cowboy* (June 1975). Albums after *Captain Fantastic* were best sellers almost automatically, which is not to say that they were not also good. Playing the part of the local lad in the 1975 movie of *Tommy* helped John's career. He is today a viable artist, and although his interests have diversified, he is still an incredible performer.

There is some debate among rock critics about Elton John's talent, but we propose the following reasons for including him among the superstars: (1) He is a very proficient piano player. (2) He writes incredibly compelling melodies. (3) His singing style is both strong and sensitive. (4) He emotes expressive qualities through his singing. (5) The song-writing team of John and Taupin has been long lasting, although it decayed toward the end of the 1970s. (6) He understood the importance of theatrical performance and played the role to the hilt. Also, he has responded to his stardom in a socially redeeming way in that he has not been afraid to enjoy his riches and indulge both himself and his friends by spending his money.

As a person, Elton John is most interesting. Physically, he is rather unimpressive, that is, without his outlandish clothes, hats, and glasses. Probably the most

Elton John   *(Photo by Geffen Records; used by permission of Ginny Cartmell and Creem Magazine Archives)*

significant part of his stage look (which pervades into his life) is the gimmick of his glasses. He has used all sorts of spectacles, including giant-sized ones. Those have become an Elton John trademark and have added immensely to his following. He has been called the Liberace of the rock world, and perhaps rightly so. Like Liberace, he also happens to be a fine musician. The extra items simply add to his aura, which is considerable.

It seems as if some critics have been so annoyed by his look that they have failed to listen to his music. Elton John has succeeded in developing a persona as a musician in order to enhance the product. However, if he had not succeeded in producing real music, he would not have been successful on the basis of the extras. Elton John is a captivating performer, either live or on record.

We will examine one tune (and suggest that readers apply these techniques to other tunes) to discover the consistent musicality of the Elton John/Bernie Taupin team. One of the songs from *Caribou* (June 1974)—"Don't Let the Sun Go Down on Me"—was nominated for a Grammy. This is extremely powerful music, and John's melodic line is well worth whatever failures the album might contain. In fact, however, he was generally criticized for the album. This particular song has been recorded by other rock artists; it has also been recorded by the Maynard Ferguson band. It would not have enjoyed this success had it not been good music. Like many of John's compositions, it is strongly written and quite compelling.

Elton John epitomizes the best of 1970s music, especially in the early 1970s. Like the late 1950s and early 1960s, this period was fairly devoid of new movement in rock. The Beatles were finished and so were the 1960s. With the exception of a few artists, the 1970s reflected a retrenching in rock, and John helped to fill the void. It was a time of commercialization, and the rise of disco from soul illustrated that rock had lost some of its purity and energy. John had a creative energy unsurpassed at that time, and he was also successful financially.

Probably the most interesting subordinate theme of John's music is the philosophical interest of Bernie Taupin in the old-fashioned, in particular the Old West of America. Although they were very English, they were both intrigued by America. Country and western influences are present in many of their collaborative works, and even if the music does not always sound like it, at least the lyrics and themes are influenced by country. It is ironic that country music maintained an active influence of rock in the 1970s including, for example, the music of Led Zeppelin.

Although John was most significant in the early 1970s, that is up to 1975, he has remained active and is not yet nostalgic. He is still progressing. Like all rock stars who pass the age of thirty, he has become old by conventional standards. He is no longer the new sensation, but he remains a genius in the context of his time. Although some critics have suggested that his singing is mechanical and nonexpressive, I believe this charge to be false. Elton John expresses his words in the context of the melodic and musical line, and within the appropriate context, his singing is both expressive and musical.

SUMMARY

In this chapter we have considered three representatives of English music in the post-Beatles era. These musicians capitalized on the attitudes of the times with the amount of taste then required, which sometimes meant that they were tasteless and antiestablishment. Artists who are on the cutting edge of the changing attitudes of society are often misunderstood, and we must be quite careful in making value judgments. The main point is whether they were successful, whether people eventually understood them, and whether they had the strength of their convictions (proven by maintaining their position over time). All three of these representatives did, and therefore they must be considered relevant.

But perhaps more important, these representatives influenced others, both in England and in America. We have traced the impact of the Rolling Stones and the Who on punk and eventually new wave. Elton John proves the lasting impact of a pianist and vocalist and the efficacy of fusion music. Underneath his music lies a solid vein of good technique, which became paramount in the 1970s. The music may be simple, but it must be played accurately.

LISTENING

The Rolling Stones, *Tattoo You*
The Who, *Tommy*
Elton John, *Captain Fantastic*

CHAPTER **13**

ART AND ECLECTIC ROCK

A number of groups in the more recent history of rock have been loosely defined as eclectic, art, or progressive rock in style. Quite often those labels are intended to be critical rather than complimentary because rock musicians and their managers and critics like to view themselves as antiestablishment. And art or snob culture in general seems to be an anachronism to many of these individuals. However, leaving that particular problem to them, music labeled as art, eclectic, or progressive is clearly different from other genres discussed in this book; this music also adds something to the dimension of rock.

Art rock is a term that loosely defines music that either has higher pretensions than standard rock or consciously imitates another style that has been recognized as art, for instance Bach or Moussorgsky. When rock artists use eastern music — such as the Beatles' use of the Indian sitar, or "Kashmir" by Led Zeppelin — it is sometimes referred to as art rock. Clearly, when a rock tune uses music from the tradition of western art music (i.e., classical music), then the definition of it as art rock makes perfect sense. However, the term is also used derisively to describe musical groups that simply view what they are doing as artistic and are trying to convey that message. That use of the term is not very helpful to our discussion.

Art rock should define music that is a creative act and is somewhat replicable. This means that most rock is art — a basic premise of this book. However, for the sake of describing groups that generally fall into the realm of art, eclectic, or progressive rock, we will use a simpler description — fusion of rock and roll with western or nonwestern art music.

Eclectic rock is a loose term that is normally applied to anything considered to be unusual. However, the actual definition of the word describes the selection of that which seems best from a particular philosophy. Eclectic rock, then, is that type of music that tries to make a point about society without any attempt to be commercial in its presentation. Eclectic rock is quite often art rock as well, although eclectic rock specifically works in opposition to commercialism. Art rock, for the most part, does not try to avoid commercial success.

It should be noted that when the term eclectic is applied to specific groups, it is a value judgment at best. Many groups that might define themselves as eclectic would fall short of their self-imposed mission by actually selling albums or occasionally becoming commercial. However, it is generally possible to describe eclectic groups and to ignore their human frailties when and if they occur. We will attempt to provide an appropriate context for including certain musicians as eclectic, whether or not the musicians themselves would accept that designation.

Some readers simply define the following musicians as bad. That is a particularly dangerous kind of provincialism, although it is perfectly normal. It is sad that most highly experimental musicians (a quality of eclecticism) do not enjoy much success. In some ways, this is their contribution to the state of the art. That is, they are doing it for the sake of the art rather than for the sake of the money they could earn if they were less dedicated.

Progressive rock is almost synonomous with art rock, but it differs in one respect. It is experimental like art rock but usually does not consciously quote or use western or nonwestern art music. It is simply music that shares the experimental quality of eclectic rock and the creative structural thinking of art rock. Progressive rock is quite often commercial music; for instance, one can speak of the progressive metal concept of a group like Rush. In short, progressive falls halfway between art and eclectic, sharing some of the characteristics of each style.

Art rock, eclectic rock, and progressive rock have been mistreated by the critics for essentially snobbish reasons. Like the critical disdain for heavy metal (although the present discussion describes music that would appear to be diametrically opposed to heavy metal in its appeal) critical comments have always centered around the lack of good hard-driving rock by art rock groups. Nothing is further from the truth. Many of the groups discussed in this chapter play very viable rock; many of the musicians have incredible technical skills; and many of them have had major influence on later musicians. Most of the groups discussed here also play some straight rock and roll; they are discussed in this chapter because part of their output has art, eclectic, or progressive elements and not because they are (as they have been labeled) tainted or holier-than-thou.

REPRESENTATIVE MUSICIANS

The groups discussed through Roxy Music represent the art rock style, and coincidentally they are all British. There is little musical distinction between progressive and art rock, but the primary one is that most art rock groups come from England; in the United States similar groups are usually called progressive. Next, we will discuss a few eclectic groups, most of which have come from the United States. We will conclude with a discussion of progressive music with examples of both American and English musicians. Although the difference between American and English groups is a significant issue, for this discussion we should view all of the musicians as playing rock and roll, and occasionally creating compositions and whole albums that take on eclectic or progressive overtones.

Probably the first album of great significance to this discussion was the Bea-

The Moody Blues   *(Photo by PolyGram Records; used by permission of Ginny Cartmell and Creem Magazine Archives)*

Procol Harum   *(Photo by Chrysalis Records; used by permission of Ginny Cartmell and Creem Magazine Archives)*

tles' *Sgt. Pepper's* album. This was a clear attempt on their part to create an album that told an entire story. Although not a rock opera per se, this conceptual framework became a trademark of their last compositional period and certainly established a model for experimentation within rock as an art form. The addition of extramusical forces, including the London Symphony Orchestra on the *Yellow Submarine* B side, provided a technique employed by other groups discussed in this chapter.

However, the first band to really establish an art rock concept was the Moody Blues. The Moody Blues, formed in 1964 in Birmingham, England, was at first a pop/rhythm and blues band. From 1965 through early 1967 they had successful singles and albums, but it was in 1967 that they changed the sound of their music. They began using a Mellotron (a primitive tape synthesizer). On their 1967 album, *Days of Future Passed,* the semi-cosmic lyrics were set to full symphonic arrangements; as a result the album finally went gold in 1970. Their album *Seventh Sojourn* (1972) was a number one hit album in the United States. The Moody Blues' style was classic art rock, especially in its use of augmented instrumentation.

Procol Harum was established in 1966 from a rhythm and blues band called the Paramounts (which began in 1963). Their only significant composition for this discussion was "A Whiter Shade of Pale" in 1967. This particular song uses an organ line derived from J. S. Bach's *Suite No. 3 in D major.* As a result of this one composition, they were the immediate leaders of the baroque rock movement; however, they may have been the only member of that movement. They were

The Kinks   *(Photo by Warner Brothers/Reprise Records; used by permission of Ginny Cartmell and Creem Magazine Archives)*

clearly important to a discussion of art rock, though, because their relationship to art music was clear, and that song was heard by many people. Therefore, Procol Harum helped to popularize the concept of art rock.

The Kinks, founded in 1962, was another group that became important to the concept of art rock, or experimentation, although that importance would not be obvious until 1969. They were hard rockers and, like the Who, set the stage for British heavy metal, especially through their theatrics. However, their importance here lies in their concept albums of the late 1960s, such as *The Village Green Preservation Society* (1969), and *Arthur, or the Decline and Fall of the British Empire* (1969), a nonstaged rock opera. They continued to perform during the 1970s and 1980s but have not been as successful. However, Kinks material is occasionally covered by other musicians, including Van Halen — "You Really Got Me."

The Who was discussed in the previous chapter. However, for the purposes of art rock they are pivotal. There is no question that *Tommy* was a significant composition for experimentalism using western art music influences. While the Who clearly had a significant career and a distinctive style, they were also successful in experiments that added to the body of music appreciated as art; they played in a progressive style.

Nice was formed in London in 1967 with Keith Emerson on organ, piano,

Emerson, Lake and Palmer *(Courtesy of Atlantic Records)*

and synthesizers. Their first single, in 1967, was called "The Thoughts of Emerlist Davjack," which also became the title of their first album in 1968. One piece on that album was called "Rondo," which was basically drawn from the music of Wolfgang Mozart, a classical musician. Nice became the training ground for Emerson, Lake and Palmer, a group pivotal for this discussion.

Emerson, Lake and Palmer was formed in England in 1970. Keith Emerson came from Nice; Greg Lake had played with King Crimson (discussed later); and Carl Palmer joined them after failing to obtain a contract to play with the Jimi Hendrix Experience. At their debut concert at the Isle of Wight Festival in 1970, they chose to play a rock transcription of Modest Moussorgsky's *Pictures at an Exhibition*. This adaptation of a later nineteenth-century piano composition clearly established their credentials and importance in art rock. They were also flamboyant in performance, employing light shows and smoke screens. Some of their albums, such as *Brain Salad Surgery* of 1973, bordered on eclectic. The group essentially broke up in late 1974, although they started up again from 1977 to

1978. Carl Palmer was partially responsible for starting Asia in 1981 (see later discussion).

Genesis started in 1966 as a collection of songwriters called Garden Wall; they changed the name to Genesis in 1968. They developed a large stage show and used elaborate costumes, in a sense making each performance an opera. From 1970 through 1976 they produced fine albums in which many compositions fit together in one long story; in essence, they produced operatic suites or collections of songs. Starting in 1978, they produced albums that contained shorter songs but had greater commercial impact. In terms of rock theater, Genesis is certainly one of the more significant groups discussed in this chapter.

King Crimson started in 1969 and was initially quite important to the art rock movement. Unfortunately, this group has suffered from incredible changes over the years, but they were important between 1969 and 1974, when the band officially broke up. They used a mellotron like the Moody Blues, but they also had a very diverse sound; they were eclectic in style although art rock in England was big business. Robert Fripp (guitar) has been the only consistent member throughout the group's history, which began again in 1981. The new King Crimson was much more complex, using African and eastern music and many new wave elements, including polyrhythms.

Yes was a progressive band that also used classical structures in their early work. Formed in 1968 in London, Yes combined hard rock, classical influences, and a folk-rock/Crosby-Stills-Nash–type of vocal ensemble. One of the most obvious examples of their art influences was the presence of Rick Wakeman in the band from 1971 through 1974. Wakeman was a classically trained pianist from the Royal Conservatory of Music. His work with Yes in the early 1970s, and his solo works, have consistently illustrated literary and mythological influences on the artistic structures of this band. However, they were generally known as a progressive band rather than as an art band, which is unusual for British groups of that era.

Renaissance was started in 1969 by two former members of the Yardbirds; their attempt was to form a fusion band—folk, jazz, classical, and rock. However, it was an album in 1972, *Prologue,* that established them as one of the commercial art rock ensembles. The name of the group certainly suggested art rock leanings, but the actual sound of Renaissance was pop in orientation. Although perhaps unfairly, some rock critics have used Renaissance as an example of the crassness of art rock. Renaissance did have good audiences in the United States, and the *Prologue* album was played on AOR (Album Oriented Rock) FM stations.

Roxy Music was formed in 1971 by Bryan Ferry and Graham Simpson. Most of the early members were classically oriented. Brian Eno was perhaps the most-discussed early member of this group if for no other reason than the significance of his "punk/new wave" career after leaving Roxy Music in 1973. Roxy Music had an unusual sound, to say the least. It could be very restrained with an emphasis on vocals—almost straight-laced to the point of being irritating. Or it could be very eclectic and unusual. They were not at all commercially successful in the United

Renaissance   *(Photo by Sire Records; used by permission of Ginny Cartmell and Creem Magazine Archives)*

States, because this particular eclectic/art band was strictly representative of British values and humor.

The Fugs was a rock band formed in 1965 in Greenwich Village, New York City; the original group was made up of nonmusicians who were part of the avant-garde of New York. They were arts-oriented—Ed Sanders also wrote a book on Charles Manson, called *The Family;* Tuli Kupferberg is a minor poet; Charlie Larkey, the bass player, married Carole King. As nonmusicians, they were somewhat like the Monkees in that they formed a rock group for nonmusical reasons. However, unlike the Monkees, the Fugs had no financial motivation for becoming a rock group; they simply felt that this was the best way to communicate their messages.

The purpose of the Fugs was simply to shock for the sake of shock. They blatantly used gross obscenity, and rock was simply a background for obscene gestures and words. Their purpose was to shock society into realizing what was truth, and the medium they chose for the message was rock. Their music is at best chaotic, but it did have some influence on other groups who carried the philosophy further and perhaps did it better. One group, MC5, was influenced by the Fugs and became the prototype punk band.

Captain Beefheart represents an entirely different concept for an eclectic musician, in that he has had virtually no effect on anyone. Don Van Vliet (Captain Beefheart) was originally from California and went to high school with Frank Zappa. He formed the Magic Band in 1964, playing mainly blues with a number of very experimental electronic sounds. His techniques are avant-garde even when he is playing blues tunes. He uses rapid-fire lyrics with no rhyme scheme, multiple phasing, and special effects. He clearly mixes contemporary electronic music, jazz, and rock, as well as other kinds of music. He had gone back and forth between contemporary composition and blues performances. His career has been tied with the Mothers of Invention, even though he has his own band. The bottom line of his eclecticism (which is very much a part of the 1970s in attitude) is that he is thoroughly unpopular and therefore successful as an eclectic.

The most significant proponent of the eclectic school of rock is Frank Zappa and the Mothers of Invention. Although he was born on the East Coast, Zappa moved to the West Coast at the age of ten and has remained there since. By the time he made his first album with the Mothers, called *Freak Out*, in 1966, he had been a lounge musician, in jail, a recording studio owner, and part of the Los Angeles underground. The first album, a complete story in itself, was biographical of the group and the scene of which it was a part. It was clearly a divergent view from the surfing scene or from that of the Byrds.

The first period of the Mothers ended in 1969, when Zappa disbanded it because of high costs and personal problems. Probably the two most important albums from the early years are *Ruben and the Jets* and *Uncle Meat*, although Zappa fans might disagree. They were chosen here because they represent the two poles of Zappa's music. *Ruben and the Jets* is considered by some critics to be a sell-out because it so blatantly imitates 1950s rock and roll. However, Zappa's musical roots are in the 1950s, so it is not inappropriate for him occasionally to use an old blues melodic passage. Underneath the words, we can hear a constant parody of 1950s music. Zappa is laughing at the style, especially on cuts like "Deseri" and "Cheap Thrills." The sense of parody in Zappa—a style shared by the Fugs—is the strength of his eclecticism.

Uncle Meat, on the other hand, is serious composition. It is a studio album and would be difficult to perform in a live setting. Zappa's music is filled with other kinds of music—everything from Edgar Varese to Thelonius Monk. Zappa is generally one of the best-educated rock musicians concerning other music, on a level with Pete Seeger. He is very progressive in the way he mixes styles and uses sound on sound, such as crashes, crowds, and speeded-up sounds all at once. In "America Drinks and Goes Home," he is making a social and musical comment through unusual sounds. In other songs, such as "Plastic People," he utterly confuses us unless we are willing to give our complete attention to the various

Frank Zappa *(Photo by Warner Brothers Records; used by permission of Ginny Cartmell and Creem Magazine Archives)*

aspects of the music. Zappa does not record background music; his studio recordings are complicated, although his live performances (seldom done) are fairly simple in comparison.

In 1970 Zappa produced a movie called *200 Motels,* for which he wrote all the music. The movie is confusing and presents a mixture of images. Characteristically, it received very bad reviews. In 1971 he appeared with John Lennon and

Rush   *(Courtesy of PolyGram Records)*

Yoko Ono in concert and put out two albums. *Waka Jawaka* in 1972 had George Duke on keyboards. After this album, Zappa returned to basic rock with strange lyrics. He predated punk by a number of years in his insistence on playing standard rock and roll of the 1950s. However, his rock and roll was not traditional because he always wrote lyrics of an antisocial nature. In 1975 and 1976 he toured again with Beefheart and then returned to studio work and touring with the Mothers.

Frank Zappa is the best of the eclectic rock musicians in that he carries through one philosophy with great care. He was and still is an excellent guitar player and a gifted composer. He is learned in other musical styles, and although he has gone through a number of musicians over the years, he has commanded a sense of respect from the industry he has condemned so soundly. In the beginning of his career he advertised his records in comic books and through the underground; he also had numerous legal problems with the industry. However, in the end Zappa has remained true to his ideals. His monumental set from 1979 and 1980, *Joe's Garage*, Vols. 1–3, illustrates that he is still creative, and he continues to influence musicians both in rock and in jazz.

Styx was established in 1963 in Chicago and put out its first album in 1972. The musical style of Styx, made up of two guitars, bass, keyboards, and drums, is reminiscent of Genesis with the volume cranked up. Interestingly, Styx was very popular with teenagers, and at times they played in almost a soft heavy metal technique. However, it is for their singles, starting with "Lady" in 1975, that they are most known. Critics have referred to this music as "pomp" rock, which suggests a certain structuring of the sound similar to what the Moody Blues, Genesis, and others have done. Styx is clearly progressive rock, in the American sense, rather than art rock. However, the name of the band (the name of a river in Greek mythology) and songs like "Mr. Roboto" from 1983 suggest other world influences ("domo arigato" is Japanese for "thank you"). They also staged a theatrical presentation on tour in 1983 for *Kilroy Was Here,* a concept album released in the same year.

Kansas (started in Topeka, Kansas, in 1970) was a progressive band of the mid-1970s that had enormous success. Clearly influenced by Genesis (Steve Walsh of Kansas eventually worked with Steve Hackett of Genesis), this band was successful at selling concept albums and had some hit singles, but it succumbed to internal strife in 1980. Probably the most obvious reasons for their inclusion in this chapter are their conscious emulation of Genesis and the presence, in Kansas, of Robby Steinhardt, a violinist.

Pink Floyd (founded in 1965 in London) might seem an unlikely candidate for discussion in an art rock chapter. Starting out as a psychedelic R & B band, they quickly became progressive because their psychedelic music became epic in length. From 1971 on, their albums were all concept albums. They also did film soundtracks from 1969 to 1972, supporting the contention that their music took on experimental aspects. Although one could easily toss off Pink Floyd as another group poised halfway between hard pop and heavy metal, that would be an error. Their music does have a sense of negative world view, such as the *Wall* image, but upon closer examination we discover that Pink Floyd draws upon many artistic sources. Besides, their 1973 album *The Dark Side of the Moon* stayed on *Billboard*'s charts for 303 weeks.

Rush, started in 1969 in Toronto, is a progressive power trio. *Rush* (1974) was a hard rock album featuring songs like "Working Man." The second album, *Fly by Night,* featured "Bytor and the Snowdog," a typical early Rush composition. The next album, *Caress of Steel* (1975), was more metal-oriented with a representative song being "Bastille Day." On the other hand, "Lakeside Park" from the same album was a song about the drummer's hometown. However, they developed a more progressive sound with *21 12* from 1976, which features a full use of electronic devices and a much mellower sound. Being a Canadian group, they combined styles of Britain and the United States and are an excellent example of progressive pop/progressive metal style. They started as a hard rock band and became more progressive by the mid-1970s. In 1982 Rush performed a small segment on the *Great White North* album of Bob and Doug McKenzie; this album was on the U.S. charts for most of 1982.

Queen was formed in 1971. The four members are very well-educated individuals who apparently decided to make money as a hard-rocking band. This band is referred to as "pomp" rock by British critics, and they do use theatricality to the hilt; they are also popular with heavy metal fans. Queen did the soundtrack to the 1980 film *Flash Gordon* and has been very successful. They could be discussed as a progressive metal band.

Boston also fits the mold of progressive metal although they have never equalled their initial success with *Boston,* in 1976. Basically a power band, made up of two or three guitars, bass, and drums, their progressive pop sound was typically American in context.

Discussion of the group Asia is a fitting close to this chapter because it represents how the art and progressive styles have evolved with the times. Formed in Los Angeles in 1981, Asia was made up of Carl Palmer from Emerson, Lake and Palmer, Steve Howe and Geoffrey Downes (both had been members of Yes), and John Wetton, who had been the bass player for King Crimson and Roxy Music. Described as the first supergroup of the 1980s, their album *Asia* was number one in the United States. The style of the first album was progressive metal, especially with its overdubbed recording technique. Intricate backup instrumental work was subdued slightly behind the lyric, which featured the vocal trio sound made popular by British groups with which some of the band members had originally played. The first cut, "Heat of the Moment," clearly represented a move toward the techno-pop sound of the 1980s. Appropriately, the second cut from the album, a ballad, started with a baroque-sounding synthesizer passage leading to a pop style vocal, which dominated over a light rock background. The song's melodic and vocal lines were very clear, although heavy metal distortion was used — especially on guitar solos.

In conclusion, this chapter has presented a mixture of styles, roughly tied together by the experimental quality of the music. While the use of the term art rock would imply an apparent contradiction to the title of the book, no such ambiguity is intended. For the most part, this music has been called art, eclectic, or progressive rock because of particular elements that make that description apt. Many of the groups discussed have had commercial success, so the terms art and progressive do not imply unpopular music. While eclectic as a descriptive term has often applied to a noncommercial philosophy, even the most noted eclectic musician, Frank Zappa, had a commercial hit with "Valley Girl" from his 1982 album *Ship arriving too late to save a drowning witch.* While Zappa may not have intended that particular song to be commercial, the point of much of this music is that it has an experimental or communicative quality to it, which clearly causes it to be unusual. It is, however, viable as a communication form and therefore succeeds as rock regardless of its structural technique.

LISTENING

Mothers of Invention, *Ruben and the Jets*
Mothers of Invention, *Uncle Meat*

Mothers of Invention, *Ship arriving too late to save a drowning witch*

Procol Harum, *Procol Harum*

Kinks, *Village Green Preservation Society*

Emerson, Lake and Palmer, *Pictures at an Exhibition*

Genesis, *The Lamb Lies Down on Broadway*

Yes, *Close to the Edge*

Styx, *Styx*

Pink Floyd, *The Dark Side of the Moon*

Rush, *21 12*

Asia, *Asia*

CHAPTER **14**

COUNTRY ROCK

In the discussion of rockabilly we alluded to a difference between rockabilly and rock and roll; that distinction should be kept clearly in mind during the preliminary discussions of this chapter. Rockabilly was the first concrete combination of country music with rock and roll and was very significant in the development of both. In fact, rockabilly still exists today and is often defined by rock musicians as basic rock or the roots of rock. Rockabilly as a technique of punk or new wave musicians serves as the focal point for rock purity. The country rock discussed in this chapter, however, has little to do with trying to preserve the primary integrity of rock and roll; it is rather a conscious amalgamation of rock and country music.

Country rock is then analogous to rock music after the middle Beatles period (1965) in that it consciously uses elements of different kinds of music. Country rock is a combination of pop, folk, jazz, rock, and country music, and although most people think of country rock as being a specific type of music, it really encompasses a diverse group of musicians. This chapter discusses the cultural influencers of country rock, some of its specific technical advancements, and its main practitioners. This chapter is also quite condensed, as one could easily write a whole book on this subject.

Country rock has a few distinct elements (although even these stylistic traits are occasionally missing from songs done by country rock groups — or groups that can be loosely defined as country rock). Country rock groups like Commander Cody and the Lost Planet Airmen usually do straight country music as well as country rock songs. The instrumentation of these groups is often versatile enough so that they can turn down the electronics, emphasize the violin or mandolin, and create mainstream country music in an effortless way. Therefore, the stylistic elements listed will define the way country rock groups play when they are doing songs in a country rock style.

A country rock band normally uses rather heavy amplification of the guitar instruments, particularly the bass guitar. The bass guitar sound is stronger than in honky tonk or any other form of country music. The drum patterns show more rock influence, although usually the country drumming style is present. But it should be remembered that even the presence of a drum set is a rock influence — very traditional country music would not use drums at all. Country rock also uses a rock-influenced style of lead guitar playing, at least in the amplification of the sound. Solo work by the lead guitar player is normally more melodic and less arpeggiated than in the standard style for country music.

The most important quality of country rock is the lyric content, lyrics which are most uncharacteristic of straight country music. The folk influence in country rock can be heard in highly political, sometimes controversial and socially aware lyrics, usually avoided by traditional country music. It is from country rock groups that we start hearing about drugs, social welfare, and ecology, and this shows a clear influence of the rock and folk worlds.

Country rock musicians usually look different from traditional country musicians. Country rock musicians grow their hair long and have beards. The rough image they project is simply a part of being modern. Since image is certainly a part of the communication of music, this difference is as important as the longer hair and beards grown by the Beach Boys after the mid-1960s. In the image sense alone, country rock musicians defined themselves as being "hip" and contemporary; and although Southern influences remain present, country rock tends to be somewhat less regional in style than traditional country music.

It is important to understand the tremendous diversity of country rock and also that it is not totally relegated to groups that recognize themselves solely as country rock groups. There are many different kinds of music that could be labeled country rock, from Bob Dylan to the New Riders of the Purple Sage. The musicians mentioned in this chapter have been included because they sang country songs, performed music that had country elements, or were influenced by country traditions. In some cases, a few of these musicians have been vastly influential, in country music and in popular music. In other cases, they have had little influence. But the main point of this chapter is to highlight some examples of musicians who were part of the general movement to amalgamate country music with other musical styles.

THE EMERGENCE OF THE SONGWRITER AS NARRATOR

The songwriter has always been important in country music, from the days of Jimmie Rodgers to today. But at no time in the history of contemporary popular music has songwriting as narration been more important. Of course, songwriters are always narrators of the human condition, and country music is one of the most conscious expressions of the human condition. But prior to the 1960s, country music was relatively limited in the scope of that narration. During the 1960s and into the 1970s the subject matter of country music diversified; the leaders of that trend were the country rock lyricists.

One of the important characteristics of country rock in this context is the expression of southern pride. Much of country music prior to the development of the Nashville sound was fairly self-deprecating, promoting the image of the southern hick. Nashville writers created a feeling of pride in their lyrics. Interestingly, one of the examples of that type of lyric writer was Willie Nelson. But it was the country rock musicians who delivered not only a sense of pride but also a diversity of message.

A good example of the southern pride expressed in country rock was Lynyrd Skynyrd's "Sweet Home, Alabama," which was designed as a rebuttal to Neil Young's "Southern Man." Crosby, Stills, Nash and Young was a highly influential folk rock group of the late 1960s and early 1970s, but "Southern Man" was not particularly complimentary of the South. Lynyrd Skynyrd's "Sweet Home, Alabama" redressed that. For the most part, country music has become more sophisticated and has lost the image of being constantly depressing.

Diversity of image is quite important in 1970s country rock, and one hears a variety of messages — social, political, moral, and others. It is in this way that the songwriter has become a more diversified narrator of life in the South. Southern music of the 1970s begins to have national impact rather than being regionalistic. Although country music has always had adherents in other parts of the United States, prior to this time fans from the Midwest liked country music because it evoked southern feeling. With the changes that occurred in the 1970s, country music began to express feelings no longer firmly tied to the South and to speak to urban issues everywhere. And probably the best proof of that is the international popularity country music has won in the last fifteen years.

The changing subject matter of country music in the 1970s has had a snowballing effect, and writers have had an increasing influence on the types of songs that are sung. Many people have followed with great interest the growth of crossover popular country tunes and the continuing growth of traditional country music. Although one could argue that marketing has been responsible for increasing the sales of and public access to country music, it must certainly be due also to songwriters who have opened up new subjects, increasing their impact to the point where they could affect trends themselves. At no time in earlier country music has the writer had so much influence on the public's thinking.

MAIN PRACTITIONERS OF COUNTRY ROCK

In this section we will consider some representative examples of country rock groups or musicians who have influenced or been influenced by country music. Some musicians mentioned in this section are known primarily as either folk or rock musicians, and most people do not recognize their country influences. They are mentioned to give credit to the country part of their performance.

Alabama

The name of this award-winning group comes from the fact that the original three members, Randy Owen, Jeff Cook, and Teddy Gentry, came from Alabama. As teenagers in 1969 they started jamming together in usual sloppy style. In 1970 they formed the group, so Alabama has actually been around for some time. Their first job was playing at a local tourist park, where they got the opportunity to back major performers who were brought in on the weekends.

In 1973 the band moved to Myrtle Beach, South Carolina, where they worked local clubs for cheap wages. They made demo records and tried to get a recording contract. They were successful and got a contract from GRT Records in 1976, recording under the name Wild Country. Their first recording of "I Want to Be with You" did not do well, but it got them a more permanent contract with MDJ Records out of Dallas, Texas. With MDJ they issued several singles that actually made the charts; in 1980 "My Home's in Alabama" made it into the top twenty. But it actually was not until 1980 that Alabama made it to the big time with RCA Records.

In 1980 RCA released Alabama's single, "Tennessee River," their first album, *My Home's in Alabama,* and another single, "Why, Lady, Why." The last single made it to the top ten on the country list in the fall. After 1981 the group had phenomenal success, with a number of gold and platinum records and numerous awards. In a day when it is rare for a country group to win awards, Alabama consistently hit the top of the charts and has collected many trophies, for example Entertainer of the Year in 1984.

This fearsome foursome fits the image of a country rock group because they are very neat looking, yet have long hair and beards. They are definitely country, and the rock part of their sound is light rock. In some ways they are folksingers, and their vocal texture is really quite soft. They do nostalgic songs and show clearly that they are Southerners. They are of course very popular in the South, but they also have a strong following in other parts of the United States.

Commander Cody and the Lost Planet Airmen

Commander Cody (George Frayne) and the Lost Planet Airmen is one of those groups that you will not find in a country encyclopedia because they are not from the South. The original members of the group were from Ann Arbor (Michigan), Boise (Idaho), Decatur (Alabama), New York, and St. Louis. When the band formed in 1968, all of them were living in Ann Arbor, where Frayne was an art student at the University of Michigan.

The campus area of the University of Michigan is very active, and Ann Arbor is a very liberal town. The town has even had an active hippie movement since the late 1960s. It was the perfect location to put together something different. But even in Ann Arbor, country rock was unusual in the late 1960s.

The group was fairly interesting in its instrumentation, using players on piano, guitars, steel guitar, and one player who doubled on fiddle, sax, and trombone. Even at its craziest, the band was made up of technically superior players. They played a combination of western swing, rockabilly, and country music. Although not highly successful, they did put out nine albums and charted three singles on the top 100 over their nine-year career. Only one album, *Lost in the Ozone,* is still available, but it belongs in every diversified country fan's library.

At times Commander Cody plays straight country music, but the band is known primarily for its novelty tunes. They do mention drugs in some of their tunes, for instance, "Stoned in the Ozone Again" or in their classic "Seeds and Stems." Novelty tunes like "Beat Me Daddy Eight to the Bar" (1972) and Tex Ritter's "Smoke, Smoke, Smoke" (1973) were good examples. It is hard to tell whether they were talking about the same kind of tobacco that Ritter was, but regardless, they did the tune in a remarkable parody.

Commander Cody and the Lost Planet Airmen may have seemed like just a bunch of crazies. But the group, whose career essentially ended in the late 1970s, was composed of very good musicians, and they did various types of music right in the appropriate style. A good example of country rock in its more unusual form, they illustrate well that even midwesterners can do country music.

Charlie Daniels Band

The Charlie Daniels Band is a more obvious example of a country rock band because it is from the South, sings about southern themes, and has a country feel to the playing and singing style. Charlie Daniels, born in 1937 in North Carolina, now resides in Tennessee. A fiddler and guitarist, he formed his first band, the Jaguars, in 1958. He toured with that band throughout the South, essentially as a honky tonker. He also did some writing during that period and in fact collaborated on a tune done by Elvis Presley — "It Hurts Me." In 1967 he dissolved the Jaguars and moved to Nashville, where he wrote songs for Tammy Wynette, among others, and played on recording sessions for Bob Dylan, Pete Seeger, and numerous country stars.

In 1971 he started the Charlie Daniels Band, which was basically an imitation

Charlie Daniels and Little Richard   *(Used by permission of Ginny Cartmell and Creem Magazine Archives)*

of the instrumentation of the Allman Brothers Band—two drummers and two guitarists. This instrumentation (which expanded over time) gives the Charlie Daniels Band a fairly heavy sound, bluesy, and strong, yet still country in orientation. Daniels recorded on a variety of levels until 1975, when he was signed by Epic. Some of his early big hits were "Uneasy Rider" and "The South's Gonna Do It." The last tune was a song of southern pride and clearly identifies Daniels with the South.

He politicized country rock when he toured for Jimmy Carter and, later, performed at the White House. Daniels, who has kept up a demanding touring schedule, won his first major award, a Grammy, in 1979. During the 1980 Iran crisis he had a major hit with "In America." This is a country rock group with a message, and Charlie Daniels, the main songwriter, functions as a narrator of the human condition in their political songs. The Charlie Daniels Band is highly respected and plays in a number of different styles, everything from country rock to traditional to Tex-Mex music.

Eagles

The Eagles were formed in 1971 and dissolved in 1981. The original four members, Don Henley, Glenn Frey, Bernie Leadon, and Randy Meisner, made up the background band for Linda Ronstadt on her *Silk Purse* album. These musicians had strong backgrounds as session players and as performing musicians, coming from such bands as the Flying Burrito Brothers, Poco, Bob Seger, and Shiloh.

The Eagles were Los Angeles – based, and although one does not think of Los Angeles as a mecca for country music, there was a thriving country rock tradition there in the 1970s. What the Eagles did was to take the country rock tradition of the Byrds and the Flying Burrito Brothers more toward the hard rock side, although they always retained some country flavor with a Tex-Mex accent.

The Eagles had tremendous success during their eleven-year career, although the awards groups did not seem to notice it. They cultivated a following of people who were halfway between country and rock and became a model for California-based country music. Hard-edged vocals pushed this particular group closer to rock than country, but the roots of country were always there.

Flying Burrito Brothers

The Flying Burrito Brothers is one of the most interesting country rock groups. The personnel changes this band has gone through in their twenty plus years of existence read like a phone book. But to make a very long story short, the Burrito Brothers use basically the following instrumentation: keyboards (electric and acoustic), guitar, bass, steel guitar, and drums. At times they have also used banjo, dobro, harmonica, and fiddle.

The Flying Burrito Brothers were only really important from 1968, when they were formed in Los Angeles, to 1970, when Gram Parsons quit the group to have a solo career (Parsons died tragically in 1973). The Parsons-led Flying Burrito Brothers was a swinging bluegrass band with perpetual rhythm and haunting lyrics that were very un – country-like. The original group was folk-rock with a bluegrass instrumentation.

After 1970 and their real success, the Flying Burrito Brothers went through numerous changes in personnel. In the 1980s they existed as a vocal duet working out of Nashville, but the original intensity of the Flying Burrito Brothers as an example of the strong country rock movement of southern California ended in the early 1970s. However, when they were hot, they were really hot.

Grateful Dead

The Grateful Dead (previously discussed in chapter ten) was formed in San Francisco in 1965 and is the only psychedelic band to survive into the mid-1980s. They have never had a hit record or a top ten single, but for true Dead Heads (Grateful Dead fans) that does not matter.

The real story of the Grateful Dead is the story of Jerry Garcia. He was born in San Francisco in 1942, started playing the guitar at the age of fifteen, and later learned to play the banjo. He began playing in bluegrass bands in 1962, and in 1964 he was a member of Mother McCree's Uptown Jug Champions (now if that does not show country roots, I give up). In 1965 the band changed its name to the Warlocks, and they were essentially the house band for LSD parties, chronicled in Wolfe's *Electric Kool-Aid Acid Test.* Then they changed their name to the Grateful Dead, were signed by MGM, and became a psychedelic band. In 1967 they changed to Warner Brothers, where their music was produced more professionally. They did start their own record label in 1973, although that really did not do any better than Warner Brothers had.

The Dead are not important for their commercial success but rather for the quality of their music. If you listen to even a smattering of Dead albums you will hear country guitar picking and country tunes (granted, you will also hear some tunes that are not country at all).

Jerry Garcia continued to work with other artists, especially the New Riders of the Purple Sage. He did session work with the Jefferson Airplane and Crosby, Stills, Nash and Young. He continues to play bluegrass banjo and peddle steel guitar (which he played when recording with the New Riders). The Dead's personnel has varied greatly over the years, but Jerry Garcia as the center of the group has kept the sound fairly consistent; and the country roots of Jerry Garcia are obvious in the sound of the Grateful Dead.

Lynyrd Skynyrd

Lynyrd Skynyrd (watch that spelling) was formed in 1966 in Jacksonville, Florida, rose to prominence in 1973, and ended abruptly in 1977 when the lead singer and a guitar player were killed in a plane crash. This band was made up of long-haired hard rockers, with a sound somewhat patterned after the Allman Brothers. They are usually left out of country rock discussions because they are mostly very loud and heavy metal.

The name of the band was a takeoff on the name of one of their school-teachers, a gym teacher who punished students with long hair. From 1966 until 1972 they played the club and bar circuit; in 1972 Al Kooper of MCA signed them to a recording contract after hearing them in a bar. From 1973 to 1980 the band, with its heavy metal brand of southern rock, had a large following in the South as well as some national exposure. Its major contribution to the cause of southern music was undoubtedly the song from 1974, "Sweet Home Alabama."

Marshall Tucker Band

The Marshall Tucker Band is made up of six musicians, the original six being from Spartanburg, South Carolina. In 1971 the Caldwell Brothers (Toy and Tommy) joined with the other four original members in what would become one of the hottest country rock bands of the 1970s. Tommy died in 1980 and was replaced by a long-time friend of the Caldwells.

The Marshall Tucker Band   *(Photo by Warner Brothers Records; used by permission of Ginny Cartmell and Creem Magazine Archives)*

Actually the Marshall Tucker Band is one of the most diverse groups in this chapter because they play everything — traditional country, blues, rockabilly, and jazz-rock. Playing a variety of musical instruments, they are capable of shifting from one style to another with great ease. They use alto sax and flute, steel guitar, and full rhythm section, but they also use combinations that give the string band flavor. The band's sound has often been described as middle-of-the-road or crossover, which perhaps explains their national and overseas following.

The Marshall Tucker Band signed first with Capricorn Records in 1972 and changed to Warner Brothers in 1978. They got their first gold record in 1975 and their first platinum in 1977. Many of the band members were fine writers, and the Caldwells in particular had many of their songs done by other artists — Waylon Jennings, Kitty Wells, and Hank Williams Jr., to mention a few. From 1977 on the band consistently put out top-selling albums and singles, and that creative impetus did not cease, even with the hard blow of Tommy's death.

The Marshall Tucker Band toured with the Allman Brothers Band in 1973, and many have said that they are simply Allman imitators. They have a strong bluesy sound, but the diversity of song styles makes them quite different from the Allmans.

New Riders of the Purple Sage

The New Riders of the Purple Sage was an invention of Jerry Garcia. He wanted an opportunity to play the pedal steel guitar, which he had taken up in the late 1960s. He joined with John Dawson, a guitarist and singer who had been in an earlier band, Mother McCree's Uptown Jug Champions. Soon the duo was joined by other Dead members and by David Nelson, who had been with Big Brother and the Holding Company.

The New Riders of the Purple Sage was a country alternative to the Dead. Their sound is folksy, with lots of country in it, although the subject matter is often fairly unconventional. Their most popular subject seems to be marijuana, in particular Panama Red. One of their songs from the first album talks about going to Mexico to collect golden "keys." A fairly short-lived band (most of the Grateful Dead members, including Garcia, dropped out of the band quickly because of time commitments), it was an interesting experiment in country rock — a band formed to allow its members to play a different kind of music.

After 1974 the initial popularity of the New Riders dwindled greatly and they ultimately lost their record contract. However, during the time they existed they were a great band, as entertaining to watch as to listen to. The sound of the New Riders was clearly country, but the subject matter of their songs was so completely out of the tradition that they were in a sense a novelty band. The novelty was very popular in liberal and college towns, and they enjoyed moderate record sales and good concert success. At one point, they served as the warmup band for the Grateful Dead.

The Nitty Gritty Dirt Band

The Dirt Band, as it has been called since 1976, was formed in Long Beach, California, in 1966. The group members are mostly from Long Beach, with one from Detroit, one from Boston, and one from West Germany. It is one of the oddest congregations of musicians you could imagine, capable of playing jug band, string band, traditional country, western swing, and country rock. They are even more versatile than the Marshall Tucker Band, which is saying something.

The original name of the band was the Illegitimate Jug Band, but by 1967 they were known as the Nitty Gritty Dirt Band. At the beginning of their career they were decidedly confused about whether they were country musicians or rock musicians; even after their first eight albums one would have been hard pressed to make that decision for them. However, with their 1973 historic recording of *Will the Circle Be Unbroken,* which featured a number of traditional country musicians such as Earl Scruggs, Maybelle Carter, Merle Travis, and Roy Acuff, they began to move more clearly into country. In 1977 they made another type of history by being the first country band to tour through Russia.

A public performance of this band was a delight to behold because they were constantly trading instruments and creating new musical textures. During the mid-1970s a young comedian named Steve Martin worked as the warmup act for the Dirt Band. Even after Martin attained star status himself, he occasionally returned to appear with the Dirt Band, playing banjo. The band's importance is that they have preserved the original integrity of a country string and jug band, while at the same time moving easily into the country rock sound.

The Dirt Band continued to sell albums into the 1980s and had some successful hits in 1980 and 1981. However, it is really mostly a historical group now. Although they have had some very lucrative recordings, probably their most important was the 1973 album with those other country stars. It received very positive reviews and helped to bridge the gap between traditional country music and the new wave of country music. Of course, many of the old-time stars were reluctant to get involved, but the ultimate result was a very pleasing experience for everyone.

Hank Williams, Jr.

Hank Williams, Jr., was born in 1949, the only son of the king of the Honky Tonk singers, Hank Williams, Sr. His father died in 1953, and Hank, Jr., was not heavily influenced by anything but his father's legacy. His mother took him to California in 1964, and he was immediately signed by MGM records, as he had shown an early talent for music. His first album, *Hank Williams, Jr., Sings* was released in May 1964; there was a hit single from that album, a song of his father's entitled "Long Gone Lonesome Blues." Although it certainly could be said that he was taking advantage of his father's songs, Hank Williams, Jr., was a bonafide star as a teenager, singing very much in the Nashville Sound style.

In the early 1970s, he reevaluated his musical style, moved to Alabama, and began searching for a unique style of his own. He did an album *Hank Williams, Jr., and Friends,* which included Charlie Daniels, members of the Allman Brothers Band, and Toy Caldwell of the Marshall Tucker Band. This album was influenced by progressive country and rock. In 1975 he had a serious accident, which broke his jaw and put him in the hospital for some time. When he emerged, he became a different kind of singer, grew a beard, and represented new wave country.

His music of the late 1970s, the 1980s, and into the 1990s is pure country rock, with traditional country subject material, such as rowdiness, drinking, and women. But he is an excellent example of country rock and its influences. He has been recognized a number of times with awards, both within the country music community and in pop music in general.

LISTENING

Alabama, *My Home's in Alabama*
Alabama, *The Closer You Get*

Commander Cody and the Lost Planet Airmen, *Lost in the Ozone*
Charlie Daniels, *Charlie Daniels*
Eagles, *Greatest Hits*
Lynyrd Skynyrd, *Gimme Back My Bullets*
Dirt Band, *Will the Circle Be Unbroken*

CHAPTER 15

JAZZ-ROCK, FUNK, AND DISCO

This chapter discusses *fusion,* the purposeful combination of two or more specific types of music. Because there were many attitudes prevailing at the same time in the 1970s, the idea of the art forms merging in something called fusion makes sense. Some people have suggested that fusion was logical because of the implications of technology, but it seems more likely that it came about because of diverse tastes. In any event, rock was heavily dominated in the early and mid-1970s by this particular concept. Rock was being influenced by and combined with other forms of music, and other forms were being affected by rock.

In some senses, rock has always been the product of other sources: first, rhythm and blues combined with white pop; later, big bands influenced the playing style. However, the intent of the performer and the desires of the audiences required a separate art form, one not tainted by certain influences. If the other forms were there, it was incidental to the rock music produced and not a part of the concept. In the 1970s, this was to change. Rock musicians became openly appreciative of other forms, studied them, and blatantly used their techniques.

This phenomenon actually started in the 1960s, although other influential musicians had previously used jazz techniques, most notably Ray Charles. However, during the experimentalism of the 1960s, many musicians worked with other music. The Beatles were interested in Indian music, which they performed on recordings. Generally, many rock groups took advantage of electronic devices that had been created for jazz, such as the electric piano and the synthesizer.

We will discuss eleven musicians or groups that identified themselves as jazz-rock musicians. Some of these musicians started before the 1970s, but jazz-rock as an important part of rock was totally a concept of that decade. In the funk section we will deal with musicians who were identified primarily with that movement. Funk as an outgrowth of soul or black music is also a concept of the 1970s. Finally, we will discuss briefly the significance of disco as a major phenomenon of that time, influential in many fields outside of rock. All three movements have strong jazz roots, although they clearly belong in the history of rock.

Fusion music of the 1970s has had enormous commercial impact, and all three types of music were financially successful. The results of commercialization in the history of rock were not always satisfying musically, but the result in the 1970s was music that both communicated and was artistically gratifying.

JAZZ-ROCK

As a jazz musician, I am biased toward this particular blending with rock. It has produced some very intriguing results, and in my opinion, the resulting music is stronger for the amalgamation. It should be remembered that jazz and rock came from the same roots, and therefore this particular marriage was one arranged from birth. The first issue to consider is why it happened at the time that it did.

The divergence of jazz and rock occurred in the early 1950s when rock and roll became identified with an entirely different audience from that for jazz. Jazz was in some ways a separatist or elitist concept in the 1950s, and it was for the most part acoustic in performance. Whereas the rock musician relied heavily on amplification, the jazz musician shunned electronic devices. Jazz was either bohemian or progressive and sought higher planes of intellectual activity. Rock was basic and was aimed at a particular type of common person—young people and rebels. When and if jazz techniques were used by rock musicians in the 1950s, they were generally used by seasoned veterans like Ray Charles; but jazz was always a subtle influence, usually through gospel and rhythm and blues. We could trace the intervention of jazz styles into rock and roll (and vice versa) through the development of electronic wizardry, as well as through the technical ability of rock musicians.

With few exceptions, the rock musician of the 1950s was not technically a good musician. The musical technique required for the style was not very complicated. Even the best of the musicians, Chuck Berry and Ray Charles, did not need technical expertise because the words were more important than the background.

The rock musician of the 1960s was not radically different in this respect, at least not until the end of the decade. The major artists were by and large singers who just happened to play an instrument. A few of the folk singers, Joni Mitchell for example, had technical ability on an instrument, but in their early recordings they did not show it. It simply was not necessary. What led to an expansion of technical ability was the experimentation of the 1960s, coupled with an expanding interest in different textures. As musicians began to experiment with different combinations of instruments, they had to learn to play them well. Occasionally, this need caused musicians to practice technique simply for its own sake. Less occasionally, it produced fine players.

Also, sometime in the 1960s there was a subtle shift in musicians' attitudes. It may be that it was caused more by the media than anything else. As rock became more and more popular as a media phenomenon, especially television, it was increasingly necessary for studio musicians to be able to play in different styles. Although studio musicians seldom had the influence on other musicians' attitudes that they probably should have, from the mid-1960s on there was a change in this respect. Many people wanted to be complete musicians, especially as the musician's role in society became more profitable and more diversified.

For many reasons, jazz musicians no longer thought it evil to play rock, and some fine jazz musicians began to do so, for example, Chick Corea, Herbie Hancock, and later, George Benson. These are musicians who in a previous generation might not have stooped to rock. However, in the 1970s they made major contributions to both jazz-rock and the world of funk-pop.

Blood, Sweat and Tears (BS&T) was a tremendously significant rock group for many of the previously stated reasons. Under the able direction of Al Kooper on organ and synthesizers, the group used a horn section (like Chicago) with a more traditional rock rhythm section. The former was initially used like a rhythm and blues horn section in that it played punctuated riffs simply to add to the instrumental texture. Started in 1967, BS&T set a standard for jazz-rock. Although it did not continue, its initial concept was to use jazz techniques under the surface of a rock band. The vocal part was very important, as it was in Chicago. However, the music's most important characteristic was that it was highly technical, far surpassing the general level of music in 1967. The most important part of jazz emphasized was the highly technical and difficult melodic line.

The Chicago Transit Authority, later shortened to Chicago, began in 1968 and was made up of musicians who were technically very competent. They used the same basic ensemble as BS&T, with only one trumpet. Chicago combined rock with jazz interludes by the horn section. It was probably the first group to make extensive use of horn melodies and solos, which were real jazz excursions. It also experimented with shifts in accent and some very fine writing for the horn section. It enjoyed continued success as a result of its technically perfect performances, its strength as a rock group, and its feel for jazz.

Billy Cobham is a jazz drummer, par excellence. He was born in Panama and raised in New York. He worked with Miles Davis during his formative years and subsequently became one of the most dynamic drummers around. He worked with

Blood, Sweat and Tears   *(Photo by MCA Records; used by permission of Ginny Cartmell and Creem Magazine Archives)*

John McLaughlin and has played in support of a diverse group of people, including James Brown and Herbie Mann. He is equally at home with jazz, funk, and rock. The combination of his technical ability and his raw power made him an important example of the emerging jazz-rock musician of the late 1960s. His major significance as a jazz-rock drummer occurred in the 1970s.

Chick Corea is a New York–raised Puerto Rican most known as a jazz pianist. However, most of his jazz is heavy funk or is Latin influenced. Corea is a very versatile musician, especially good at improvisation; he makes extensive use of electronics and synthesizers. He has experimented heavily with unusual meters and chord changes. Although he is perhaps not well known to the rock world, in his jazz performances he plays some of the best rock around. Primarily a phenomenon of the 1970s, he continues to influence people in this decade.

Earth, Wind and Fire is slightly different from the previously mentioned musicians, but it is quite clearly a jazz-funk group. Started in Chicago in 1971, the group uses an expanded rock ensemble — multiple percussion and extensive keyboards (organ, piano, and synthesizers) — and one horn player doubling on flute, tenor sax, and soprano sax. Again, these are very technical players who use the funk sound to great effect. Although many of the jazz-rock groups are clever in their use of dynamics and staging, Earth, Wind and Fire is one of the best. One of the most delightful characteristics of this group is its ability to keep the feel going, changing from loud to soft instantaneously.

Earth, Wind and Fire   *(Courtesy of Columbia Records and Bruce W. Talamon, photographer)*

Electric Flag had the shortest career of any significant jazz-rock group. It was formed in 1967 and established itself at the 1967 Monterey Festival. It was the first group to use two horn players in a rock context, and although it lasted less than two years, it was very influential because of the musicians' technical virtuosity.

Herbie Hancock is another jazz musician who has bridged the gap between jazz and rock, primarily through funk. A concert pianist, Hancock was classically trained and schooled in the real world at the same time. He was the pianist for Miles Davis between 1963 and 1968 and is highly regarded for his improvisational ability. He is equally at home with electronic keyboards or synthesizers and with the acoustic piano. He is probably most famous for his composition "Watermelon Man" and has been voted the best pianist by *Downbeat, Playboy,* and other polls. He and Chick Corea are the two most important pianists in the jazz-rock tradition.

John McLaughlin is an English guitarist who first succeeded as a virtuoso jazz guitar player. He played with Miles Davis on his *Bitches Brew* album of 1971. In the latter part of that year he converted to a Bengali mystical religion and subsequently developed two different avenues of musical communication. One was Indian music, played mainly on acoustic guitar; the other was a pulsating jazz-rock. He formed the Mahavishnu Orchestra, which was an expanded ensemble reaching symphonic proportions at one time. His jazz-rock music is very powerful, and even within the context of traditional Indian music, his virtuosity is obvious. Of the jazz-rock guitarists, perhaps only George Bensen is a rival.

Jean-Luc Ponty is a French violinist who was classically trained. He became a

Herbie Hancock *(Courtesy of Columbia Records)*

significant jazz violinist in Europe and ultimately performed in the United States, where he played with the Mothers of Invention. As the amplified violin is rather a rarity, Ponty is without rival, with the possible exception of Papa John Creech.

Santana is an important representative of the jazz-rock school, especially in its blending of Latin-American elements. Carlos Santana was the son of a *mariachi* musician and spent his formative years playing in Tijuana, Mexico. He moved to San Francisco during the height of the youth culture and firmly established his band in the late 1960s. He employed many Latin-American musicians, and his major compositions were Latin in flavor. Probably his most important album was

Santana   *(Courtesy of Columbia Records)*

Abraxas in 1970. In the mid-1970s he worked with John McLaughlin and later with Alice Coltrane, John Coltrane's wife. Santana himself was a competent musician, and within the context of his various bands the sound was effective, with obvious Latin and funk overtones.

Weather Report was formed in 1970, and the two important members of this group are Josef Zawinul on keyboards and Wayne Shorter on saxophone. Both musicians are alumni of Miles Davis. Zawinul is a classically trained pianist from Vienna, Austria, and Wayne Shorter is a black saxophonist from the East Coast. Both are phenomenally good jazz musicians who moved slowly into the jazz-funk school while retaining their excellent improvisatory abilities. *Heavy Weather* in 1977 was a smash hit with both the rock and jazz audiences; several tunes from that

Weather Report   *(Courtesy of Columbia Records)*

album have been covered by other jazz musicians, Sonny Rollins and Maynard Ferguson, for example.

The significance of jazz-rock is as follows:

1. Some very competent musicians began to make contributions to rock technique.
2. Rock became more complicated as a result.
3. The commercial value of rock was made broader by the inclusion of an audience that previously would have shunned it.
4. At times, the message of the lyrics was stated better because of the expanded support mechanism.
5. Many electronic devices became commonplace in both jazz and rock.
6. Studio musicians set the standard for musical development as the media demanded more of this type of music.
7. Jazz influences began further to legitimize rock as a serious form of communication.

Rock improvisation had been quite static until this period. Even though the result of the jazz-rock merger was more commercial music, watering down the basic prototypes, the music became technically more proficient in general; and in particular, rock improvisation began to take on aspects of jazz improvisation. It became more melodic, more expansive, and generally just more interesting. Whereas the guitar had been almost the only instrument to play solos, in the jazz-rock era the solo function was expanded to include keyboards and other melodic instruments. Saxophone solos of the 1970s (which were important in the 1950s) were more like jazz solos, and the technique required to play them was much more demanding. In all, jazz-rock has had an exhilarating effect on the development of rock musicality.

FUNK

The word *funk* can be defined in several ways, all of which are illusive. The most common way is to think of it as a four-letter word having various sexual and social meanings. Funk evolved from music called *soul,* a euphemism for black music. Soul was the term that replaced rhythm and blues in the black community, and soul music was most certainly centered in Detroit and the Motown (Motor Town) complex of the 1960s and 1970s. Early soul music was personal and spoke clearly to black constituents and concerns. Funk did the same in its early stages.

The first soul recording containing the word funk was Dyke and the Blazers' "Funky Broadway" in 1967. Of course earlier tunes contained the word, but this was the first recording successful enough to be played on the radio. As soon as the word was used, it was legitimized and any evil implications were glossed over. Funk became a way of life, a feel for existence, especially within the black community.

However, funk is also definable musically, and it was not long before the style was copied by white musicians. By the early 1970s funk was probably the most significant style in rock, and maybe in pop music in general. Funk certainly began as an expression of black consciousness, and the funk vocabulary is a specialized black vocabulary. Even with the separation of the black and white communities at that time, funk became a bridge between them.

The funk style does not depend on any particular chord progression, although it was quite often played in the blues style. Some funk pieces do not change cords at all because funk is a musical and rhythmic texture. Funk can be totally instrumental, although at first it was primarily a musical background for narrative songs. The funk style requires a particular rhythmic ensemble—percussion and bass line—and either sustained chords or rhythmic interpolations by other instruments. Like rock in general, it uses evenly spaced beats rather than a swing jazz feel and syncopation. Quite often, once the basic feel is established, it simply repeats the music over and over. The best general description of funk is the concept of "street feel" or the way one walks. Funk is an attitude, which when expressed musically transforms the listener into a particular mood, usually described as laid-back or mellow.

Funk can be aggressive, and its message can be bleak or depressing, depending on the times. However, the musical structure combines both softness and harshness. Backup instruments often come in as punctuated short riffs. The most common beat pattern for these punctuations is an accent on beat four of a four-beat measure (usually short-short-long). The beat pattern of the percussion group, the simplest being just a drum set, is rather constant but clipped short most of the time. Sustaining is the responsibility of either the voices or a keyboard instrument. Funk is electronic because it is an urban style.

Probably its most important musical feature is the bass line, and depending on the player, it can be quite complicated or relatively simple. To fully appreciate the funk style, we must sort out the bass line. In simple styles the bass line will set up a repetitive rhythmic pattern based on one and five of the musical scale; many funk tunes don't change chords at all, so it is easy to analyze them. If the tune is really complicated it will usually be the result of a complex bass line. Stanley Clarke has enormously complicated funk bass lines, and in this style he is the undisputed master.

The history of black attitudes can certainly be heard in funk tunes, which are a minichronicle of black attitudes in the last twenty-five years. In this sense, funk is very relevant to what the black community perceives as its position in life, and it is an interesting study in itself. The latest stage in the evolution of funk was probably the *rap,* a phenomenon starting in the late 1970s. This was a free-form conversion with lightly textured funk music in the background.

Kool and the Gang is a very successful East Coast group that put together all the funk elements into one unit. Its greatest success was in the early 1970s (especially 1974) with songs like "Funky Stuff" and "Jungle Boogie," although in the late 1970s it scored big with "Celebration." The funk background is remarkably versatile, and the voices sort of flow through the varied background. In general, the group is optimistic and always very mellow.

The Commodores started in the late 1960s, and in 1970 they were the opening act for the tour by the Jackson Five. Their first album was called *Machine Gun* (1973); one of the songs, "Do the Bump," was a crossover in that it was quite successful with a basically white audience. The Commodores use a standard rhythm section, saxophone, and trumpet. It is definitely a funk band, although its music fits nicely into the disco concept as well.

Parliament was a vocal group founded in the mid-1950s. The leader of this group and the one that evolved from it (the Funkadelics) was George Clinton, who is the purest of funk musicians. He believes in raw energy, which both Parliament and the Funkadelics had. Their style was mainstream funk with no commercial softening at all, and the vocal line was most important. They did little crooning like Kool and the Gang, and even funk-rock groups like Earth, Wind and Fire were criticized by Clinton as sell-outs. For real funk people, the Funkadelics (or Parliament-Funkadelic, as it is sometimes called) is the model for the form.

Like many of the different forms of music in America, funk has become a part of the necessary repertory of a musician. We cannot imagine professional musicians today not being able to play at least five or six funk riffs. However, once they know these five or six riffs, they can survive indefinitely. Funk is enjoyable to play

Kool and the Gang *(Courtesy of PolyGram Records)*

but is quite simple. Unless it is mixed with jazz, it is technically not demanding. On the other hand, it can be rigorous, as played, for example, by Stanley Clarke.

DISCO

Disco, a movement of the 1970s, was very important — at least until the new wave — because it provided a central focus for the return to dancing. Other than Donna Summer, however, not many people have become successful solely from disco music. John Travolta, in *Saturday Night Fever,* established himself as a sex symbol based on his disco dancing as well as his image. Even though a number of musicians — Kate Smith, James Brown, Diana Ross, Chuck Mangione, and the Bee-Gees, for example — have made disco recordings, the form has been unproductive

Funkadelic *(Used by permission of Ginny Cartmell and Creem Magazine Archives)*

for the creation of new, exciting music, although it has had some commercial success.

Disco is simply dance music with an even tempo and a light rock feel (in fact, it is played rather consistently at one tempo—about 130 beats per minute). It often has funk undertones, but it is not as obvious or compelling as funk. Many of the funk performers have made disco recordings that lacked the smoothness disco

Donna Summer   *(Photo by Geffen Records; used by permission of Ginny Cartmell and Creem Magazine Archives)*

requires. In some senses, disco is the Muzak of the rock world, and like Muzak it was at one time very successful.

The subject matter of disco is optimistic and without social comment. It is simply good-time music, sexually unobtrusive in the sense that all real emotions are guarded. Disco has returned to the platonic relationships of ballads in the late 1950s, although some of Donna Summer's disco songs have overtly sexual lyrics, such as "Love to Love You, Baby," "Hot Stuff," "Bad Girls," and "Dim All the Lights." It often suggests relationships or nostalgia toward some place, but always with a hint of optimism. It is a clear reaction to the growing complexity and sadness of the 1970s, and many people seek refuge in it.

There is no question that disco was the most commercial venture of the

1970s, a musical formula that could be applied evenly to anything. All a musician had to do was add a rock beat and smooth out the lyrics — the result was disco. Many types of music were changed into disco tunes, even some of the favorite cartoon songs of Walt Disney.

Disco has also had far-reaching implications for other types of music and the social scene. It has become part of the standard repertory, and we can expect to hear it in certain social settings. It has affected jazz; the opening song of Chick Corea's *Secret Agent* (1979) is a disco tune. The jazz-funk trumpeter Tom Browne uses disco very tastefully and effectively on his album *Tom Browne* (1980). Disco complements jazz nicely, as it bears much resemblance to the fast samba form. In fact, we might even argue that the disco beat, with accents on beats two and four, might have come from the samba and/or bossa nova.

Few stars emerged from disco because the form was not sustainable, except for dancing. It was difficult, if not impossible, to reproduce its total effect in a concert because disco was designed for dance halls, with the lights, the action, and the people. It had become a DJ's art form in that what mattered was continuous music, and not necessarily recognizable music. Records were produced for discos that simply required a specific musical style and nothing else. Disco was responsible for taking away jobs from live musicians, so naturally it was not favored by professional musicians. However, all that aside, it was a valid response to a confusing world, and it did provide escape.

LISTENING

Chicago, *Chicago V*
Weather Report, *Heavy Weather*
Santana, *Abraxas*
James Brown, *Original Disco Man*
Funkadelics, *Uncle Jam Wants You*
Donna Summer, *Bad Girls*

CHAPTER **16**

HEAVY METAL

INTRODUCTION

Heavy metal is commonly described as being loud music, or just plain loud noise. While there can be little doubt that it is power-oriented, the genre certainly has more diversity to it than just loud noise. The elements of heavy metal consist of heavy use of electronic devices, in particular distortion, high volume, a thick cluttered sound where all musical elements combine to establish the sense of power, and a sound mix where the vocals are typically buried within the texture rather than being dominant as they are in other forms of rock and roll. At times, heavy metal–oriented bands have relied heavily on the lead guitar solo, and the pyrotechnics of that solo for a sense of propulsion, although the bass line becomes more important in later work. In addition, vocals have become more significant in later heavy metal, as it becomes a more specialized genre.

The term was first used by William Burroughs in his novel *Naked Lunch,* and

Alice Cooper   *(Used by permission of Ginny Cartmell and Creem Magazine Archives)*

first used in music by Steppenwolf in the song "Born to Be Wild." The most noted expert on the subject, Lester Bangs, popularized the term in the heavy metal fan magazine *Creem*. Some of the first musicians to play in this style were the Who, Jimi Hendrix, Iron Butterfly, MC5, Cream, and Blue Oyster Cult. During its formative stages, heavy metal was simply part of the development of rock and roll; only later did it become a specialized form for certain groups. Theatrics clearly had a great deal to do with the development of that specialization, through musicians like Alice

Cooper, Kiss, and Black Sabbath. Later heavy metal has been heavily marketed and has become identified with particular lyric and philosophical traits. However, the one thing we must remember in this brief description of a relatively important phenomenon in contemporary rock is that it is not just loud music — it is diversified in its subject matter and communicates a wide spectrum of ideas.

In its development, heavy metal basically has two traditions. The British/ European style is riff-oriented and blues-based; the American version is more melodic in orientation and less blues-based. There are hybrids of this concept, most notably Loudness, which tends to follow Los Angeles–type heavy metal, and others such as Scorpions and Krokus. One of the more interesting phenomena in the United States is the mid-1980s connection of heavy metal with professional wrestling. Heavy metal tends to be album-oriented rather than single-oriented, although there are occasional hit singles. In any event, as we trace through the following musicians, one should keep in mind the difference between British and American heavy metal, and the general characteristics of the style. What we will point out, in essence, are interesting cases and differences from the basic characteristics.

The representative musicians have been classified under the following subgroups: pre-metal, classic metal, mainstream metal, thrash/speed/death, and neo-punk/funky. These are basically chronological groupings although in the later cases, there are distinctive musical characteristics that separate those styles from a continuation of mainstream metal or hard rock, which continues through to the 1990s.

ATTITUDES OF THE 1980s

As this edition goes to press, the 1980s are recent history. Although the twenty-first century is close at hand, anyone would be hard pressed to predict what the cultural attitudes of 2001 will be and for that matter what configuration the world will be in the next century. Unfortunately, many of the manifestations of physical, cultural, and political history in the 1980s continued the pessimism of the 1970s and although one can always hope, the optimism of the 1950s and the commitment of the 1960s seem very far behind us.

As we entered the 1980s in the United States, Ronald Reagan was our president and served with some distinction through 1988, to be replaced by his vice-president, George Bush. Clearly a conservative era, although the balance of power was maintained by a Democratic Congress, the power and prestige of centralized government was brought into question many times. Startling events throughout the world caused the 1980s to be a time of retrenchment for the United States and the world economy in general.

The OPEC nations and the Middle East became important influences during the 1980s, as well as activity in Central America. Major economic failures, such as the savings and loan debacle of the late 1980s, significant changes in the price of oil and its availability, and the late-1990 occupation of Kuwait captured the attention of the world. And as usual, the United States was right in the middle of everything.

Political changes occurred in Europe as well, with socialist parties gaining great power, Soviet bloc countries vying for freedom, and the falling of the Berlin wall. By 1990, the United States and Russia were edging closer and closer to each other, in mutual support seemingly against a world that had lost its reason.

In the United States, the 1980s represented a time for great concern over the viability of the family, race relations, honesty or lack of honesty in governing officials, the drug war, AIDS, world starvation, and the viability of the economic institutions of the United States and the world. The stock market crash of 1987 was almost worse than Watergate because the threat of recession became a reality. Although we had economic concerns before, the economic problems of the late 1980s were more real and continued into the 1990s. The American reaction was gallows humor, such as the stock market and broker jokes; the world reaction was lack of trust in America as the land where the streets were paved with gold.

If we weren't trusted or believed in the 1970s, we really weren't trusted in the 1980s. Bankruptcies occurred in greater numbers; people had less morality toward debt; and pessimism abounded and for good reason. However, the 1980s also brought out the best in Americans and people throughout the world, a silent reaction to troubled times.

The troubles produced a schizophrenic society, which manifested itself in pessimism and negativity, but also in very positive ways. The dreaded disease AIDS became a rallying point for diversified people to join together in a common goal. America became concerned about the environment and protecting the farmer (Willie Nelson continued to be one of the best spokespeople for this cause). Many politicians, writers, actors, and artists became involved in publicly advertised activities designed to help correct problems. In short, the pessimism of the 1980s sometimes created the psychological need for people to act as they would have in the 1960s.

American business has weaknesses, but it also had strengths. Out of the ashes of economic hard times came new ways of doing business. Economic activity in emerging free-market economies from the Soviet Bloc created the fodder with which new ventures occurred. So while one would generally paint a pessimistic picture of the 1980s, that decade had both positive and negative aspects. And nowhere was that proved better than in the arts, music, and in particular rock and roll.

Although we will say a bit about this at the end of the book, the 1990s seem to be heading on the same path as the 1980s. We are still in a conservative frame of mind, but the schizoid character of cultural attitudes continues to reflect both positive and negative activity. As happened at the end of the 1970s, I see no reason to believe that the events of the 1980s will not continue to influence the 1990s. However, like every decade some new catastrophe will probably occur that will impel the world in a different direction. And with that, rock and roll will continue to reflect those changes in an accurate if not oblique manner.

PRE-METAL REPRESENTATIVES

The pre-metal stage is made up of musicians who were called rock musicians, sometimes hard rock musicians. Although they played music that would have heavy influence on metal style, they were mainstream hard rock musicians. Some continued on to be known as metal musicians and some remained outside the style of classic metal. Jimi Hendrix was born in 1942 in Seattle, Washington, and died in London in 1970. He was influenced by Muddy Waters, B. B. King, Chuck Berry, and Eddie Cochran. He played guitar from an early age and in 1959 enlisted in the army. Although he played during his army stint, his career really began in 1961, after he was discharged because of injuries. In 1964 he moved to New York City, where he became a working musician. He played behind numerous musicians, including Sam Cooke, B. B. King, Little Richard, Ike and Tina Turner, the Isley Brothers, and King Curtis. His stage name at the time was Jimmy James.

In 1965 he formed his own band, called Jimmy James and the Blue Flames. At a Greenwich Village club, he was heard by Chas Chandler of the Animals, who arranged for him to move to London. It was there that the Jimi Hendrix Experience was formed, with Noel Redding on bass and Mitch Mitchell on drums. His first hit, "Hey Joe," was quickly followed by the first album, *Are You Experienced?*, which also contained "Purple Haze." However, he was still unknown in the United States. Interestingly, it was Paul McCartney who suggested that the Experience be added to the program of the Monterey Pop Festival in June 1967. That performance made Hendrix a superstar.

His first American tour was as the warmup band for the Monkees, one of the more unlikely pairings in rock history. The Experience was not retained on that tour. Their second tour, in 1968, was not met with universal approval either. Throughout his very short career, Hendrix was mired in difficulties, and he always felt that the best forum for his music was the recording studio. In fact, he built his own studio in New York, called Electric Lady.

Many musicians, however, were impressed with Hendrix, both during his lifetime and afterwards. Such notables as Miles Davis, Bob Dylan, and John McLaughlin showed their appreciation by performing Hendrix-styled compositions. In August 1969 the original band was no more. At this point, Jimi formed a new band called the "Band of Gypsies," which put out one important album. The formation of this band was a partial response to constant pressure he received to play black music with black musicians.

Although his short career was not successful on a case-by-case analysis, his influence was incredible. His playing style, all of his compositions, and even unreleased tapes have been analyzed, re-recorded, and discussed by many rock critics and, most importantly, significant musicians. His lasting legacy is his continued popularity; and he has had pivotal impact on the style and development of heavy metal.

The Who has been discussed in a previous chapter, so biographical and discographic information will not be repeated here. They are included in this chapter because they used some particular techniques before they became fashionable. The high use of distortion as a tension-building device would later become very important to rock in general and heavy metal in particular; the Who started using heavy distortion at approximately the same time that Hendrix was active. Also important are the destructive stage antics they used. Like Hendrix, the Who (primarily Pete Townshend) destroyed guitars and amplifiers on a regular basis. It was part of their stage routine and they were certainly made more visible as a result of it. But while the Who did not continue to develop as a heavy metal band—they already had a rather unique sound—they used techniques that would later become staples of heavy metal.

The Yardbirds was originally formed in 1963 as the Most Blueswailing Yardbirds; Eric Clapton joined the band four months after its formation. At first they were a pure blues band, although ultimately they served as an important link between British rhythm and blues and the psychedelic/pre–heavy metal rock of the late 1960s. Interestingly, when Clapton was with the Yardbirds the band was not really very progressive, although at the time they were recognized as being at the forefront of British rock. Clapton actually quit the band in 1965 because he felt it was becoming too pop in orientation; he joined John Mayall's Bluesbreakers (another seminal band known for its influence on the blues revival, and for the roster of superstar musicians who belonged over the years).

When Clapton quit the Yardbirds, he was replaced by Jeff Beck. In 1965 the Yardbirds put out one major album, *Having a Rave-Up with the Yardbirds* (with Jeff Beck), on which there was at least one song with heavy metal implications. "Heart Full of Soul" contained electric guitar riffs with heavy use of fuzz sound. In 1966 Jimmy Page joined the group, first on bass, then guitar. While the pairing of Beck and Page did not last long, that particular sound was to have lasting implications, if only because of what the two musicians did afterwards.

The Yardbirds disbanded in July 1968, although the name was kept by Page for the formation of the New Yardbirds (he soon changed the name to Led Zeppelin). Although the Yardbirds was a short-lived group, it was highly significant because of the lasting influence of its members. It was also significant because the heavy guitar style that occasionally emerged would be amplified by some of the same musicians and turned into heavy metal.

Led Zeppelin was an incredibly important band from 1968 until 1983. The two most important members were probably Jimmy Page, recognized by everyone for his influence on rock guitar players, and the vocalist Robert Plant. While Jimi Hendrix may be credited as rock's most significant guitar player and the first influence leading toward heavy metal, Led Zeppelin should be considered the first great heavy metal band. Led Zeppelin has also influenced the mythology of heavy metal, since Jimmy Page believes in exotic philosophies; this clearly comes through their song lyrics and playing style.

As previously mentioned, Led Zeppelin was formed first as the New Yardbirds, to complete bookings for which the old group was still obligated. They changed their name to Led Zeppelin after completing a Scandinavian tour; Led

Led Zeppelin   *(Courtesy of Atlantic Records)*

Zeppelin was recommended by Richard Cole (later their road manager), who got it from either Keith Moon or John Entwistle of the Who. Their first album (1969) reached the Top Ten in *Billboard* and their second album went to number one. Their first U.S. tour in early 1969 was with Vanilla Fudge.

Led Zeppelin has had phenomenal success. They were clearly the most successful band of the 1970s, both on the basis of record sales and concert proceeds. For instance, in 1976 their album *Presence* went platinum on advance orders alone; they are the only band ever to do that.

While I am certain that nobody doubts the heavy metal roots of Led Zeppelin, the group quite often does tunes that depart from a traditional heavy metal approach. However, in the sheer power of their playing they remain true to the tradition. For instance, on stage Jimmy Page uses four 200-watt Marshall amps; he also uses a wah-wah pedal, an MXR unit, a harmonizer, a violin bow, and an Echoplex unit. He has used a steel guitar, a banjo, and a mandolin on various albums, which at times give the music a country- or folk-rock sound. In short, Led Zeppelin is an extremely diversified group, massively important in impact, and musically one of the most significant groups discussed in this chapter. Interestingly, for the first few years of their career they received excessively bad reviews. However, since about 1973 they received their deserved credit, although with drummer John Bonham's death in 1980, the group disbanded.

The music of Led Zeppelin is rather diverse and contains a number of elements beyond traditional heavy metal characteristics. This of course furthers the argument that heavy metal is much more heterogeneous than many critics maintain. For instance, some of the following songs illustrate other qualities: "Whole Lotta Love" is an ABA form; "The Rain Song" is a ballad; "Tangerine" is country in orientation and features a steel guitar; "Immigrant Song" and "D'yer Mak'er" illustrate international influences; and "Kashmir" has a rhythmic feel that poses three against four. Even "Stairway to Heaven," which is probably their most popular hit, is not in a heavy metal style. (See the appendix for an analysis of "Whole Lotta Love," which is prototypical heavy metal despite its unusual form.)

Jeff Beck was another alumnus of the Yardbirds who eventually went on to form his own group, The Jeff Beck Group (started in 1967). Although each new incarnation of the Jeff Beck Group would end quickly, the first group, with Ron Wood and Rod Stewart (who later formed Faces), was probably the most exciting from a musical point of view. From 1972 to 1974 Beck joined with Tim Bogert and Carmine Appice, formerly of Vanilla Fudge, and Cactus, for a different style of music from the first group with Wood and Stewart. The first group was blues-based; the second was funk-oriented. However, the one underlying stylistic trait of either group was the dominance of Jeff Beck's heavy metal guitar.

Beck's playing style has been very important to heavy metal as he was an early exponent of distortion, note bending, and power playing. However, he also had the technical skill of a John McLaughlin, with whom he toured during 1975 and 1976 as co-headliner. This third group was more jazz-oriented in style, perhaps because of the melodic influence of McLaughlin. However, the major significance of Jeff Beck is the highly technical style he brought to early heavy metal.

Cream is mentioned here because it is another group through which Eric Clapton passed; after Cream's demise in 1968 he and Peter (Ginger) Baker went on to Blind Faith, then solo. Cream is not a prototypical heavy metal band, but it did influence heavy metal guitar playing through Eric Clapton. This band played high-intensity blues in which the extensive improvised solos set models for later heavy metal guitarists. The music was loud, especially in public performance. However, in the studio their music was somewhat more diversified and was reasonably popular. They had two top ten hits in 1968, and one number twenty-eight U.S. hit in 1969, after their demise. However, even after that they continued to put out Cream albums, because the band's sound was really significant.

Deep Purple was formed in 1968 and was at first a fairly light-textured group with some technical wizardry. They were somewhat successful in 1968, but with their 1970 album *Deep Purple in Rock,* the guitar playing of Ritchie Blackmore began to dominate. By this time, and with the next album, *Fireball,* they had become pure heavy metal. Of course, the chief quality of Deep Purple's heavy metal sound is Blackmore's guitar playing. In one sense, Blackmore may have established the overpowering style of heavy metal, because Deep Purple was long known as the loudest rock band in existence.

The last statement points out an interesting incongruity in heavy metal music; that is, the critical statement often made that it is *just* loud music. Often it is quite loud, but beneath that loudness usually lies good playing technique. Blackmore is a good example of that. He plays the guitar with a very light touch and uses the tremolo bar to a great extent, for instance on the song "Highway Star." However, even with the light touch and quick passages, his Marshall amp is turned up high and seems to put out 1000 watts. Therefore, the screaming quality of his playing is done totally through electronics; in fact, he has been quoted in several articles as preferring lower volumes for playing because he says he plays better.

Blackmore left Deep Purple in 1975 to form Rainbow, another significant heavy metal group. Deep Purple, however, was terribly important in its time. From 1970 to 1975 they were consistently recognized as the premier heavy metal band. While Led Zeppelin did not firmly plant itself in that style, Deep Purple did and attracted many of the cult fans of early heavy metal. Interestingly, many heavy metal fans who have been around for a while think that Deep Purple, and other groups of that vintage, were better than what we have today.

Rainbow is an extremely important group in this discussion because of its longevity and diversity. Although clearly rooted in the powerhouse playing of Ritchie Blackmore, Rainbow also uses musical influences of a broader variety, such as older classical music and nonwestern music. Formed in 1975 in Los Angeles, Rainbow has gone through its share of musicians from both the United States and England. However, the continuing influence of Ritchie Blackmore is apparent throughout.

Iron Butterfly was formed in San Diego, California, in 1966, and although they did not last past 1971, they had one major hit, which was to influence heavy metal (and rock in general): "In-A-Gadda-Da-Vida," from the 1968 album of the same name, sold three million copies and made the group famous. The significance of that tune was that it was seventeen minutes long, featuring a two-and-a-half-minute drum solo. Also, its style, while not powerful in comparison to today's sound, was really unusual in 1968. Anyone listening to that tune has to recognize the distorted, fuzz tone playing style so clearly associated with heavy metal.

Blue Oyster Cult is another interesting example of how rock bands are formed. The original group that formed this band were students at the State University of New York at Stony Brook. They decided to form a rock band in 1969, to communicate somewhat unusual ideas through that medium (in some senses like the Fugs, who were also from New York). After several name changes, they settled on Blue Oyster Cult, and they subsequently toured with Alice Cooper for several years in the early 1970s. They did not really have a commercial hit until 1976 with the album *Agents of Fortune* and the single "Don't Fear the Reaper." Certainly a great deal of this band's success can be attributed to their consistent use of satanic images, so popular with heavy metal bands, although they probably did not believe in it. Also, Blue Oyster Cult was powerful in style, sometimes using three guitars, and of course, extensive amplification. They also used lasers, popping lights, and ear-splitting guitar solos as early as 1971. They toured with Black Sabbath in 1980, on what was called the Black and Blue Tour.

MC5 was a relatively short-lived group from Detroit, Michigan. Two of their three albums were classics, or at least are remembered as such. "Kick Out the Jams," from the 1969 album of the same name, is a prototypical heavy metal song. Although highly riff-oriented, and basically heavy blues, it features a massive amount of electronic distortion and a powerful singing (almost shouting) style. Some have called this music early punk, but I think heavy metal is more appropriate. Their second album, *Back in the USA* (1970), was acclaimed by critics, and even called the greatest hard rock album of the year by some. In 1970s parlance, that meant heavy metal.

MC5 was quite political in a revolutionary sense, and they also made rather extensive use of profanity. In their short career they used heavy amplification, and, at least at the beginning, they were involved in the White Panther political party and performed at the riots outside the Democratic Convention. The band broke up in 1971 and frankly was a commercial failure. However, their albums have been re-released (in 1977 during the punk era, and again in the early 1980s).

ZZ Top is probably the heaviest country rock band and interestingly enough has been around for a long time. Billy Gibbons, the leader of ZZ Top, was with a band called Moving Sidewalk, which did a totally psychedelic album in 1966. By 1970 Moving Sidewalk had broken up and the trio called ZZ Top was formed. A Texas band, ZZ Top has consistently walked the line between Southern rock (Texas style) and heavy metal. Before forming ZZ Top, Billy Gibbons opened for Jimi Hendrix, who later called Gibbons one of the best guitar players in America. The Gibbons style is classic heavy metal/blues revival. Both the Allman Brothers Band and Lynyrd Skynyrd could be mentioned in this context because of the double guitar, double drums instrumentation of the Allman Brothers, and the triple guitar instrumentation of Lynyrd Skynyrd. But while they both properly belong to country rock, ZZ Top is a heavy metal band, Texas style.

Returning to mainstream heavy metal, Black Sabbath was formed in 1968 in England, with at least two of the original members being significant heavy metal musicians — Ozzy Osbourne, vocalist, and Tony Iommi, guitar. Always leading the list of rock groups hated by those who feel rock sometimes influences in an evil way, Black Sabbath had all the elements of heavy metal. The name of the group, changed from Earth in 1969, clearly indicated what the band was conveying. Black Sabbath purposefully played upon satanic worship, demonology, and a general state of gloom. Within these subject matters, represented by songs like "Paranoid" from the album of the same name in 1971, they played and sang in a typical heavy metal fashion (European style). The music was heavily riff-oriented and had a strong midrange mix. Although Black Sabbath's main market was the United States, their playing style retained some English characteristics. Ozzy Osbourne quit the group in 1979 and went solo with the Ozzy Osbourne Group, which

ZZ Top *(Photo by Warner Brothers Records; used by permission of Ginny Cartmell and Creem Magazine Archives)*

contained Randy Rhoads. He continued in the earlier style of Black Sabbath, although he expanded his horizons by biting the heads off small animals, including one bat.

Grand Funk Railroad is one of those bands that deserves to be in this chapter although most rock critics have panned them for years. They were formed in 1969 in Flint, Michigan, and disbanded in 1976. The original group was made up of guitar, bass, and drums, and like other trios used a variety of electronic effects and massive amplification to produce a heavy metal sound. In 1972 they added a keyboard player. Grand Funk's style was typically American and served as a good model for other American heavy metal musicians. Their music was heavily melodic in orientation, featuring guitar solos that were powerful but also very expressive. Although not generally given proper credit, this was probably the most successful

American heavy metal band during their era. Two of the original members later joined the Bob Seger Band.

Mountain was a very important American heavy metal band formed in 1969 with Felix Pappalardi (former producer of Cream) on bass and Leslie West on guitar. Although the original group was a quartet — bass, guitar/vocal, drums, and organ, the organ playing of Steve Knight was eliminated in 1971. Therefore, Mountain was essentially a power trio, with Leslie West's guitar playing being the central focus.

Leslie West was influenced primarily by British guitarists like Eric Clapton and the Who's Pete Townshend. In actuality, his great technical ability was influenced by a variety of styles, including classical and jazz guitar playing. However, he plays without the benefit of technical training or knowledge and this makes his playing all the more amazing. His use of hyper-amplified lyric lines makes him an excellent example of American style heavy metal, and he has clearly carried the blues revival concept throughout his music. He is best known for his solo in "Mississippi Queen." He has been most innovative in using the guitar strings to produce unusual effects — harmonies in "Theme for an Imaginary Western"; hammering techniques on the album *Flowers of Evil;* and bottle-neck style through an Echoplex on "Pride and Passion." Ultimately, however, he fits clearly into the heavy metal school with his powerhouse technical playing. Although the band terminated for all practical purposes in 1973, they have done reunions several times. During their heyday they were quite influential and served as a good model for later American groups.

Although Alice Cooper is not generally considered in heavy metal circles, there can be little question that Alice Cooper, along with Michigan's Iggy Pop, have influenced the lyric style and subject matter of American heavy metal. Bizarre stage antics and outlandish costumes (influential on Kiss) symbolize both of these musicians. Most of the time their music is hard rock, bordering on heavy metal. Distortion in electronic sound and stage antics suggest the philosophy if not always the sound of heavy metal.

With Ted Nugent we have a quintessential heavy metal musician from the United States. From Detroit, Michigan, Ted Nugent started playing professionally in the early 1960s and opened for early Detroit groups such as the Supremes. His family moved to Chicago in 1965, where he formed the Amboy Dukes. Until 1975 he had minor successes playing a strong heavy metal guitar sound like MC5 and Iron Butterfly. In 1975 his career took off with a new record company, and the same playing style suddenly became more popular.

The personal image of Ted Nugent is fascinating because it predates some of the more current images of heavy metal. He is a tough guy, macho, and personal supporter of the National Rifle Association — relatively conservative positions. Several of his big hits of the late 1970s were "Dog Eat Dog" and "Cat Scratch Fever." His playing style is complicated, melodically oriented, and shows the influence of jazz styles and nonrock music. He has used many of the traditional techniques of heavy metal — heavy distortion, wall-to-wall feedback, playing with his teeth, and equipment destruction. His solo career since 1975 has been much more influential than his time with the Amboy Dukes. He remains one of the better and more flamboyant guitar players to come from the United States.

CLASSIC METAL REPRESENTATIVES

Classic metal started in the middle of the 1970s, when musicians were first called heavy metal musicians. It was during this period that the rather definitive split between British and American metal styles occurred, and it was during this time that heavy metal became a separate style of rock and roll, with its own fans and magazines. It was also at this time that heavy metal left mainstream rock and roll and although there were a few musicians, like Led Zeppelin, who were recognized as metal and not-metal, most bands either got on the bus or got off.

The raucous style of classic metal distinguished it from mainstream rock and theatricality became part of the "gig." Demon worship and the continuing focus on the lead guitar player distinguished this period. It was also at this time that classic heavy metal, like its contemporary, punk rock, earned the disgust of traditional society. And of course, this ensured its lasting success.

AC/DC *(Courtesy of Atlantic Records)*

Judas Priest *(Photo by Columbia Records; used by permission of Ginny Cartmell and Creem Magazine Archives)*

The Scorpions is a German band that began in 1971. Since that time they have undoubtedly been the most significant continental European heavy metal band. A variety of important European musicians are alumni of the group, including Michael Schenker. Both Iron Maiden and Van Halen, among others, have played Scorpions' material, so their influence has been felt. Most attractive about the Scorpions is that they have been relatively uninfluenced by other styles; therefore, they have added something distinctive to the heavy metal story.

As a result of the relative lack of influence on the Scorpions their sound is an interesting cross between riff-oriented English heavy metal and melodically influenced American heavy metal. There is a roughness and bombastic quality to their playing that goes beyond a simple show of amplified power. German rock fans are heavy consumers of heavy metal music.

AC/DC is an Australian band first formed in 1973. However, this group did not achieve real popularity until 1979, when they charted with the album *Highway to Hell.* The instrumentation of AC/DC is two guitars, bass, and drums. Bon Scott was the vocalist until he died in 1980; Brian Johnson replaced him. This particular heavy metal band is known more for their live performances than their studio technique, although their albums since 1981 have done well. In live performance

Kiss   *(Photo by Casablanca Records; used by permission of Ginny Cartmell and Creem Magazine Archives)*

they regularly make obscene gestures; their songs are sexual, and often about drinking; and they have also discussed eternal damnation. Obviously, the name of the group implies certain deviant sexual activity, and their image certainly fits that. The lead guitar work of Angus Young is not as flashy as others mentioned in this chapter, but he is certainly a solid player.

From a commercial point of view, Aerosmith was the top heavy metal band of the mid-1970s. Formed in New Hampshire in 1970, from 1973 with their first album *Aerosmith* to 1977 with *Draw the Line* they were very successful. Their tours were sold out in the mid-1970s and their albums all went platinum. A rather typical American instrumentation of vocalist, two guitars, bass, and drums accommodated a high-energy, high-volume output. The band was very blues-oriented and the dual-guitar work was strong even if it may not have been as technically satisfying as that of some other groups.

Judas Priest is from Birmingham, England; the group was formed in 1969. The guitar duo of Tipton and Downing began in 1974, but the group did not really prosper until the late 1970s in England, and the early 1980s in the United States. Given the almost state-of-the-art quality of their amplification system and the way they create the heavy metal sound, one is hard pressed to understand why they did not peak sooner. However, it may have been because other people did satanic

The Ultimate Sin

Ozzy Osbourne *(Courtesy of Columbia Records)*

music better than Judas Priest. Since the *British Steel* album in 1980, their lyric content has changed slightly. However, one of their earlier albums illustrated all of their musical characteristics — the 1977 album *Sin after Sin*. One of their most visible stage antics was Rob Halford's riding a Harley on stage. Judas Priest presents a fairly typical image of heavy metal — leather and all.

It is clear to me that Kiss does not deserve a tremendous amount of musical recognition. Their main claim to fame is their look, the rather extensive use of fire breathing, and other extramusical effects. The theatricality of their costumes and their painted faces impressed fans, and they gained a rather large following in the mid-1970s. By the end of 1976 they had moved slightly toward pop/preteen music and their audience changed considerably toward younger fans. An American group that was always heavy metal in sound and volume, they influenced heavy metal groups in stage presentation during the first part of their career. However, once they changed to a pop orientation, they stopped having much influence.

Quiet Riot started in Los Angeles in the mid-1970s, and ultimately it was the guitar playing of Randy Rhoads that was most important to that group. In fact, it was probably the personal charisma, good looks, and guitar ability of Randy Rhoads that made the group popular. His playing and the style of Quiet Riot were prototypical American heavy metal — heavy concentration on long, virtuosic melodic passages and flashy stage routines. However, Quiet Riot was essentially finished musically when Randy Rhoads went to play with Ozzy Osbourne. Unfortunately, Rhoads died in a plane crash one year later. Interestingly, the biggest success of Quiet Riot was in the 1980s, with what is rare for a metal band — a number one album entitled *Metal Health*.

MAINSTREAM METAL REPRESENTATIVES

Mainstream metal is a term that describes metal from 1980 through 1987 and delineates a style that is fully developed, evolves into equal strength in all instrumental and vocal aspects of the band unit, and settles into a very acceptable level of musical competence. In short, mainstream metal satisfies its audience with specific music styles that are presented in a somewhat predictable although highly skilled manner.

Heavy metal became more mainstream in its audience share in the 1980s, although it was still highly album-oriented in production. The theatricality of metal became somewhat downplayed although the message and strength of the lyric message was certainly still strong. Interestingly, as one moved through the 1980s, some alternative and neo-punk bands moved more toward metal style. Although one could argue that the pre-metal musicians were the creators who established the method of playing that would have lasting impact, one must admit that the consummation of the metal style really occurred in the 1980s.

Def Leppard was started in 1977 and put out their first album in 1980. All of their work has done well financially, and some have described them as the new wave of British heavy metal. While that may be overstating the issue, Def Leppard does have a heterogeneous sound. Clearly conceived in heavy metal terms, they quite often use techniques that do not belong to heavy metal at all. At times the twin guitar players play straight bluesy lines, and at other times they play contemporary high-velocity lines. Their sound is powerful but their albums show a tremendous mixture of styles. Some critics have derided them for being merely a conglomeration of other styles, but it seems to work with their fans. Of great note were the 1983 album *Pyromania*, and its hit single, "Photograph." Even more successful was a 1987 album, which peaked at number one on the charts, entitled *Hysteria*.

Def Leppard *(Courtesy of PolyGram Records)*

The Van Halen brothers, Eddie and Alex, moved to the United States from the Netherlands when they were teenagers. They established their first band soon after, settling on Van Halen as a name in 1974. They played the bar circuit in Los Angeles until they did a demonstration tape for Warner Brothers in 1976. Their first album in 1978 sold quite well, and since 1980 they have been very successful. The singing style of former lead singer David Lee Roth is hard rock/heavy metal in orientation, but the lyric content is really more diversified. David Lee Roth left Van Halen for a solo career in 1986 and has been replaced by Sammy Hagar.

However, the really significant part of this group is Eddie Van Halen's guitar playing. By virtue of the rather circuitous route he followed to get to the forefront of West Coast heavy metal, Eddie Van Halen's guitar playing is neither strictly American nor British. He plays with equal intensity in both melodic and rhythmic, or riff, terms. Like most heavy metal experts, he uses feedback extensively within the context of his solos. He also uses vibrato quite effectively. He controls harmonics quite well; in fact, one suspects a little Randy Rhoads influence there. However, it is in the incredibly tasteful way that he makes solos fit the song's lyrics and style that he stands apart from most heavy metal guitarists. Van Halen is at home at high volumes, but Eddie and his group are also at home in other styles.

Motley Crue was formed in Los Angeles in 1980. Starting out as Kiss imitators, Motley Crue has become reasonably popular and actually had a top forty hit with "Smokin' in the Boys Room" (from their third album). They have had growing success with albums in the 1980s, *Too Fast for Love* (1982), *Shout at the Devil* (1984), *Theatre of Pain* (1985), and *Girls, Girls, Girls* (1987), which went to number

Van Halen   *(Photo by Warner Brothers Records; used by permission of Ginny Cartmell and Creem Magazine Archives)*

two on the charts. Their lead singer, Vince Neil, was heavily influenced by David Lee Roth.

The symbol for Motley Crue is the pentagram, but their music is not totally about devil worship. At the beginning of their career they wore lots of leather, spikes, and Kiss-type makeup. Since their first album, though, they have dressed more stylishly—almost new wave mod. A fairly simple band whose music appeals to younger audiences, particularly females, they did some rather interesting syn-

Krokus *(Photo by Arista Records; used by permission of Ginny Cartmell and Creem Magazine Archives)*

thesizer work on their last album, although in the first years of their career they relied almost totally on theatrics.

Twisted Sister, formed in New York in 1976, was heavily influenced by Alice Cooper's stage presentation. Dee Snider, their vocalist, has a very low and growling voice which gives Twisted Sister a sound that matches their name. Their look is obviously influenced by the women's clothing they wear. Their albums are *Under the Blade* (first in England, in 1982), *You Can't Stop Rock and Roll* (1983), *Stay Hungry* (1984), and *Come Out and Play* (1985). They had a top forty hit with "We're Not Gonna Take It" from *Stay Hungry*. On their 1985 album they did two parodies, one of "Be Cruel to Your School" (including Alice Cooper and Billy Joel), the other being "Leader of the Pack."

Krokus, from Switzerland, is another significant European band. Their albums are *Pay It in Metal, Metal Rendevous, One Vice at a Time, Headhunter,* and *The*

Blitz. The lead singer, Mark Storace, has a scratchy voice, and the band was more riff-oriented, in the European style, at the beginning. However, *The Blitz* is quite melodic, and more American in style. Some rather unique tunes are "Screaming in the Night" from *Headhunter,* a slow blues screamer; also, "Midnight Maniac" from *Blitz,* uptempo in a traditional heavy metal style, but more pop-oriented.

WASP is a Los Angeles band that started in 1981. The vocalist, Blackie Lawless, is probably the dominant force in the band, which is mainstream heavy metal. Lawless toured with the New York Dolls toward the end of that group's career. WASP's most popular, or at least best known, song is called "Animal," and has the subtitle "F . . . Like a Beast." Their live shows are called electric vaude- ville, and they feature things thrown into the audience, for instance , raw meat and hamburger. "Animal" was banned in England, and this may account for some of their popularity. Their musical style features crashing chords, heavy bass drum and backbeat, and rudimentary guitar solos. The music is vocally oriented, thus the suggestion that Lawless is the center of activity.

RATT was started in 1980 with a combination of Los Angeles and San Francisco musicians; the band works out of Los Angeles. Their albums are *RATT, Out of the Cellar,* and *Invasion of Your Privacy.* "Round and Round" from *Out of the Cellar* was a number two pop hit, and the band has been heavily influenced by Aerosmith. Warren DeMartini, the lead guitarist, is influenced by Hendrix and Van Halen. He has excellent technique and is, in my estimation, the most exciting thing about the band, which is musically solid.

Loudness is a Japanese band featuring the musicians Akira Takasaki (guitar), Minoru Niihara (vocal), Masayoshi Yamashita (bass), and Munetaka Higuchi (drums). Their albums are *Birthday's Eve, Devil Soldier, Law of the Devil's Land, Road Racer, Disillusion,* and *Thunder in the East.* The albums through *Road Racer* are sung in Japanese; *Disillusion* is in English but a Japanese release; and *Thunder in the East* is a U.S. release. The last album contains a pop hit called "Crazy Night." Loudness is very popular in Japan, which actually has many heavy metal fans. Takasaki, the guitar player, has superlative technique and sounds a lot like Van Halen. Niihara, the vocalist, has a strong singing style, although when he sings in English his pronunciation and phrasing of words leaves a bit to be desired. Loud- ness is a good band technically, and they certainly fit the style of heavy metal; however, their English songs wane in comparison to other bands because of lan- guage difficulties.

Queensryche started in 1982 in Seattle, Washington. Their album *The Warning* illustrates a growing tendency in heavy metal for the messages of songs and albums to be more diversified. This particular album is about a person trying to find his identity. Although much heavy metal music is uptempo, this particular album is fairly slow in tempo, for example "Take Hold of the Flame." This song features a slow, heavy sound with the drums creating extended tension. It is dense and there is distortion, but the feeling is one of ponderousness, rather than a barrage of the senses. Their vocalist, Geoff Tate, probably creates the most signifi-

Loudness   *(Photo by Atco Records; used by permission of Ginny Cartmell and Creem Magazine Archives)*

cant part of the texture; however, the sound of Queensryche contains different textures. They also had fairly good success with an album from 1989, entitled *Operation: Mindcrime.*

Iron Maiden was left for the end of this chapter because by the time I researched and listened to the music of the other musicians, I began to develop a sense of personal taste about heavy metal. After all was said and done, Iron Maiden struck me as the most musical, and most representative, of the heavy metal style. They started in 1977 in England, and although they have changed personnel a number of times, Iron Maiden has always had good technical musicians. The reason I feel they deserve special recognition is that this is a balanced musical

Iron Maiden   *(Used by permission of Ginny Cartmell and Creem Magazine Archives)*

ensemble; each of the musicians contributes to the technical quality of the band, and that makes their music all the more interesting.

Albums

1. *Sound House Tapes* (Extended Play — four songs) Independent.
2. *Iron Maiden* EMI
3. *Killers*
4. *Maiden Japan*
5. *Number of the Beast*
6. *Piece of Mind*
7. *Powerslave*
8. *Live After Death*
9. *Somewhere in Time*

10. *Seventh Son of the Seventh Son*

11. *No Prayer for the Dying*

This band represents the pure British heavy metal technique of playing. It is neither hard rock in orientation nor is it blues revival. It is powerhouse technical playing with a heavy bass line, intertwining guitar solos and fill patterns, and powerful singing. The subject matter of the compositions is really quite diverse, often historical or literary, or derived from poetry or science fiction. Less often is a song about devil worship than even the title might suggest. Generally speaking, Iron Maiden does not enjoy radio airplay because the music is not top forty. However, among heavy metal fans Iron Maiden enjoys a healthy sales market for their albums, which are based on excellent musicianship and interesting subject matter. They were also the first heavy metal band to tour in communist countries (Poland, Hungary, and Yugoslavia). Of special interest are the compositions "Run to the Hills," from *Number of the Beast*, "Trooper," from *Piece of Mind* (analyzed in appendix), and "2 Minutes to Midnight," from *Powerslave*. The last tune is interesting because it really is more pop-oriented; most Iron Maiden is very uptempo, but "2 Minutes to Midnight" is slower.

1980s AND 1990s METAL— THRASH/SPEED/DEATH

By the late 1980s, the terms *thrash, speed,* and *death* were used in connection with heavy metal. While there are some heavy metal bands from previous eras that continued to be called just heavy metal or even hard rock, newer bands were classified in one or more of these categories.

Thrash is essentially heavy metal instrumental style with neo-punk lyrics. The singing style has qualities of both traditional heavy metal singing and punk. The lyric tends to be buried in the mix of the musical totality as in traditional heavy metal. Slam dancing has always been associated with thrash, although it probably came from neo-punk bands evolving toward heavy metal. In fact, some neo-punk bands like Suicidal Tendencies evolved from a relatively pure punk style into thrash metal. Other significant bands who play in this style are Exodus, Nuclear Assault, Slayer (see also death metal), and Overkill.

Speed metal is the logical evolution of mainstream American heavy metal, incorporating long melodic phrases by the guitarists and relatively fast tempos. Although many bands in the late 1980s and 1990s tend to move back and forth between thrash and speed styles, speed metal remains the mainstream style of heavy metal, with the biggest market share. Some bands have evolved into speed metal style from the underground; others evolved naturally into this style from mainstream metal of the early to mid-1980s.

Megadeth is a good example of a neo-punk band that evolved into speed metal, or from eclectic to commercial. The ever-popular Metallica is a mainstream speed metal band, which has wider recognition because it has been around since 1983. Anthrax, with "Metal Thrashing Mad" and "Madhouse," also fits into this category, even though it at times fits into the thrash category as well. Death Angel (an Asian band) has an interesting evolution, in that its first two albums, *Ultra Violence* (1987) and *Frolic Thru the Park* (1988) were in the thrash style; its third album, *Act III* (1990), is speed metal. Similarly, Testament started with a thrash album, *Legacy* (1987), and then did two albums that are a combination of thrash and speed—*New Order* (1988) and *Souls of Black* (1990).

In actuality the dividing line between thrash and speed is rather thin. Thrash fits as a defining title when the lyric is very rough in quality and the music is almost overly distorted; speed is relatively clean in vocal and use of distortion by comparison to thrash. One might say that the difference is really attitudinal and somewhat artificial. If a band creates a lyric and instrumental composition that calls for heavy distortion and a rough singing style, then it's thrash; it if asks for a melodic and cleaner presentation, then it's speed.

Death metal is a particular style and groups are clearly identified as being death metal bands. The style is clearly defined by its lyrics, with words like death, burning, hell, suicide, gore, blood, pestilence, and brutality indicating clear themes. Death metal is the logical conclusion of satanic rock and what many heavy metal haters point out as the evil in heavy metal. While we are not taking up that argument, there is brutality in death metal and its origins come from hard rockers, eclectic musicians, punkers, and alternative musicians.

The musical style is very rhythmic, in that the drummer plays constantly in a steady beat, somewhat similar in style to punk drumming. There is not a tremendous amount of melodic playing, but rather the bass guitar and guitar are used as rhythmic instruments and as texture fillers. The voice is all important, as the lyric is the most significant part of the style. Often the lyric is not really sung but shout-sung. One might say that it was heavy metal or alternative rapping, but there are none of the funky voice rhythms present as there are in rap. The best way to describe it musically and culturally is to say that it is brutal. Perhaps not designed for commercial impact, death metal has a relatively small but devoted audience. Generally, death metal is the alternative music of metal heads and has a small market share. Like more traditional heavy metal, it is album-oriented music.

Some have argued that the roots of death metal go back to Blue Cheer, Black Sabbath, and more importantly Motorhead. Slayer is sometimes mentioned in an evolution of death metal, but clearly this band was really a mainstream heavy metal band and still is. An English band, Venom, is often cited as the first death metal band, with their debut album, *Welcome to Hell.* However, the most reasonable premise is probably that Napalm Death, a slightly more current band, was the real focal point for the beginning of death metal. Regardless of who started the style, the most important thing to understand about death metal is that it really is a hybrid form (another type of fusion) in that most of its constituent groups started in the underground, were called either neo-punk, alternative, or hardcore, and that the form has more recently been confirmed as being part of heavy metal. Some of the more current death metal groups are Carcas, Malevolent Creation, Atrocity, Obituary, Death, Deicide, Pestilence, and Morgoth.

NEO-PUNK/FUNKY METAL

Last but not least, a new phenomenon in 1990 was a neo-punk/funky style of heavy metal, represented by bands like the Red Hot Chili Peppers and Faith No More. Both of these bands came from the underground all the way to mainstream. Their style is clearly commercial and has only peripheral heavy metal traits. The playing style is still strong, but the lyrics are very clear, not buried in the mix and the subject matter is definitely not hardcore. And the bass playing style is more funk-oriented, popping bass, than it is power bass, which is so traditional in all heavy metal styles. This may very well suggest the future for heavy metal as it moves more and more toward mass appeal.

LISTENING

Jimi Hendrix Experience, *Are You Experienced?*

Led Zeppelin, *Soundtrack from the Film . . .*

Black Sabbath, *Paranoid*

Grand Funk Railroad, *Grand Funk Hits*

Mountain, *Mountain*

Kiss, *Double Platinum*

AC/DC, *Highway to Hell*

Quiet Riot, *Metal Health*

Judas Priest, *Screaming for Vengeance*

Motley Crue, *Theatre of Pain*

Ozzy Osbourne, *Diary of a Madman*

Loudness, *Thunder in the East*

Def Leppard, *Pyromania*

Iron Maiden, *Piece of Mind*

Def Leppard, *Hysteria*

Metallica, *. . . And Justice for All*

Megadeth, *Rust in Peace*

Napalm Death, *Scum*

CHAPTER **17**

PUNK, NEW WAVE, AND ALTERNATIVE MUSIC

Like anything relatively new, punk and new wave had many detractors. However, we should approach this music with an open mind, the same as we have with older music. Although both punk and new wave were progressive movements, they have some common elements with more traditional rock; thus, much of what we have learned up to this point can help us understand the newer music. Because we do not have all the listening skills necessary to understand it completely, however, a proper assessment will undoubtedly have to wait until punk and new wave are a part of history.

PUNK

The term *punk* is usually applied to a child or teenager who acts in an antisocial way. It was also used to describe a particular clothing style in London in the 1970s, and updated version of the Teddies of the 1950s and the mods of the 1960s.

Somewhat analogous terms in the United States were *beatniks* and *hippies*. Punk was slightly different because it suggested being outside the law. However, the common element of all these types was that they were unconventional and anti-establishment.

Punk certainly started much earlier than the mid-1970s. There were punk attitudes about Elvis Presley in his individualistic clothing styles and particularly in his hairstyle. In the 1960s there were many prototype punk musicians—the Rolling Stones, the Who, Frank Zappa, and others. Anyone who made strong statements and did outlandish things could be labeled a punk, before that term was applicable musically. Jimi Hendrix could be seen as punk because he was destructive, occasionally smashing a guitar on stage. However, these musicians were incipient punkers; they were not thoroughly dedicated to punk, which was simply a part of their entertainment package.

Punk was a form of rebellion, like other styles of rock; it turned against all other musical forms of the 1970s. Some critics saw it as an artistic movement, in this case antiart similar to that of the Fugs in the 1960s. It was the ultimate in sensationalism and should be seen as a philosophy of musical production, wherein the total statement was more important than the music and any constituent part of the performance.

Although punk was named after an English clothing style, the first real punk musician was Iggy Pop (James Jewel Osterburg), who was born in Ann Arbor, Michigan, in 1947. It is interesting that Iggy Pop and the Stooges, MC5, John Cale, and the Velvet Underground were all performing at the end of the 1960s. Each reemerged in the 1970s as a new group. Iggy Pop and the Stooges was consistent in its punk style before that style became codified. It was established by *The Stooges* in 1969 and *Fun House* in 1970 and eventually served as the model for punk groups. In these albums the group used abstract lyrics and a repetitious background. Over the years, Iggy Pop has remained a crazy if not exciting musician, who more than once has been assisted by David Bowie, who many people feel is the godfather of punk.

Punk was the third rock revolution—the formation of rock and roll itself came first; the Beatles started the second revolution in 1964; and the punk movement started the third in 1976. Clearly the punk movement was cultural as much as musical. It was anarchic, against society, and against everything in the established order. It was nihilistic (destructive), pessimistic, and presented a bleak outlook on life. Punk also stood for the frustration of British youth, many of whom were out of work. Also, mid-1970s society in general faced possible nuclear destruction, and there were American weapons and missiles in Europe. Musically, punk was a reaction against the boredom of rock, and, in particular, the boredom of American rock. Early punk bands clearly opposed the commercialization of rock—disco, art rock, jazz rock (everything rock had done in the 1970s). In short, punkers wished to take rock and roll back to the 1950s style and sing lyrics that accurately communicated reality.

Essentially, punk philosophy is dadaist or antiart. In a sense punk bands were "disposable"; punkers often formed groups in order to record. They really did not practice very much because technique was not a part of the point they were making. They were political and had a very definite message; their performing style reflected that. Whereas many of the groups discussed in previous chapters produced technically precise recordings, punk bands did not want technically precise recordings. Punk was rejected by the mass media and therefore created its own underground media. Punk bands used independent record labels, cheap instruments, and created "garage" recordings. A few punk bands, like the Clash, viewed themselves in different terms; therefore, the Clash went on to become new wave and continued to mature musically. However, the essential point of punk was probably best presented by the Sex Pistols.

The Sex Pistols, established in 1975 with its leader Johnny Rotten (Lydon), became the leader of the British punk movement. Sid Vicious joined the group on bass in 1977, and the combination of Vicious and Rotten set the group's tone, if only by their names. In short, these were very nasty people.

It is interesting that many punk groups featured musicians who were mainly lyricists rather than strong instrumentalists. Before joining the Sex Pistols, Johnny Rotten had never sung in a band. Two groups mentioned earlier started out from the same perspective, the Fugs and the Monkees. The Fugs, you may recall, were basically poets who came together to express the values of Greenwich Village. They were new wave musicians because of that one factor.

The music of the Sex Pistols was raw and uncontrolled. The background music was reiterative, and the music itself was reminiscent of 1950s rock and roll, straight continuous sound and four-beat drumming. Rhythms tended to be even and just slightly clipped off, a staccato effect (short). However, the musical background was not the primary element; the image was all important, and perhaps even the words were secondary. The purpose of punk was to shock, to hurt people's feelings, and generally to lay all emotions open, like a wound. Two representative songs from the Sex Pistols, from their album *Never Mind the Bollocks Here's the Sex Pistols,* were "Anarchy in the UK" and "God Save the Queen." "God Save the Queen" was probably their most important tune; it was banned by the BBC for its antimonarchy statement. They became fairly popular as a result; they were signed by EMI Records, but later dropped.

This was a conscious reaction to the 1970s, and it was perhaps a more honest reflection of it than any other kind of music at the time. In the mid-1970s the world seemed to be falling apart. Economic disasters, hijackings, terrorism, and the threat of imminent war were all at hand. These, combined with run-away technology and the lack of individual control over events, caused great anger and frustration. Some people sought refuge in nostalgia (Sha-Na-Na and big bands), whereas others expressed themselves through punk rock.

The Sex Pistols were made popular by the indignation of polite society and the hatred of the press. They were banned from the radio and many public per-

The Clash *(Used by permission of Ginny Cartmell and Creem Magazine Archives)*

formances; this gave them cult status. They had learned their lessons from Mick Jagger very well. Like rockers as far back as Bill Haley, the Sex Pistols were successful because so many people hated them.

In England they were followed by the Clash, the Damned, and others who copied their concept. Punk rock was primarily an urban concept, and at least in England, it had significant impact. The chordal style and straight rhythms allowed the image and the lead singer to project the fundamental premise of punk rock — straight, ugly truth. Even the melodies were not highly significant, and although there was a blues influence, it also was incidental to the image. What was important was the way the musicians accosted their audiences. They danced around, quite often just jumping up and down (called the *pogo*), screamed, and made obscene gestures. They used extensive feedback and distortion.

The lead singer usually spit the words at the audience, and there was little or no rhyme scheme. The clothing and hairstyles were somewhat like those of the 1950s, although more style-oriented — leather jackets, short hair, and mean visages. Punk rockers were not known for their social graces and quite often built their reputations by nasty actions outside of their performances (especially in

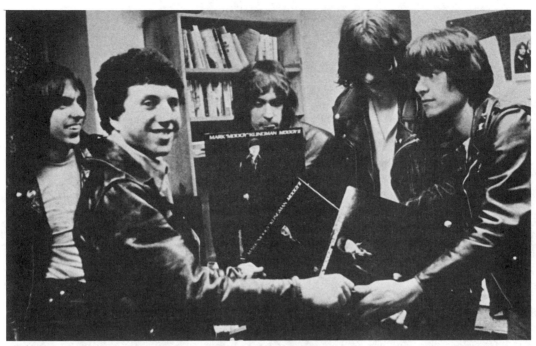

The Ramones   *(Used by permission of Ginny Cartmell and Creem Magazine Archives)*

public places). For punk, they wore their hair with the wet look; for new wave, the dry look was in.

The Clash was slightly different from the Sex Pistols although at first their musical style was quite similar. A mainstream punk band, the Clash started with a rather traditional punk image, which is certainly reflected in the song "I'm So Bored with the USA" from *The Clash* of 1977. However, the Clash was political in different ways from the Sex Pistols. By 1979 they were called new wave with their *London Calling* album, and their 1981 *Sandinista* illustrated strong reggae and British ska influences. The Clash consistently tied themselves to British political causes, including the Rastafarians (see reggae discussion), Sandinistas, and others.

Women became much more significant in the punk movement (X-Ray Spex), as the tough image of punkers was actually relatively nonsexist. Other significant punk bands included the Ramones, the Tubes, and the Buzzcocks. The United States had its share of punk groups, and for that matter, still does. The New York Dolls was managed by the manager of the Sex Pistols, Malcolm McLaren. The Ramones was a significant U.S. punk group. Although its success was not major, it was purely punk; it did not become new wave, which most other punk groups eventually did. More recently, conservative political views have been expressed by West Coast groups like the Dead Kennedys.

The Dead Kennedys *(Photo by Alternative Tentacles Records; used by permission of Ginny Cartmell and Creem Magazine Archives)*

REGGAE

Reggae is the general name of pop music from Jamaica and is Jamaica's version of soul music. Interestingly, reggae has not influenced rock except in the late 1970s and 1980s even though it has been around for some time. The original folk music of Jamaica was called *mento,* played by "acoustic" bands made up of homemade instruments; it was similar to skiffle in that sense. There was a syncopated quality to the music. By the late 1950s Jamaica became more urbanized, especially in West Kingston where many rural blacks had moved to the city. These urban blacks immediately began listening to radio, in particular, radio stations from New Orleans and Miami. This cultural addition caused the creation of Jamaican *ska,* which was a clear synthesis of *mento* and American R & B.

By the mid-1960s further changes in American black music created a new Jamaican sound called rock-steady. From 1966 to 1968, rock-steady was the dominant style with the local disk jockeys, many of whom operated from the back of trucks. Rock-steady featured a slower tempo than ska, heavier bass line, plucking guitar, and a soloist with background singers. There was clearly a strong soul influence (Memphis style).

In 1968 reggae was established. Reggae was essentially a faster rock-steady with electric organ. However, the soul influence was more political in nature and reggae eventually became a political tool. The first important reggae tune was the Maytals' "Do the Reggay." Probably the most important reggae musicians from Jamaica were Bob Marley and Jimmy Cliff.

A very important part of the reggae scene is the Rastafarian religious movement. Essentially a form of black Christianity, Rastafarians believe in a unique interpretation of the Old Testament. Marcus Garvey, a protestant minister from Jamaica, was the philosophical leader of Rastafarianism and preached one of its fundamental principles — blacks must return to Africa, in particular Ethiopia, as the homeland. He prophesied in 1927 that a black king would be crowned and that he would bring blacks home to Africa; in 1930, Haile Selassie was crowned in Ethiopia and Selassie became the black messiah. Rastafarians believe Ras Tafari (Selassie's original name) is the second coming of Christ and support that contention with biblical quotations. They also support with biblical quotations practices such as communal living, vegetarianism, not cutting the hair (dredlocks), and using marijuana.

Rastafarianism has not been transplanted to the United States and its religious principles are not subscribed to by many American blacks. Interestingly, reggae is not terribly popular in urban black communities, but rather in liberal college towns. However, Rastafarians received sympathy and support in London in 1979, most notably through the music of the Clash. The real significance of Rastafarianism and reggae is the influence it had in creating British new wave music, sometimes called British ska.

NEW WAVE

When new wave music started in the late 1970s, no one really knew what it meant. As a result, many types of music were called new wave in the late 1970s and early 1980s; it will be the purpose of this short section to discuss some representative bands that were called new wave or British ska. New wave style is clearly still around, but the new wave movement was only really in vogue through about 1983. Therefore, we can see new wave as having a distinctive period even though some of the groups that were called new wave and will be mentioned in this chapter ultimately do not live up to the final definition of the style.

New wave referred to new music, like *ars nova* referred to music in the fourteenth century as opposed to *ars antiqua*, which referred to music of the thirteenth century. New wave sometimes simply meant contemporary music, although it was often reserved for music that was contemporary in message and had an experimental quality to it. It was sometimes used to refer to music we would classify as being progressive, or art rock.

New wave described many different styles of music, but generally it was a philosophy of life that manifested itself in certain kinds of music. It encompassed

Elvis Costello   *(Courtesy of Columbia Records)*

music that was both simple and complex, old and new in structure, and positive and negative in feeling. If it was described as having "older" characteristics, it must be understood that those characteristics existed within the context of the modern studio and technology of the 1980s. Although it was at times repetitious and also contained certain punk elements, it was more diverse and complex than older music or punk. New wave music had an abstract quality that set it apart from other styles. Also, new wavism was thought to be broader than a musical style, a philosophy of living in today's or tomorrow's world.

Britain was the leader of the new wave movement, even though we may have heard more new wave bands from America. Two important English musicians were Elvis Costello and Graham Parker. They both made the transition through

Gang of Four   *(Photo by Warner Brothers Records; used by permission of Ginny Cartmell and Creem Magazine Archives)*

pub music and punk to new wave. They brought to new wave an energy that included the anger of punk and the sophistication of other musical styles. The Clash was important for the same reasons, because it was able to ride through the punk era and come out the other end as a formidable ensemble with its own unique sound.

Some other important new wave bands from England are the Undertones, Stiff Little Fingers (Irish political music such as ''Barbed Wire Love''), Gang of Four (actually Scotsmen), Magazine, the Buzzcocks, XTC, Stray Cats, and Wire. One aspect of new wave is called ska, which is Jamaican reggae music combined with a contemporary rock band. Some of the important ska bands are Madness, the

The Stray Cats *(Photo by EMI Records; used by permission of Ginny Cartmell and Creem Magazine Archives)*

Beat, the Selector, and the Specials. Ska bands usually contain both white and black musicians. The Specials had a big hit with a tune called "My Town Is a Ghost Town," which talked about the riots in London. Although some of these bands may not be well known in America, they are all good musical groups with an amazing amount of creativity.

Probably the best American new wave group is the Talking Heads. Although

The Specials   *(Courtesy of Chrysalis Records)*

there are many new wave bands in the United States, the Talking Heads is an especially attractive ensemble. Many of its compositions are African-derived with very complex rhythmic structures underlying a monochordal and monothematic singing style. Its lyrics have a contemporary message, and the music is the ultimate in fusion. Some other important American new wave bands were the B-52s, the Cars, Blondie, and Devo. The Police were quite significant in new wave as early as 1980 with their album *Zenyatta Mondatta,* especially with the song "Canary in a Coalmine."

The Talking Heads *(Photo by Sire Records; used by permission of Ginny Cartmell and Creem Magazine Archives)*

ALTERNATIVE MUSIC — NEO-PUNK, HARDCORE

Alternative music is by definition music that represents another option to what is already commercially viable or has already been classified. Heavy metal is therefore not alternative; it is heavy metal. However, as it is usually used, the term *alternative* is applied to music similar to that of the eclectic musician. In other usages, it is applied to anything that is wierd, unusual, or gross.

There was a short-lived attempt to recreate punk style in the 1980s, with groups like the Dead Kennedys, mentioned previously. Group names, such as Bad Brains, Big Black, The Cure, Danzid, Fear, the Butthole Surfers, and the Revolting Cocks, seem to imply the concept of neo-punk, when in fact most of these groups are alternative groups searching for an identity.

Other groups like P.I.L. (with Johnny Rotten from the Sex Pistols), Ministrys, Skinny Puppies, Nine Inch Nails, Cabaret Voltaire, and others have been alternative bands who have broken through to the other side to become dance music groups with thrash overtones. The skinhead movement suggests punk overtones but in fact usually takes in groups who are moving toward thrash/metal. Bands like REM eventually became country alternative/progressive and even groups like the Cramps and the Violent Femmes moved more toward commercial music.

Although clearly there are alternative groups that have a short-term following, there are very few alternative groups that in fact last very long as alternative groups. They either become more mainstream or they get other jobs. Therefore, alternative music will always be around, have relatively little lasting impact on rock and roll, have little commercial success, but will occasionally have real impact. Like the eclectic musicians from the 1960s, alternative musicians are usually trying to make a statement from a noncommercial point of view. But the best of them slip up, like Frank Zappa, and become cult heroes.

LISTENING

Sex Pistols, *Never Mind the Bollocks*

Iggy Pop, *Soldier*

Elvis Costello, *Taking Liberties*

Graham Parker, *Squeezing Out Sparks*

Talking Heads, *Fear of Music*

CHAPTER **18**

TECHNO-FUNK/POP, RAP, MTV, DANCE MUSIC, AND THE FUTURE

INTRODUCTION

This concluding chapter contains a collection of musical types from the 1980s and early 1990s, starting with techno-pop/funk, then rap, and finally dance music. At the end of the chapter there is a chart that models rock history in a purist to commercial continuum. As the concluding chapter in an update of a book on a form that will continue growing (hopefully to a fourth edition), please keep in mind that groups discussed are relatively current as of 1991 (when the manuscript was finished).

TECHNO-FUNK/POP MUSICIANS

The early 1980s saw a slow shift away from new wave. Some important subcategories of rock were the *new romantics,* represented by Visage, Ultra-Vox, and at times Adam and the Ants; the *blitz* (essentially disco/new wave) was electric-chic-

Blondie   *(Photo by Chrysalis Records; used by permission of Ginny Cartmell and Creem Magazine Archives)*

disco and was antipunk, represented by Flock of Seagulls, Men at Work, Soft Cell, and the German band Kraftwerk; *punk-jazz,* represented by its spiritual leader Ornette Coleman, and bands like Material; and *blue wave,* a combination of blues and new wave, represented by the Fabulous Thunderbirds (Texas), the Blasters (California), and the Stray Cats (originally from New York, moved to London, and returned to the United States).

By 1984 we saw a clear dominance of the musical style defined as the *blitz,* although it was no longer referred to by that name. In 1984 the term *techno-pop* or *techno-funk* was the standard way of defining what was happening. The big names in 1984 were Prince ("1999," which was upbeat funk, "Purple Rain," which was psychedelic, and "Raspberry Beret" of 1985, in the same style as "Purple Rain"); Michael Jackson (for both singles and video—see analysis of "Billy Jean" in the appendix); Lionel Richie (slow ballads in the crooning Motown tradition of the Commodores); Madonna; and Cyndi Lauper. A number of other musicians remained popular through this era, for instance Bruce Springsteen (a constant hard rocker), and Sting of the Police, who by this time had embarked on a very successful solo career.

The video craze began in 1984, although the concept had existed prior to

Men at Work *(Courtesy of Columbia Records and Laura Levine, photographer)*

that time. The technology of the time created the means by which to market rock—through videotapes—and there developed a whole recording technique for videos. Many songs were written specifically for videos, so that the music and words would fit visual images. An especially delightful example of that is *Girls Just Want to Have Fun* by Cyndi Lauper. That particular video is an excellent example of visual images and musical communication fitting together. It is a contemporary example of word painting—the communication is much more effective as a result

The Fabulous Thunderbirds   *(Courtesy of Chrysalis Records)*

of an intelligent combination of aural and visual images. Videos in 1984 were strong statements, and MTV in the United States became a dominant power in rock, sometimes to the chagrin of British rock critics.

However, by examining some of the big hits and significant groups of 1985 we discover a slightly different story. For one thing, videos were made a bit tamer in 1985 because of strong censorship—the traditional reaction against overstatement. Also, a majority of U.S. songs became more pop-oriented and less techno-funk. Violent and strongly sexual lyrics began to abate. Even bands like the Talking

Michael Jackson, *Thriller*   *(Courtesy of Columbia/Epic Records)*

Heads, the last vestige of new wave, did more pop-oriented tunes, on their album *Little Creatures.* Sting started recording with a black backup band in 1985; "Set Them Free" is a medium funk tune, and "Fortress Around Your Heart" is a slow pop tune.

Other examples of this phenomenon in 1985 were Lionel Richie ("Say You Say Me," a slow ballad with an upbeat middle section); Wham! ("Careless Whisper," a mellow ballad, and "Wake Me up before You Go-Go," an upbeat pop tune); Simple Minds ("Don't You Forget about Me," a mid-tempo movie theme song, and "Alive and Kicking"); 'Til Tuesday ("Voices Carry," a mid-tempo pop tune); Phil Collins ("Billy Don't Lose My Number"); Huey Lewis and the News ("Power of Love," and "Back in Time," both upbeat pop tunes); and Stevie Wonder ("Part

Time Lover" of late 1985, a mid-tempo pop tune). Even Aretha Franklin had a pop tune hit in 1985 with "Who's Zoomin' Who?" Aretha had always been relatively pure gospel in style.

Therefore, we should be able to conjecture that we saw a noticeable shift between 1984 and 1985. Of course, some musicians carried through both years. We also have the continuation of rap, funk, heavy metal, rockabilly, and other styles. But the dominant style in 1985 was clearly less techno-funk and more straight pop music. The popular music of 1985 illustrated the commercial side of rock and roll, which has often meant that change is about to occur.

RAP

Rap is the logical extension of the development of black music in the United States and its constituent parts were developed from African slave music, the blues, gospel, and more currently soul and funk jazz rock. It is a form of music that features a strong rhythm section, with the slap bass so important to funk, soul, and reggae. On top of the continuous rhythmic background, often monochordal, the rapper/singer sings/speaks his or her message in a punctuated style that has become as varied as any other form of poetry set to music. Further, rap chronicles the changing societal views of black Americans as well as Africans in other countries. Of course, the most fascinating thing about rap from the point of view of the evolution of music is that there are Japanese, white American, Hispanic, and other nationality rappers as well.

There are many theories about the origin of rap and consistent with the author's general viewpoint, we take the position that it started a long time ago with natural word rhythm in black dialect, rather than with some modern musical group. However, the most obvious antecedents to the contemporary style are in rhythm and blues utterances and screams, like those of Little Richard, Ray Charles, and others. Clearly, the music of soul musician James Brown in the 1960s had incipient rap qualities to it as well. The musical background of rap has been around a long time, although the strengthening bass line and the popping style of playing certainly derived from funk musicians of the late 1960s and early 1970s, to be fully cultivated by the time of Stanley Clarke (see chapter fifteen).

The speech song vocal technique of rap was not recognized as a separate style until the late 1970s, but its antecedents certainly started in a full-blown sense with George Clinton and the various musicians involved in the Parliament(s)/Funkadelic grouping, with William "Bootsy" Collins. The rhyming pattern of Parliament is clearly rap, even before the time when it was so recognized.

Further, rap started from the underground, which is to say that it was a regional style, appreciated by audiences of particular musicians/groups, that had very little national exposure (i.e., there were no hit records). Recognized simply as a part of funk music, rap developed into a recognizable style when it became commercial. In fact, most of the groups/musicians mentioned in this section started as underground musicians, only reaching commercial viability when the rap style became such a big hit.

Other aspects of the rap style that are important are the following: the scratching style, dance steps, mouth beat box, and breakin'. Scratching style is the dragging of the needle across a record on a turntable to produce a steady rhythm. Dancing is very significant in rap for punctuation of particular words and messages and for contrast between verbal communications. Using the mouth as a rhythmic instrument (mouth beat box) is another technique specific to rap, creating a rhythmic back beat with the rhythm section. The whole break dance phenomenon is tied to rap and some have even argued that it was the break dance that created a market for rap. Eventually the break dance popularity created clothing styles that became popular and then particular ways of dressing for rap musicians, which further delineated the style and message from other types of music.

Of the earlier rappers, the following groups include most of the important musicians: Kool Moe Dee with the Treacherous 3 from 1977, the Sugarhill Gang, Kurtis Blow and the "Christmas Rappin' " of 1979, and Grandmaster Flash (mentioned in a previous chapter). Generally Blow, Grandmaster Flash, and the Sugarhill Gang developed the rapping style in New York clubs, between 1976 and 1979. Sugarhill Gang's "Rapper's Delight" became the first international rapping pop hit, having much more success in England than in the United States; it reached number thirty on the UK charts. In 1980, Kurtis Blow charted number eighty-seven on the U.S. charts with "The Breaks"; it reached number four on the R & B chart. That record was done with Davy D on backing tracks, scratching on his turntables. This is still the early history of rapping as far as commercial viability is concerned, but having a million-selling record certainly established Blow as one of the pivotal figures in rap music. Blow continued to have success through about 1986 with his novelty rap "Basketball" in 1985 and "If I Ruled the World" in 1986.

The techno-funk development of the early 1980s, using synthesizers and electronic devices, actually contributed to the accessability of rap, because it was possible to create the rhythmic background for rap without having a complete rhythm section. But it was probably the creation of break dancing, the beat box (portable radio), and eventually the rise of music videos, "black" films, and the realization of the record companies that black music was more than just Motown that caused rap to really take off. There is little question that the groups that contributed the most to this middle period of rap development were LL Cool J and Run DMC.

Run DMC started in 1982 in New York as a specialist rap group, made up of Joseph Simmons (Run), Darryl McDaniels (DMC), and DJ Jason Mizell (Jam Master Jay). They signed their first recording contract in 1983 with Profile Records. The first rap LP *Run—D.M.C.* stayed on the U.S. charts for over a year and became the first U.S. gold rap record. They toured with LL Cool J in 1983. In 1985, they appeared in the first rap movie, *Krush Groove* and they were involved in the Artists Against Apartheid song and video entitled *Sun City*. In 1986 they were the artist representative for Adidas. The association of rap groups with commercial products, such as running shoes, had a significant impact on the commercialization of rap in general. Their dance routine (sometimes called hip hop style) was a significant part of their image and had an impact on later groups. Although Run DMC was successful, rap remained a specialist style in the mid-1980s, occasionally having commercial impact. Touring activity, such as the "Run's House" U.S. tour (1988) with Jazzy Jeff and Fresh Prince (who had a TV show in 1990 called "Prince of Bel-Air"), Public Enemy, and others contributed to their lasting impact in the late 1980s. Continuing in popularity into the 1990s, they became mainstream rappers and had national recognition and commercial success, with raps like "The Ave" (1990).

LL Cool J (James Todd Smith) was also from New York and developed at the same time as Run DMC. He was less mainstream than Run DMC in the beginning, although by the mid- to late 1980s, he was having quite a bit of commercial success,

M.C. Hammer   *(Compliments of Capitol Records)*

Bell Biv Devoe *(Compliments of MCA Records)*

with "I Need Love" in 1987 and "Going Back to Cali" from a film in 1988. Like many other rappers, he recorded for Def Jam Music. He developed a harder hip hop style in his early recordings and was the first to do a slow rap, which was essentially a love song — "I Need Love."

Another interesting group from the mid-1980s is the Fat Boys, somewhat comical because of their size but commercially viable. They had two hits that started them toward commercial success, "Wipeout" in 1987, a remake backed by the Beach Boys and "The Twist," a remake of a Chubby Checker hit from 1960 and 1962. The Fat Boys was partially responsible for making the beat box and the drum rhythm vocal technique so important to rap.

Moving toward the end of the 1980s, there is no question that rapper M.C. Hammer was the most significant commercializing factor in rap. His first two albums *Let's Get It Started* and *Please Hammer Don't Hurt 'Em* topped the charts June through October 1990. An electrifying performer, Hammer was sometimes criticized for being too soft and romantic. There is no question that he has had more

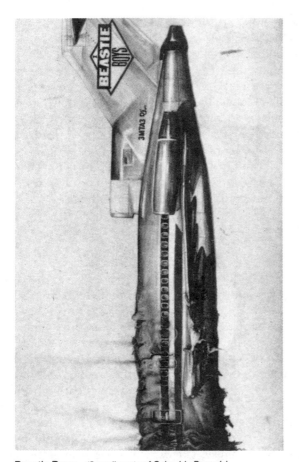

Beastie Boys   *(Compliments of Columbia Records)*

crossover success than most rappers. Although the message of his raps is optimistic and generally not hardcore, it is still rap. It just isn't raw enough for black purists. His second album sold close to six million copies, and he won a number of music awards, including the MTV Music Award. He has also endorsed soft drinks, footwear, and other products. Therefore, Hammer is important and the message he conveyed about not using drugs and staying in school is certainly socially redeeming. He also connected himself with the history of rap by performing with many other rappers, such as Kool Moe Dee, Public Enemy, and others.

In the late 1980s and early 1990s, rap was one of the most significant forms of black music and certainly conveyed a wide gamut of human expressions. In addition, a number of rap groups were popular with white audiences, to the point where it was sometimes impossible to separate rap from dance groups (see later section). The first white rappers were the Beastie Boys (1987) and Vanilla Ice, receiving notoriety as the opening act on the M.C. Hammer/Vanilla Ice tour of 1990. Vanilla Ice's album *To the Extreme* went to number one in November 1990.

Underground groups abounded through the 1970s and 1980s, such as Schooly Dee and Dana Dane. In the late 1980s into the 1990s, there also existed purist rap groups that conveyed black-oriented messages not designed for white audiences at all, such as Public Enemy, Ice T, X Klan, Boogie Down Productions, D/Nice, MC Lyte (female black-oriented rapper) and Professor Griff, who was with Public Enemy. Great controversy surrounded rap groups who presented their message with little concern for the use of profanity, such as 2 Live Crew, NWA (ask somebody what that means; it can't be printed in a book), Kool T, HWA (female group). But like previous groups discussed in this section, some of these groups will break out of their underground status and become mainstream.

MTV AND ITS INFLUENCE

Rather than present a complete discussion of particular videos over the 1980s into the 1990s, we will simply point out the rather incredible impact of MTV on the industry during that period. In fact, music videos have been around for a long time, starting as film shorts in the late 1920s. However, starting in 1983, MTV in combination with videos became part of the total package of particular artists, perhaps focused the best in the developments around Michael Jackson in 1984. We have already mentioned earlier in this chapter the rather remarkable impact that Michael had in 1984 and 1985, which of course continued through the "Bad" Tour in the late 1980s. Also discussed previously was the impact that censorship had in that period, basically causing videos to lose some of their hard edge between 1984 and 1985. Subsequent activity by various censorship groups during the 1980s had a monitoring effect on music videos, which became more and more commercial in orientation.

Music videos cover the entire gamut of rock history in the 1980s, with some of the major categories being metal/hard rock, dance/rap and mainstream, or easy listening. Some of the most popular videos for purchase were those by artists like Kenny G and Barry Manilow, both hardly part of mainstream rock and roll. On MTV itself, videos in various categories are played at different times to different audiences. Production of music videos for country music, country rock, teenage rock, and virtually every kind of music one could imagine have been created as a necessary part of the marketing package of music.

MTV has also had an impact on the relative success of various kinds of music as well as the buying habits of younger Americans who watch it. Interestingly, it has also had an impact on the buying tastes in other countries, like England. At first, MTV was condemned by many as a marketing hype and also because of its "evil" influence. Although the marketing hype argument is certainly fair, MTV has become a barometer of the music business and the MTV awards are very valuable to the career of individual musicians who are trying to break out of the underground or who simply wish to advance their careers.

DANCE AND POP/ROCK MUSICIANS

In the late 1980s and into the 1990s pop/rock music was generally called *dance music*, a title that could easily have been applied to similar music in previous eras of rock history. What it actually represents in terms of attitude is a growing commercial period in rock, a softening of the basic form for commercial impact. Also a fusion music, this particular category fits nicely into the chart describing rock's cyclical development (see next section).

Another intriguing factor about dance music is that the category encompasses a wide variety of artists — Paula Abdul, Phil Collins, and Linear are examples. Another excellent early example of contemporary dance music would be Whitney Houston (see analysis of "I Wanna Dance with Somebody" in the appendix). This is of course similar to the developments discussed in chapter seven (Broadening of the Style). Like the previous periods in rock history where rock diversified its definition for commercial reasons, this music is most successful in terms of record sales and dollars. Dance music is not universally respected by rock purists and rock critics, although it is important to understand that these highly visible and commercially viable groups are fundamentally responsible for creating the fiscal base that allows the support of less commercial recordings.

The last statement as a justification for commercial music can certainly be argued. The question is: Do record companies stick solely to formula approaches to record success or do they truly allow noncommercial music because they are successful with certain other types of recordings? Obviously we take the position that if the record industry is financially viable, then underground material is recorded for either historical or charity reasons. But the bottom line is that the music business is part of the free enterprise system, and the emphasis in the late 1980s and early 1990s was dance music.

As representatives of this particular phenomenon, we have chosen to discuss the following: Janet Jackson, Billy Joel, Madonna, Miami Sound Machine with Gloria Estafan, George Michael, and the New Kids on the Block.

Janet Jackson is the youngest of the Jackson family, born on May 16, 1966. She appeared with her brothers in a Las Vegas show in 1973. She was a child actress, appearing in various television series — "Good Times" and "Different Strokes." She signed a recording contract in 1982 and her first LP was produced, *Janet Jackson*. Throughout the 1980s, she had great success, such as with *What Have You Done for Me Lately* (number four in 1986), *Nasty* (number three in 1986), *When I Think of You* (number one in 1986) and *Control* (number five in 1986). *Control — The Videos* was released in November 1986. In *Billboard*'s year-end survey of artists, she was in the number one position in six categories. In 1987 *Control — The*

Whitney Houston   *(Compliments of Arista Records)*

Videos Part II was released. Her video *Nasty* won an award for its choreographer, Paula Abdul, who ultimately developed into a major singer in this genre of music in the late 1980s.

Billy Joel was born on May 9, 1952, in New York. In the late 1960s he started playing piano for several rock groups and signed his first soloist contract with Family Productions. Like Elton John and Barry Manilow, Billy Joel is essentially a pianist/songwriter who seemed to slip into rock through the back door. By the mid-1970s, he was a successful recording musician, but he still was most significant as a songwriter. However, in 1977, his album *The Stranger* moved up to number 2 on the U.S. charts and ultimately became Columbia's second biggest selling album after Simon and Garfunkel's. He won countless awards in the 1980s, became an ambassador for the United States in 1987 by touring Russia, and was involved in a variety of activities, including the "We Are the World" single of 1985 and Disney movies.

Janet Jackson   *(Compliments of A & M Records)*

Madonna (Madonna Louise Ciccone) was born on August 16, 1959, in Detroit. As a child she was involved in dance, music, and acting. Starting in 1979 as a dancer, she spent three years trying to get a hit. In 1983, her first album, *Madonna,* was successful in the United States and a video for *Lucky Star* was released in England. But it was really *Like A Virgin* (1984) that definitively made her a superstar. With an ever-expanding musical and acting career, Madonna remained through the early 1990s a vibrant performer, concertizing in provocative costumes. Some have criticized her for lip-synching, which doomed Milli Vanilli in 1990, but with her energetic performances, one is really hard pressed to criticize that. She does her own singing on the albums and has a full-bodied voice. Her video performances have also been successful, from *Like A Virgin* to *Vogue* in 1990. She has been compared to Marilyn Monroe in presence and is certainly one of the stars of the dance music category.

Miami Sound Machine with Gloria Estafan is another superb example of a

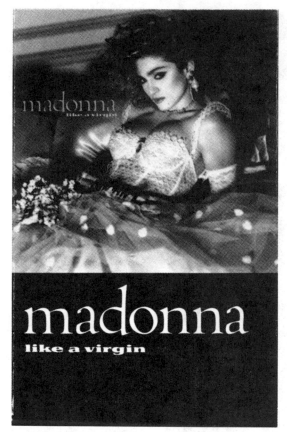

Madonna *(Compliments of Sire Records)*

group that grew toward this particular category at just the right time. The band formed in Miami as the Miami Latin Boys (Emilio Estefan, keyboards; Juan Avila, bass; and Enrique Garcia, drums). Gloria joined the group as a singer in 1974 and married Emilio in 1978. All four members were born in Cuba and raised in Miami. They performed solely in Spanish until 1984, recording on the *Audio Latino* label; their first single was called "Renecer." In 1986, they did music for a Sylvester Stallone movie and for Tom Cruise's *Top Gun*. From 1986 on, they had phenomenal success, doing most of their recordings in English, and they were named the Top Pop Singles Act of the Year in 1986 for *Billboard* magazine.

George Michael was born in England on June 25, 1963. In 1981, Michael and Andrew Ridgeley formed Wham, one of the most successful British pop groups of the 1980s. One of his first hits, "Careless Whispers," was written in 1981; this would later become his first number one song in 1985. This ballad has become a model for middle-of-the-road pop music in the 1980s. Somewhat like Phil Collins, Michael was both part of a pop band that had enormous success and a solo singer as

New Kids on the Block   *(Compliments of Columbia Records)*

well. His lyric voice, dreamy looks, and love-song style make him another good example of the dance music phenomenon.

Last but not least, The New Kids on the Block close out this representation of dance music groups. Formed in the summer of 1984 as a Boston teen quintet, Joe McIntyre, Donny Wahlberg, Danny Wood, and brothers Jordan and Jonathon Knight were probably the most successful act of 1990. Originally named NYNUK by Maurice Starr, their producer, they were put together as a teen group. Columbia Records signed them in 1986, and they quickly produced their first album, called *New Kids on the Block*, after a rap that Donny had written. The songs on that first album were mostly songs that Maurice had written. "Be My Girl," from that album, was the first single that made it to the Top 100 singles chart, although it never moved up the charts from number ninety.

Their second album was released in 1988, *Hangin' Tough*, and a single from that album, "Please Don't Go Girl," made it to position ten on the charts in August

1988 and remained on the charts for twelve weeks. They also did videos of "Please Don't Go Girl," "(You Got It) The Right Stuff," "I'll be Lovin' You (Forever)," and "Hangin' Tough" for that album. They followed that album with *Merry, Merry Christmas* and the incredibly successful *Step By Step* (1990) song, tour, and video. Songs from that album include "Where Do I Go From Here?," "Valentine Girl," "Let's Try It Again," and "Games" (see appendix for analysis). *Step by Step* was the album that replaced M. C. Hammer's *Please Hammer Don't Hurt 'Em* as the number one album for one week in June 1990. *No More Games* was released in 1990 with songs from prior albums remixed with new instrumental backgrounds.

The New Kids on the Block is a perfect example of dance music, although there are elements of rap in its music and exclusively rap songs. Their stage performances are filled with dance routines, love songs, and nonstop action. Their message is optimistic and positive about life, expressing values that are clearly different from other forms of rock and roll. One can clearly understand the lyrics and although in 1990 they became for the most part nonteenagers, they still sing about the joys of youth, having fun, and platonic relationships reminiscent of early 1960s music. Although in the 1990s it remains to be seen whether they will evolve like the group to which they are sometimes compared, the New Kids on the Block may very well become more and more like the Beatles as they grow up and move toward the twenty-first century.

THE CYCLIC GRAPH OF ROCK HISTORY

The following graph illustrates a principle that has emerged from this author's study of rock and roll. I became aware of a tendency for rock and roll to follow societal changes, roughly analogous to changes in political thinking from conservative to liberal, Republican to Democrat, good times to bad times (not necessarily in that order). Although I could never really ascribe specific movements in rock and roll clearly to these ideas, I did discover what I perceived as a tendency for rock and roll to follow a cyclical pattern of development, swinging back and forth between relatively pure forms of rock to more commercial fusion-oriented music. In the chart, I have identified the peaks I believe exist and described that cyclical movement.

This chart does not take into consideration all the forms of rock discussed in this book, but the point of the graph is that there has been a tendency for rather pure forms of rock to lead to imitations and then to fusion in styles. There is also a tendency for commercial periods of fusion music to lead to another relatively pure form of rock and roll. Our contention is that one could predict the future of rock and roll given this cyclical chart, although it would be impossible to predict what form the new development would take, only its relative degree of commercial or purist character.

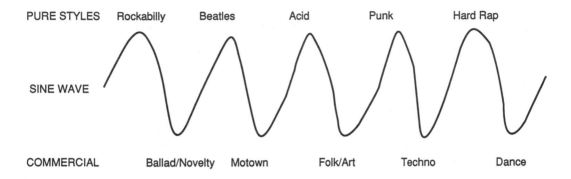

DATES: '51-'55 '56-'62 '62-'65 '66-'69 '67-'69 '70-'75 '76-'79 '80-'83 '84-'86 '87-

PURE STYLES Rockabilly   Beatles   Acid   Punk   Hard Rap

SINE WAVE

COMMERCIAL   Ballad/Novelty Motown   Folk/Art   Techno   Dance

CONCLUSION

In predicting a return to the 1960s liberal folk-rock as the next pure form, we are doing so with the realization that it may never happen. However, all indications are that rock and roll does follow political cycles, and there is a polar nature to that cyclical activity. The mid-1980s illustrated a miniversion of that cyclical development. Of course, the pop music of 1985 was well done, but it clearly represented an amalgamation of the styles available, coupled with a growing commercialization. We also saw a softening in the style of videos, which was the fusion form of the mid-1980s. I would like to think that my prediction of the return of the philosophical thinking and music of the 1960s is based on a solid cyclical view of our cultural history. On the other hand, it may be just wishful thinking. Obviously, the history of rock is not over. However, we have established some basic premises, with which we will conclude:

1. Rock is a legitimate art form, with its own technique and its own complexity.
2. Like any art form, it has its highs and lows. However, whenever things seemed static, someone came along to breathe vitality into the tired body.
3. We can trace cycles in rock, which seem to correlate with societal views.
4. Rock has had a major influence on society and on other art forms. This is perhaps the best proof of its effectiveness as an art form.
5. Although it began as a way for youth to rebel against their parents, rock is now a universal art form and a means of communication, spanning the gamut of generations all over the world.

LISTENING

Sex Pistols, *Never Mind the Bollocks*
Iggy Pop, *Soldier*
Elvis Costello, *Taking Liberties*
Graham Parker, *Squeezing Out Sparks*
Talking Heads, *Fear of Music*
Michael Jackson, *Beat It*
Madonna, *Like A Virgin*
Miami Sound Machine, *Anything for You*
NKOTB, *Step by Step*
M.C. Hammer, *Please Hammer Don't Hurt 'Em*
Vanilla Ice, *To The Extreme*

APPENDIX A

TECHNOLOGICAL TERMS AND DEFINITIONS

Changes in electronic technology over the last thirty years have been phenomenal. Scientific change in general has had a major influence on our society, in terms of both its viewpoint and its physical life. Technological change has, throughout history, had a massive effect on human society. No matter what the technological advancement, there has always been a corresponding reaction to it, sometimes positive and sometimes negative.

However, since World War II the world has experienced technological change at a seemingly impossible rate. Although it is certain that other eras have felt such changes as much as we have, somehow our reaction has been stronger, if for no other reason than the speed of change. We have less and less time to get used to each change before the next advance is upon us.

Although technology has affected everything in our society, it has been especially important to rock music. Music has become an electronic art in the last thirty to forty years, and rock has been the leader in that movement. In this appendix we will define various electronic devices and terms. However, it should also be understood that there were nonelectronic devices created during the history of rock and roll that significantly affected its ability to proliferate. An example of this would be the invention of high speed record-producing machines, whereby thousands of records could be produced quickly in order to meet the demand created by the marketing techniques discussed earlier.

Clearly, an understanding of these devices is important in helping the reader grasp the techniques by which rock musicians have created their music. Their presentation in this appendix allows the reader to consult the terms when they come up in the book, or they can help those who wish to have scientific explanations of how specific devices work. It will be useful for some readers to go to a rock record or music store to view particular devices, and to try them if they are applicable to their interest.

DEFINITIONS

A-B test   Testing the performance of two or more amplifiers or speaker systems by switching back and forth between systems.

Absorption   The ability of a room to absorb acoustic energy.

AC power   110-120 volts of alternating current (in the United States, the wall plug).

Acoustics   The science of sound, sound heard, hearing ability, and the production of sound.

Active   Circuitry that can increase the amplitude of a signal.

Additive synthesis   See Synthesis.

Ampere   A unit of measurement of electrical current.

Amplifier   A device that accepts a signal from a sound source and increases the loudness or power level of the waveform without distorting its original sound. It raises the signal level so that it can be driven through speakers.

Attenuation   Reduction in level of a signal.

Audio chain   Describes the order of connection of components for the reproduction of sound; typically sound source, microphone, preamplifier, special effects, graphic equalizer, amplifier, and speaker(s).

Audio range   20 cps (cycles per sound, or hertz) to 20,000 cps. The frequency spectrum of sound perceptible to humans.

Baffle   The panel on which a speaker is mounted in a speaker box.

Balanced cable   A shielded cable.

Balanced line   A transmission line (cable) capable of being operated so that the voltages at both ends are equal.

Bandwidth   The definition of a range of sound frequencies that can, for example, be controlled by one switch. See also Graphic equalizer.

Bass reflex   A speaker enclosure in which the speaker's rear sound waves come out of an opening, thus reinforcing the bass sounds.

Boost   Indicates an increase in gain of a frequency, or a band of frequencies.

Bus   A conductor that services two or more signal sources, used in a mixer board.

Capacitor   An electrical part that reduces heat loss in the conducting of electrical energy. It blocks direct current and allows the passage of alternating current.

Cardioid   A microphone whose construction picks up sound from the front rather than the back. A unidirectional microphone.

Chorus   A pedal device that makes the sound bigger through a simple flanger without regeneration control. See also Flanger.

Clipping   Amplifier overload that causes a change in the waveform resulting in distortion.

Compression   Reduction in amplifier gain corresponding to increased input level.

Compressor   A type of pedal that automatically turns down the level of a signal going into it as that level increases and turns the level back up as the signal dies away, thus creating a sustain effect.

Conductor   A wire or cable that carries electrical current.

Continuous power   The power rating of an amplifier, measured at 1000 Hz for a specific amount of time. Rated in watts.

CPS   Cycles per second, the historic way of describing the number of vibrations per second a simple tone produces. In modern terminology, cps is called Hertz (Hz).

Critical distance   The point in a room where the sound level produced by a speaker equals the reverberation field of the acoustic properties of the room.

Crossover   An electronic device that divides electrical power sent from amplifiers to speakers into various bandwidths corresponding to different sized speakers. See also Bandwidth.

Current   The rate of flow (measured in amps) of electricity in a circuit.

Cut   Describes a reduction in level of a frequency, or band of frequencies, when using an equalizer.

Decibel   A term used to describe the relative strength or power of a sound source. Typically understood to be loudness.

Digital delay   Also referred to as Echo, this is a pedal-controlled device that allows for a controlled repeat of the original sound from one millisecond to two seconds. On some devices one can also control the number of repeats.

Digital sampling   See Synthesis.

Dip   A reduction in gain at certain frequencies.

Directivity   Area of coverage of a speaker or microphone.

Dispersion   The spread or distribution of sound coverage produced by a speaker. If the sound decreases in volume as you move away from a point directly in front of the speaker, it is a directional speaker.

Distortion   Undesirable change in a waveform.

Dynamic range   The decibel range capable of being produced by an instrument, or the range of acceptable volumes produced by electrical equipment (from softest to loudest).

Echo   See Digital delay.

Efficiency   The relationship between power usage and power output.

Electronic drums   A reasonably recent development, electronic drums are essentially membranes or drum heads with sensors built into them, which trigger individual circuits. This allows for a variety of electronic drum sounds, and also can be used in connection with a drum synthesizer.

Enclosure   An acoustically-designed housing for a speaker.

Equalization   Control of various bands of frequencies so as to enhance or modify the total sound. See also Graphic equalizer.

Excursion   Movement of the cone of the loudspeaker.

Exponential horn   A high-frequency speaker shaped like a horn.

Feedback   In electronic terms, a return of some of the signal back to the circuit. In acoustic terms, the return of the signal to the original microphone.

Filter   A device that allows certain frequencies to pass through the circuit while blocking others.

Flanger   A pedal device that creates a millisecond delay, or a moving sine wave. It is not the same as a phaser, rather, it creates a chorus effect. The delay rate is controllable by a knob on the pedal, as is the regeneration, which controls a change in intensity of the harmonic structure. The flanger is a very popular device.

Frequency   The number of cycles per second that a basic oscillator or instrument produces; determines the high or low quality of the sound.

Frequency response   A measure of the effectiveness of a circuit, device (microphone, amplifier, or speaker), or electronic system to produce equal intensity across the frequency bands between a lower and upper limit.

Fuzz   Another pedal effect, the fuzz box produces distortion by introducing a square wave, in which positive energy peaks and then immediately becomes negative.

Gain   Increase in strength of a signal, usually expressed in ratio of input to output voltage, or power increase in decibels.

Graphic equalizer   A set of controls that allows one to lower or raise the decibel level of specific bands of frequencies, typically built into mixer units and power amplifiers. See also Equalization.

Ground   A non-power-carrying wire in an electric circuit, connected to a metal part of the frame, or to the junction box.

Harmonic   Describes particular frequencies in relation to a fundamental pitch. These frequencies are determined by the harmonic series of a fundamental pitch or sine wave. Harmonics, and their relative intensity, determine the timbre, or tone quality, of a complex sound. Harmonics can also be produced on acoustic instruments by lightly stopping the string or overblowing.

Headroom   The difference between optimal power level and the level at which clipping or distortion occurs.

Hertz   A unit of sound frequency measurement that replaced the older term cycles per second (cps).

High pass   A filter that allows frequencies above a certain point to pass through it, and cuts off frequencies below this point.

Hum   Distortion from the power line that typically impedes listening to the sound source.

Impedance   Opposition to alternating current flow from a circuit, expressed in ohms. High and low impedance cords and microphones are used to match the resistances of various devices.

Inductance   Generated force of a circuit, or two circuits, as an opposition to a change in current.

Input overload   Distortion created by too strong a signal coming into a device.

Integrated   Multiple components or functions combined into one unit.

Jack   A receptacle into which something is plugged.

Kilohertz (kilocycles)   1000 hertz or 1000 cps (KCPS).

LED   Diode or small bulb that emits light when a specific current is applied to it.

Limiter   A circuit that limits the amplitude, or level, of a waveform from exceeding a certain present limit, and also maintains waveform shape.

Line out   An output connection that will drive an amplifier or allow reproduction.

Low pass   A filter that allows frequencies below a certain point to pass through it, and cuts off frequencies above this point.

Loudness control   Controls the volume of the output of an amplifier.

Loudspeaker   A reproduction device that translates electrical energy into acoustic energy after the original sound source has been amplified, and sometimes modified, through the audio chain. See also Tweeter and Woofer.

Loudspeaker efficiency The ratio of signal input to signal output.

Master Main control for gain or volume level.

Microphone A transducer that receives acoustic energy and transmits it as electrical energy through wires to the rest of the audio chain. See also Unidirectional and Omnidirectional.

MIDI A universal connection used on many contemporary electronic keyboard units and synthesizers that allows computer control of multiple keyboard and synthesizer units.

Mono Monophonic sound; one single source emitting from speakers.

Noise Any signal that adds distortion, hum, or other undesirable signals to sound output.

Notch filter A filter that substantially lowers the gain of a very specific spectrum of sounds.

Octave The interval between two frequencies with a ratio of 1 : 2, for example, low C and the C above it.

Octave divider The octave divider is usually a small unit hung on the belt of the musician but controlled by a pedal. It adds a sound an octave below, and/or two octaves below, the basic sound sent through it. The relative intensity of the reproduced sound can be adjusted by a volume control on the unit.

Ohm A unit of electrical resistance. It takes one volt of potential to drive one amp of current through one ohm of resistance.

Omnidirectional Microphones that pick up sound from all directions.

Overtone harmonic Multiples of a fundamental waveform.

Palm Pedal The Palm Pedal is actually not a foot pedal, but a lever screwed into the body of an electric guitar. Popularized by Duane Eddy, the Palm Pedal is an adaption of the Knee Pedal used by steel guitarists; recently it has been adapted to the organ (Farfisa). The Palm Pedal is a mechanical device that stretches the guitar's strings, thus raising the pitch. In some senses, it is the predecessor to electronic pedal effects.

Parallel Devices connected directly to a circuit; current flows through each device independently, and back to the circuit, rather than one after another, as in series.

Peak Maximum value of a signal's amplitude.

Pedal devices Electronic circuits that create various effects, and can be controlled by a foot pedal, which often turns them on or off. Occasionally the pedal allows one to control the actual device. They are plugged in between the instrument or microphone and the preamplifier. See Chorus, Compressor, Digital delay (Echo), Flanger, Fuzz (Distortion), Octave divider, Phaser, Wah-Wah. See also Palm Pedal (mechanical device).

Phase Time interval between two events. Two signals are in phase when their waveforms overlap exactly. When sine waves (or other waves) are separated by part of the entire wave, they are out of phase.

Phaser   A pedal device that creates a sine wave opposite to the basic sound being sent through the pedal.

Polarity   Opposite magnetic or electrical poles (plus and minus).

Power   Electrical energy in watts.

Power amplifier   The final amplification in the audio chain, just prior to the speakers.

Preamp   An amplifier that increases the total gain of a source, such as a microphone, so that it has sufficient level to drive a power amplifier.

Real time analyzer   An instrument that measures the response of an audio system to the room in which it is operating.

Reflection   Sound waves bouncing off of walls and other obstacles.

Resistance   Opposition to flow of current (ohms).

Resistor   An electrical component designed to create resistance, or to provide a voltage drop.

Resonance   The tendency of all electronic parts to vibrate.

Response   The range of frequencies within which an amplifier or speaker will respond, and the relative intensity of those frequencies.

Return   An input that accepts a signal after it has been sent to special effects. See also Send.

Reverb   Sound that continues to be heard after the actual source has ceased. Sometimes thought of as echo, reverb is actually repetition of a sound, although the repetitions are indistinguishably close to one another.

Ring mode   Sound that lies just below the threshold or occurrence of feedback.

Roll off   Attenuation or reduction in sound level above or below certain frequencies; measured in decibels per octave.

Send   An output to an external processor or effect. See also Return.

Sensitivity   Minimum input signal required to produce output.

Series   A series of components connected in a line, which forms one signal path for current; the opposite of parallel.

Sine wave   A wave that follows the mathematical sine of time, shifting from positive polarity to negative polarity and back again. It looks like an S on its side.

Snake   A shielded, multiconductor input cable that allows for the connection of many microphones to a mixer or amplifier at some distance from the stage.

Solid state   A type of circuitry in which all components are placed on circuit boards, rather than being connected by wires. Typically using transistors to replace vacuum tubes, solid state circuitry is a technique for miniaturization, and it avoids the bane of electronics — heat build up.

Speaker   See Loudspeaker, Tweeter, and Woofer.

Splitter   A box or connector that can break one sound input into two or more output signals.

Stereo   A system in which two separate power amplifiers create control over different inputs; the speakers reproduce the spatial effect of the sound more accurately than monophonic reproduction.

Synthesis   Synthesis is the process by which sounds are electronically created. The *synthesizer* is essentially a collection of interconnected *oscillators* (sound producers). Later, *filters* and *envelope controls* were added to primitive synthesizers. Synthesizers were first designed for studio production of electronic music, and later were adapted for live performance and pop music.

> **Subtractive synthesis**   was the first type of synthesis used, in which a basic waveform created by an oscillator was modified by notching out harmonics and articulating the sound over time. *Filters* were used to control harmonics and to vary the intensity of the wave's harmonics. *Envelopes* were used to control the attack of the sound (starting of a pitch), the sustain (over time), the decay (dropping intensity or ending of a sound), and the release.

> **Additive synthesis**   is a relatively new method since about 1982, in which a pure sine wave is modified by a carrier modulator, i.e., sounds are added together. Envelope is used in a manner similar to subtractive synthesis, the earlier process.

> **Digital sampling**   is perhaps the newest and most exciting development in synthesis. By using the standard binary storage techniques of computer technology, one takes a basic sound (through a direct connection to an instrument, a microphone, or a recorded source) and reduces it to 256 units per page of material (determined by the type and sophistication of the sampling device). This allows for looping and control of sampled sounds through traditional subtractive synthesis techniques. Most units are essentially a computer within a keyboard unit. Usually a *MIDI*-connected device, this allows for computer control, storage, reproduction through a printer, and overdubbing by the basic device, and even studio overdubbing through external computer storage and manipulation.

Subtractive synthesis   See Synthesis.

Timbre   The complex waveform of sound including the basic pitch (pure sine wave), and the harmonics produced by the instrument or sound producer, i.e., sound quality.

Transistor   A nonvacuum electronic device that replaces vacuum tubes in function. They are very small, do not produce heat, and are used in solid state circuitry. See also Solid state.

Transducer   A device that changes energy from one form to another, such as acoustic energy to electrical energy.

Transformer   A component featuring a coiled wire to transfer alternating current from one circuit to another. It can either increase or decrease voltage, depending upon the ratio of turns of wire to the diameter of the coils.

Tweeter   A high-frequency speaker.

Unidirectional A term normally applied to microphones (although it can be associated with speakers), it defines a narrow spectrum of sound reception. Unidirectional microphones pick up sound from only one direction, and therefore do not pick up crowd sounds, feedback, and other interference.

Volt The unit of electromotive force.

Voltage Measure of electrical pressure.

Volume Intensity or loudness of sound.

VU meter A test unit that indicates the frequency power level, or volume, of a complex waveform.

Wah-Wah A pedal device that has been around for some time, also called a Cry-Baby because of the sound it creates. Most often used by blues-oriented musicians, the wah-wah creates full treble sound by moving the pedal forward, and full bass by moving it back (toe is treble and heel is bass). Moving it back and forth creates the plaintive, and at times funk, sound of the wah-wah pedal.

Watt A unit of power. The electrical wattage of an amplifier describes the power with which it can drive a speaker.

Woofer A low-frequency speaker for bass notes.

APPENDIX B

ANALYSES OF REPRESENTATIVE COMPOSITIONS

List of Compositions

1. Stick McGhee and his Buddies — "Drinkin' Wine Spo-Dee-O-Dee" — *Hist. R & B Vol. 1*
2. Bill Haley — "Rock Around the Clock" — *Bill Haley Scrapbook*
3. Elvis Presley — "Heartbreak Hotel" — *Worldwide Gold Vol. 1*
4. Little Richard — "Rip It Up — *Original Rock Oldies Vol. 1*
5. Chuck Berry — "Roll Over Beethoven" — *Echoes of Early Rock Vol. 1*
6. Ray Charles — "What'd I Say?" — *Rock Begins Vol. 1*
7. Supremes — "Baby Love" — *Where Did Our Love Go*
8. Beatles — "P.S. I Love You" — *Early Beatles*
9. Beatles — "Eleanor Rigby" — *Revolver*
10. Beach Boys — "Surfin' USA" — *Best — Beach Boys*
11. Jefferson Airplane — "White Rabbit" — *Worst of JA*
12. Rolling Stones — "Satisfaction" — *Out of Our Heads*

13.	Who	"Pinball Wizard"	*Tommy*
14.	Elton John	"Border Song"	*'Live' Collection*
15.	Mothers of Invention	"Mother People"	*Mothers of Invention*
16.	Chicago	"25 or 6 to 4"	*Best of Chicago*
17.	Weather Report	"Birdland"	*Heavy Weather*
18.	Kool and the Gang	"Celebration"	*Celebrate*
19.	Parliament	"Dr. Funkenstein"	*Clones of Dr. Funkenstein*
20.	Jimi Hendrix	"Purple Haze"	*Essential Jimi Hendrix*
21.	Led Zeppelin	"Whole Lotta Love"	*Led Zeppelin II*
22.	Iron Maiden	"Trooper"	*Piece of Mind*
23.	Clash	"I'm So Bored with the USA"	*Clash*
24.	Police	"Canary in a Coal Mine"	*Zenyatta Mondatta*
25.	Talking Heads	"Burning Down the House"	*Speaking in Tongues*
26.	Michael Jackson	"Billy Jean"	*Thriller*
27.	Bruce Springsteen	"Born in the USA"	*Born in the USA*
28.	Whitney Houston	"I Wanna Dance With Somebody"	*Whitney*
29.	M. C. Hammer	"U Can't Touch This"	*Please Hammer Don't Hurt 'Em*
30.	New Kids on the Block	"Step by Step"	*Step by Step*

Introduction

This section adds a dimension to the book needed by students taking a class in rock music. The following information is the result of struggling with analysis for nonmusic majors during my eighteen years of teaching.

You will notice quickly that the charts of the compositions are not complete. I do not feel it is sound teaching to provide the student with everything. If I were to provide melody lines, complete transcriptions of all instrumental and vocal parts, and the lyrics, some might be tempted to ignore the results. Here we have provided a skeleton for the complete analysis; the student or reader will have to fill in the lyric lines where they fit, so that the analyses are complete, and to a certain extent personalized. That was one of the fundamental assumptions of this book, mentioned in chapter one. The only way analysis becomes meaningful is if the reader does it; therefore, only partial information has been provided.

The basic structure shows phrase lengths, such as twelve-measure units (blues form, for example). Measures contain four beats unless otherwise marked. Where appropriate, the chord changes will be placed at the rhythmic points where they actually happen. In a few cases, a pseudo-notation is used to describe the change more fully. A symbol like $1/4 = 168$ (as in the first piece) means the quarter note gets one beat, and there are 168 quarter notes, or beats, per minute; this tempo marking indicates the speed of the composition. Some descriptive remarks preface selected compositions to explain anomalies of this system.

Lastly, I decided to present the chord changes in letter notation rather than traditional roman numerals. It was my feeling that it would be more useful to those readers who might wish to play the changes, or listen to the recordings and follow the changes, to have them in this form. The chord changes are, for the most part, correct; however, there are alternate chords that will work, and sometimes the rhythmic placement of a chord might strike you as being earlier or later. Those of you who do use these chord changes might consider transcribing the vocal melodies, bass lines, guitar solos, and so on, if that would be useful to you, to do a more complete analysis.

The pitch center, or key, of a few of these compositions is at best questionable, especially items 1, 5, 6, and 7. Older pieces have usually been re-mastered by record companies. Item 1 was a minor hit in 1949, and appears in my transcription in F natural (although the actual pitch is a little sharp of F). It seems most likely that the original recording was in E, because that key makes use of the guitar's open strings. Chuck Berry's "Roll Over Beethoven" is probably not in E♭ but in E; however, my audio system says it is in E♭. Ray Charles's "What'd I Say?" has always been in F, but appears in E in my transcription. The Beach Boys' "Surfin' USA" is probably not in E♭, but again, that is what my record player produced.

Fortunately, the pieces where the keys are questionable are fairly old ones, and for the most part the chord changes and structures are easy to hear. If you are playing along with the recordings, make sure you use a guitar or a tunable electric piano or synthesizer. If you try to play all these pieces without having the capability of either tuning your instrument or tuning the turntable, you will be frustrated. I have pointed out this difficulty so that you will be aware of the problem, although most people who use this appendix material in a complete manner will have to confront these problems themselves. Solving that problem is the biggest part of the learning process.

Drinkin' Wine Spo-Dee-O-Dee by Stick McGhee   1/4 = 168   F

This rhythm and blues recording from 1949 is a novelty tune, and is especially easy to begin our analysis with because of the clear chord changes. The changes are supported by very distinct breaks in the singing. However, the phrase lengths are old fashioned urban blues, because of the irregularity of the seventeen-measure verse length, and the thirteen-measure refrain (one version is twelve and one half). This particular structural style simply establishes instrumental accompaniment for as long as the verse takes although each verse appropriately takes seventeen measures.

Instrumental intro
D♭9 C9 C7
1   2

Verse 1/Verse 2

F						break|		Bb7			F7	C7		F7	F C		F C
‖:1	2	3	4	5	6	7	8	9	10	11	12	13	14	15	16		17:‖

Refrain

F				Bb		F		C		F	F C F C
1	2	3	4	5	6	7	8	9	10	11	12	13

Verse 3

F						break|		Bb7			F7	C7		F7	F C		F C
1	2	3	4	5	6	7	8	9	10	11	12	13	14	15	16		17

Refrain

F				Bb		F		C		F	F C F C
1	2	3	4	5	6	7	8	9	10	11	12	13

Guitar solo

F				Bb		F		C		F C F C
1	2	3	4	5	6	7	8	9	10	11	12

Verse 4

F						break|		Bb7			F7	C7		F7	F C		F C
1	2	3	4	5	6	7	8	9	10	11	12	13	14	15	16		17

Refrain

F				Bb		F		C		F C F C F
1	2	3	4	5	6	7	8	9	10	11	12 + 1/2

Verse 5

F					break|			Bb		F		C		F	xDbC DbC	C F
1	2	3	4	5	6	7	8	9	10	11	12	13	14	15	16	17

Rock Around the Clock by Bill Haley   1/4 = 188   A major

This particular piece is fairly straightforward, and is in a straight blues style. It starts with an eight-bar introduction after one measure of guitar chords and then into seven blues progressions (the last one has a two-measure extension). The ending is an old cadence, or ending formula, from country music. The guitar solo is straight hillbilly picking. Also notice the band call response between verses 4 and 5.

Instrumental intro (guitar chords)
A E7 A x
1

Vocal introduction

A(inst. out. . .)E7	A(out) . . .	E7 A	. . . .	x E7 x E7
1	2	3	4	5	6	7	8

Verse 1/Verse 2/Guitar solo/Verse 3/Verse 4/Band call and response
6 times

A7				D7		A		E		A		
‖:1	2	3	4	5	6	7	8	9	10	11	12 :‖

Verse 5

A				D		A		E		A A/C# D	D#°	E7	A
1	2	3	4	5	6	7	8	9	10	11	12	13	14

Heartbreak Hotel by Elvis Presley   1/4 = 92   E major

This piece is interesting in its presentation, although the structure is a rather straightforward eight-measure country blues form. The most interesting quality is the stop time singing at the beginning and end. There are also bass and piano solos that break up the phrases in verses 1 and 3. It has a standard ending for pop songs of the 1940s and 1950s. Certain aspects of the song are not rock and roll, but the black urban blues style is clearly apparent. The chord changes are rather straightforward.

Verse 1 (vocal alone)   +bass

	F F		F F	F	Bb		C7	F
1		2		3 4	5	6	7	8

Verse 2   +guitar

F				Bb		C7	F
1	2	3	4	5	6	7	8

Verse 3   piano

F				Bb		C7	F
1	2	3	4	5	6	7	8

Verse 4

F				Bb		C7	F
1	2	3	4	5	6	7	8

Guitar solo   Piano solo

F7				Bb7		C7	F
1	2	3	4	5	6	7	8

Verse 5   Bass solo hold

	F F		F F	F	Bb		C7	F	Gb + 7	F + 7
1		2		3 4	5	6	7	8	9	

Rip It Up by Little Richard   1/4 = 98   F major

This piece is a fascinating example of 1950s rhythm and blues. It has one of the great screams in rock history, and the sax solo is representative of the honking saxophone style. You will notice that I have analyzed the piece in ten-measure blues phrases with a six-measure saxophone solo between verses 3 and 4. You could count this with twice as many beats, calling the four verses twenty measures in length, with twelve measures for the sax break; the choice is yours. Notice again the stop time style of the very beginning (the singer is by himself except for chords on beat one in measures 1, 3, 5, and 7). The ending is another formula rhythm ending (see notation). In the original recording this song was probably in F major because Little Richard played piano, and his back up group was not guitar-oriented.

Verse 1/Verse 2

F	F	F	F	B♭7	F	B♭7	F	C	F	
‖:1	2	3	4	5	6	7	8	9	10	:‖

Verse 3   Sax break

F	F	F	F	B♭7	F	B♭7	F	C	F
1	2	3	4	5	6	7	8	9	10

Sax solo

F		B♭7	F	C	F
1	2	3	4	5	6

Verse 4

F	F	F	F	B♭7	F	B♭7	F	C	F
1	2	3	4	5	6	7	8	9	10

Verse 5

F	F	F	F	B♭7	F	B♭7	F	C	F
1	2	3	4	5	6	7	8	9	10

Roll Over Beethoven by Chuck Berry   1/4 = 174   E♭ major

This is a good example of the classic singing style and guitar playing that made Chuck Berry one of the greatest of the 1950s rockers. The piece begins with a stop time guitar solo that keeps going for the length of one blues progression based on an E♭ (E) chord. Then there are four verses, followed by a guitar solo, and three more verses. The last verse has a two-beat measure in the middle of it, and the song concludes with a held ninth chord. The only other thing worth mentioning is that this song represents the worst quality of mastering of the old records. My transcription is in E♭ because that's what the record is in; however, the song was probably in E major because that was Chuck Berry's style (guitar-based instrumental background).

Guitar solo

Eb		Eb		Eb							
1	2	3	4	5	6	7	8	9	10	11	12

Verse 1/Verse 2/Verse 3/Verse 4/Guitar solo/Verse 5/Verse 6
7 times

Eb	Ab7	Eb		Ab7		Eb		Bb7		Eb	
‖:1	2	3	4	5	6	7	8	9	10	11	12 :‖

Verse 7 (refrain like repeating title)

Eb			Ab7			Eb		Bb7		Eb	⌢ Eb9
1	2	3	4	5	6	7	8 2/4 9	4/4	10	11	12 held‖

What'd I Say? by Ray Charles   1/4 = 170   E major

This particular piece is quite interesting, and when it came out in 1959 it was very unusual. Of course, you can tell by the chart that it is longer that what you have seen so far. It also features audience participation, and is one of the more obvious examples of African retentive quality in rhythm and blues; the call and response is quite apparent. The stop time quality is present throughout the composition, the electric piano solo is quite experimental and virtuosic for its time, and the structural tension achieved is remarkable. Again, I do not believe this song is in E, but rather in F. However, it is transcribed here in E to accurately represent available recordings.

Piano solo

E7				A7		E7		B7	A7	E7		
‖:1	2	3	4	5	6	7	8	9	10	11	12	:‖

continued piano solo/// stop time first four measures
4 times
bass (4th time)   piano (4th time)

E7		E7		A7...		E7		B7	A7	E7		
‖:1	2	3	4	5	6	7	8	9	10	11	12	:‖

Verse 1/Verse 2

♩ 𝄽 - -   ♩ 𝄽 - -

E7				A7	E7		B7	A9	E7	B7	
‖:1		2	3	4 5 6	7	8	9	10	11	12	:‖

Verse 3

♩ 𝄽 - ♩ 𝄽 - ♩ 𝄽 - -

E7			A7	E7		B7	A7	E7	B7	
1	2	3	4 5 6	7	8 9	10	11	12		

Verse 4

E7				A7		E7		B7	A7	E7	B7
1		2	3	4	5	6	7	8	9	10	11	12

Piano solo/piano solo/Verse 5/Verse 6
4 times
bass (second time)   piano (second time)

E7		E7		A7		E7		B7	A7	E7	B7	
‖:1	2	3	4	5	6	7	8	9	10	11	12	:‖

Refrain with horn responses
3 times

E7				A7		E7		B7	A7	E7		
‖:1	2	3	4	5	6	7	8	9	10	11	12	:‖

Audience talk with Ray saying
"What?"

Call and response
Yeah   Oh   YeahYeah Oh   Oh   YeOhYeOh . . . .
no chords

1	2	3	4	5	6	7	8

Refrain/Call and response/Refrain/Call and response/Refrain/Refrain/Refrain
7 times

E7				A7		E7		B7	A7	E7		
‖:1	2	3	4	5	6	7	8	9	10	11	12	:‖

Baby Love by the Supremes   1/4 = 132   C

The Motown style is perfectly exemplified by this tune by Diana Ross and the Supremes. It starts with an instrumental introduction, four verses, a two-measure modulation up a half-step to Db, and then three more verses with a fade-out ending. The vocal style is predominant, backup singing is tasteful, and the structure is easy to follow. This is a straightforward piece that illustrates the techniques for which Berry Gordy, Jr., became famous.

Instrumental intro   Ooh by Ross

Dm	Bb		G	F C	
1	2		3	4	5

Verse 1/Verse 2/Verse 3/Verse 4
4 times   instruments on melody (verse 3)
Sax background (verse 3)

C	C/Bb	A7	Dm		C	F	C	F	C	F C/E	Dm G7	
‖:1	2	3	4	5	6	7	8	9	10	11	12	:‖

Modulation
Db

1	2

Verse 5/Verse 6/Verse 7   fade out (verse 7)
3 times

Db	Db/B	Bb7	Ebm		Db	Gb	Db	Gb	Db		Gb Db/F	Ebm Ab7	
1	2	3	4	5	6	7	8	9	10		11	12	:|

PS I Love You by the Beatles   1/4 = 134   D major

"PS I Love You" ideally represents the early Beatles' pop style. This lovely ballad communicates a very simple lyric idea. The verse structure is ten measures long and the refrain is eight measures long. There is a four-measure phrase derived from the ending of the first verse that concludes the piece. However, the chord changes are quite unusual and represent influences on the Beatles totally unlike the influences felt by the U.S. musicians. This particular piece has less rhythm and blues influences; both the phrase structure and the chord changes illustrate the stylistic difference the Beatles provided even in their earlier period.

Refrain

G Db	D	G Db	D	G Db	D	D A7	D
1	2	3	4	5	6	7	8

Verse 1/Verse 2

D	E minor	D	A7	Bm	A7	Bb		C	D		
:|1	2	3	4	5	6	7	8	9	10		:|

Refrain

G	D	G	D	G	D	D A7	D
1	2	3	4	5	6	7	8

Verse 3

D	Em	D	A7	Bm	A7	Bb		C	D	
1	2	3	4	5	6	7	8	9	10

Refrain

G	D	G	D	G	D	D A7	D
1	2	3	4	5	6	7	8

Verse 4

D	Em	D	A7	Bm	A7	Bb		C	D	D Bb C
1	2	3	4	5	6	7	8	9	10	

Vocal ending

D	Bb C D	D
1	2 3	4

Eleanor Rigby by the Beatles   1/4 = 128   **E minor**

From the *Revolver* album, "Eleanor Rigby" represents the middle compositional period of the Beatles. Its lyrics are very complicated, and are certainly good poetry. It would be very instructive to analyze the lyrics separately from the music, and then discover how the music supports the words. Musically, the piece is very interesting because of the use of a full string section and the predominate cello line. Structurally, the musical phrases fall into eight- and eighteen-measure units; the refrain is eight measures and the verse is eighteen. However, the eighteen-measure phrase is further subdivided into two five-measure units and two four-measure units (5 + 5 + 4 + 4).

Characteristically in the Beatles' ballad tunes, there is a preponderance of flat sixth relationships in this tune — E to C. Also, the extended Em chords are colored by the added flat seventh, sixth, and flatted sixth. Another tune that does the same thing is "Taste of Honey." However, once you get the chords for the refrain and the verse it does not change.

Refrain

C		Em		C		Em	
1	2	3	4	5	6	7	8

Verse 1/Verse 2

Em		C	C Em|Em				C	C Em|E-7	E-6	E♭6 Em	E-7	E-6	E♭6 Em	
‖:1	2	3	4	5	6	7	8	9	10	11	12	13	14	15	16	17	18	:‖

Refrain

C		Em		C		Em	
1	2	3	4	5	6	7	8

Verse 3

Em		C	C Em	Em				C	C Em	E-7	E-6	E♭6 Em	E-7	E-6	E♭6 E	......
1	2	3	4	5	6	7	8	9	10	11	12	13	14	15	16	17	18	19

Surfin' USA by the Beach Boys   1/4 = 170   **E♭ Major**

My recording is in E♭ but the correct key is E. This is the Beach Boys' theme song, appropriately, a Chuck Berry composition. Its structure is a sixteen-measure pharse that begins on the dominant or five chord, although it is really not blues-like in character. The dominant feature is the smooth group singing style characteristic of the Beach Boys. There is a primitive organ solo after the fourth verse and a short guitar solo. The vocal ending of that sixteen-measure unit is then repeated three more times for the traditional Beach Boys fade-out ending.

Inst.	Vocal
E♭	B♭7
1	2

Verse 1/Verse 2/Verse 3/Verse 4
+drums and bass and background vocals in harmony in Verse 2
Ooh in harmony in Verse 3
Vocal Background harmony in Verse 4
4 times

B♭7		E♭		B♭7		E♭		A♭		E♭		B♭7	A♭	E♭	
‖:1	2	3	4	5	6	7	8	9	10	11	12	13	14	15	16 :‖

Organ solo

B♭7		E♭		B♭7		E♭		guitar A♭		E♭		Vocal ending B♭7	A♭	E♭	
1	2	3	4	5	6	7	8	9	10	11	12	13	14	15	16

Vocal ending · Vocal ending · Vocal ending (fade out)

B♭7	A♭	E♭		B♭7	A♭	E♭		B♭7	A♭	E♭	
1	2	3	4	5	6	7	8	9	10	11	12

White Rabbit by the Jefferson Airplane   1/4 = 112   A

This song is fairly typical of the Jefferson Airplane's softer psychedelic sound. The lyric is based on *Alice in Wonderland,* and certainly deserves some analysis. Musically, the lyric is supported in a through-composed manner, although there is one consistent chord progression based on the F♯ to G chord change, an old Spanish or Latin American device. In musical style this piece is not blues-oriented but is much more folk-like in quality. There is a twelve-measure instrumental introduction, followed by two twelve-measure verses and a twenty-four measure unit that I called verse 3. Verse 3 uses a different melody and is then concluded by a five-measure extension. Once the piece gets started it maintains the same texture to the end.

Intro (bass)   +drums (first time)
Guitar (second time)
3 times

F♯		G		
‖:1	2	3	4 :‖

Verse 1/Verse 2

F♯		G		F♯		G		A		C C♯ A		
‖:1	2	3	4	5	6	7	8	9	10	11	12 :‖

Verse 3 (different melody)

E		A		E		A	
1	2	3	4	5	6	7	8

F♯						G	
1	2	3	4	5	6	7	8

F♯		G		A		C C♯ A	
1	2	3	4	5	6	7	8

Extension conclusion   held chord
A   E7   A   A
1   2   3   4   5

Satisfaction by the Rolling Stones   1/4 = 132   E minor

"Satisfaction" by the Rolling Stones is lyric-dominated; the musical structure and lack of chord changes both support this premise. The distorted sound of this piece creates an instrumental background, or milieu, for the meaning of the words. Clearly one would want to write in the lyrics here, because it is not very interesting without them.

Instrumental introduction (fuzz sound)
E   A(+4)E   A   E   A   E   A
1   2   3   4   5   6   7   8

Verse 1/Verse 3
E   A7   E   A7   E   B   E   A   E   A(+4)E   A
:|1   2   3   4   5   6   7   8   9   10   11   12   13   14   15   16   :|

Verse 2/Verse 4
E   A   E   A   E   A   E   A   E   A   E   A   drums
1   2   3   4   5   6   7   8   9   10   11   12   13   14

Interlude (like beginning)
E   A(+4)E   A(+4)
:|1   2   3   4:|

Verse 5
E   A7   E   A7   E   B   E   A   E   A+4   E   A
1   2   3   4   5   6   7   8   9   10   11   12   13   14   15   16

Verse 6
E   A7   E   A7   E   A7   E   A7   E   A7   E   A7   drums   E   A7
1   2   3   4   5   6   7   8   9   10   11   12   13   14   15   16

Refrain ending (four measure phrases)
E   A7   E   A7 |E   A7   E   A7 |E   A7   E   A7 |E   A7   E   A7|
1   2   3   4   5   6   7   8   9   10   11   12   13   14   15   16

Refrain ending to fade out
E   A7   E   A7
1   2   3   4

Pinball Wizard from *Tommy* by the Who   1/4 = 120   Bm

If you have already read the section on *Tommy* you probably realize that I think quite highly of the work; this piece is my favorite from the entire opera. The lyric is compelling and thought-provoking, but I appreciate the musicality of the setting as well. You will notice that the first nine-measure phrase sets up the beginning of the song. Characteristically for the Who, the chord changes are basically a dominant chord (F# seventh) with suspended notes, and other chords clustered on top of the bass dominant note. The Who has used this device excessively but to great advantage. It creates a drive toward the beginning phrase, and the beginning of the chorus. Also interesting is the use of an acoustic guitar in this phrase. Most phrases from this point on are fairly regular, except for the instrumental interlude after the third verse. Of great interest is the chord progression in verse 2, which goes B-A-G-F#; this is also called the Andalusian (Spanish) cadence. This type of cadence creates tension and pushes the music toward the next phrase.

Instrumental opening (acoustic guitar)

Bm/F#	B+4/F#	B+2/F#	F#	A/F#	Em/F#	Em/G	F#	F#7
1	2	3	4	5	6	7	8	9

Instrumental (stronger)   +bass
B(sus. 4)

1	2	3	4	5	6	7	8

Verse 1   Refrain

B+4		A+4		G		F#	
1	2	3	4	5	6	7	8

Instrumental interlude

B	A	D	E	B	A	D	E
1			2	3			4

Verse 2

B+4		A+4		G		F#	
1	2	3	4	5	6	7	8

Instrumental interlude

B	A	D	E	B	A	D	E
1		2		3			4

Refrain   Vocal call and response

E F# B	E F# B	E F# B	G	D7					
1	2	3	4	5	6	7	8	9	10

Verse 3

B+4		A+4		G		F#	
1	2	3	4	5	6	7	8

Instrumental interlude

```
B  A  D  E      B  A  D  E
1         2  3            4
```

Refrain

```
E F♯ B   E F♯ B   E F♯ B   G        D7
1        2        3        4        5        6
```

Second instrumental phrase from beginning in D

```
D+4                 +bass
1        2        3        4        5        6        7        8
```

Verse 4

```
D+4                 C+4              B♭              A
1        2        3        4        5        6        7        8
```

Refrain closing to fade out and into next song

♪♪ ♩ ♩ 𝄾

```
D    A  F   E7   E7+4 repeat and fade
1        2  3        4        5        6        7        8
```

Border Song by Elton John   1/4 = 70   C major

This composition is in many ways like the previous one; its style is basically through-composed. That is, the music clearly follows the words (which, in this case, were written first). This particular song illustrates the compositional and playing styles of Elton John, with its acoustic piano beginning, long melodic lines, and textural arc formed by the entire composition. The piano solo occurs right after the build up to the strong, funk bass (an Elton John characteristic). The song begins and ends with the acoustic piano. Please take note of the chorus refrain at the middle of the seventh measure in the verses; it is the structural "hook" of the piece.

Piano intro

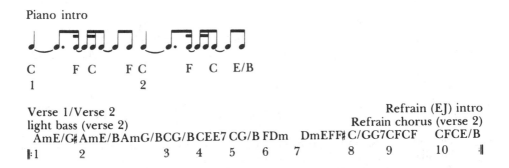

```
C    F  C    F C      F  C  E/B
1                2
```

```
Verse 1/Verse 2                                      Refrain (EJ) intro
light bass (verse 2)                                 Refrain chorus (verse 2)
  AmE/G♯AmE/BAmG/BCG/BCEE7 CG/B FDm   DmEFF♯C/GG7CFCF    CFCE/B
‖:1      2            3   4   5  6  7        8        9        10       :‖
```

Verse 3 (different melody) Strong bass   Intro
line
C	F	G7+4	C		C F7 D7/F♯ G7+4CFCFCFCE/B	
1	2			3	4 5	6 7

Piano solo (bass out at beginning)   Chorus refrain
AmE/G♯AmE/BAmG/BCG/BCEE7 CG/B FDm   DmEFF♯C/GG7CFCF   CFCE/B
1   2   3   4   5   6   7   8   9   10

Verse 4 (strong bass returns)   Refrain   Refrain
Refrain
AmE/G♯AmE/BAmG/BCG/BCEE7 CG/B FDm   DmEFF♯C/GG7CC/EFF♯C/GG7CC/EFF♯
1   2   3   4   5   6   7   8   9   10   11

Conclusion (ritard) intro
C/G G7 2/4F   Intro   Octave C-tremolo!
1   2   3   4

Mother People by the Mothers of Invention   various tempos and keys

This is classic Frank Zappa, and reveals the many kinds of music he uses in what we have referred to as art, or eclectic rock. In this piece will be found a very fast rhythmic figure for the singing part, orchestral music, a record scratching sound, electronic music, and chance piano, in that order. For this piece we have used a different technique. This time line for the fast central theme is meter signatures only; it combines various 1/8 and 3/4 note meters. For the other sections we have simply indicated what happens without giving tempo, key, or chord changes. If any of you want a real experience, try to figure out the meter changes for the fast theme without using my chart.

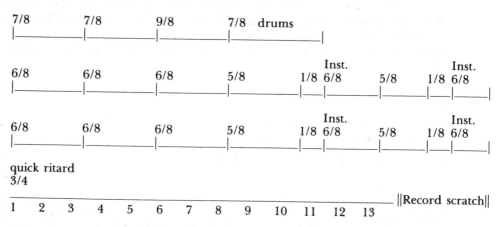

||Orchestral music in nineteenth-century style—slow and indeterminate in tempo but diatonic in quality|| Return to fast theme (first three measures)|| Electronic sounds—distortion|| Chance piano (a la John Cage)||.

25 or 6 to 4 by Chicago   1/4 = 152   B♭ minor

One of Chicago's biggest hits, this song illustrates the jazz-rock ensemble and the use of expanded horn sections, especially in the second eight-bar phrase. Also, the guitar is used extensively in a long solo passage (sixty-four measures). The harmonies of this particular piece are fairly simple, a descending four note scale; there is also a harmony refrain that has a more diatonic chord progression. The five chords that conclude the piece, in a dramatic slowing of the tempo, are unique and deserve attention.

Intro rhythm section—bass dominant/intro + horns/Verse 1/Verse 2
4 times

B♭m	B♭m/A♭	B♭m/G	G♭	F	B♭m	B♭m/A♭	B♭m/G	G♭ F	
‖:1	2	3	4	5	6	7	8		:‖

Refrain in harmony

G♭		D♭		A♭		G♭	
1	2	3	4	5	6	7	8

Horns plus guitar solo/Verse 3/Verse 4
3 times

B♭m	B♭m/A♭	B♭m/G	G♭	F	B♭m	B♭m/A♭	B♭m/G	G♭ F	
‖:1	2	3	4	5	6	7	8		:‖

Refrain (harmony)

G♭		D♭		A♭		G♭	
1	2	3	4	5	6	7	8

Guitar solo for six choruses/Intro rhythm/Intro rhythm plus horns/Verse 5 + 6
10 times

B♭m	B♭m/A♭	B♭m/G	G♭	F	B♭m	B♭m/A♭	B♭m/G	G♭ F	
‖:1	2	3	4	5	6	7	8		:‖

Refrain (harmony)

G♭		D♭		A♭		G♭	
1	2	3	4	5	6	7	8

Guitar solo

B♭m	B♭m/A♭	B♭m/G	G♭	F	B♭m	B♭m/A♭	B♭m/G	G♭ F
1	2	3	4	5	6	7	8	

Chordal conclusion with horn section

E♭m6+9	G♭9	C6+E♭	A♭/B	C/B♭
		ritard		held chord
1	2	3	4	5

Birdland by Weather Report   1/4 = 156   G major

Weather Report normally plays complex and jazz-influenced music. They also use a variety of electronic keyboards and synthesizers, as you can see in the following analysis. The music also tends to be rhythmic, so rhythms are carefully notated where they are substantive. As there are a few complicated chord changes we have designated certain phrases A, B, and so on, so we can refer to them more simply.

Introduction Arp synthesizer
G
1 2 3 4 5 6 7 8

A—Bass melody in harmonics + drums

G   Gm
1 2 3 4 5 6 7 8 9 10 11 12

B—add sax

    F F   E♭   F Dm   F E♭   F Em   Gm F
  1   2   3   4   5   6

Em F F♯ G Em Gm F
7   8

Rhythm interlude
G
1 2 3 4

C—Rhodes piano melody
F/G   G   F/G   G   F/G   G   F/G   G13
1   2   3   4   5   6   7   8   9   10   11   12 13 14   15   16

D—Sax   Bass solo piano

G C A♭13 G13   G13 A♭13 G13 Bm7♭5   G
  1 2   3 4 5 6   7   8 9 10 11 12 13 14 15 16 17 18

E—Main melody sax/harmonized melody/harmonized melody
3 times

G Bm7 Em7 C6   Bm7   E7♭9 Am7 G6 Am7 C   G Bm7 Em7 C6   Em7   C9

‖:1   2   3   4   5   6   7

G Am CM7   Am7

8   ‖

Interlude (rhythm) C—Rhodes melody
G   F/G
1   2   3   4   5   6   7   8

Sax solo
G G♭ F E E♭ D D♭7 repeat........................G7
1   2   3 4 5 6 7 8 9 10 11 12 13 14

Interlude (rhythm)
G
1   2   3   4

A—Bass melody
G   Gm
1   2   3   4   5   6   7   8   9   10 11 12 13 14 15 16

B—Ensemble melody
 F   F   E♭   F Dm   F   E♭   F Em Gm   F   Em F F♯ G Em Gm F
1   2   3   4   5   6   7   8

C—middle section of rhodes
melody
 G   F/G   G   F/G   G
 1   2   3   4   5   6   7   8

E—Main melody sax/Harmonized melody/Harmonized melody
3 times
 G Bm7 Em7 C6   Bm7   E7♭9 Am7 G6 Am7 C G Bm7 Em7 C6   Em7 C9 G Am CM7
Am7
‖:1   2   3   4   5   6   7 8   ‖

Vamp on part of main melody to fade out

G6 Em/B Em   Bm7   E7   Am G Am C   G
1   2   3   4

Celebration by Kool and the Gang   1/4 = 132   A♭

This piece begins with an eight-measure introduction that establishes the funk feel. The song is in A♭ because of the use of the horn players, although that particular key is rather unusual. The following three phrases (sixteen measures, sixteen measures, and six measures) constitute the main melodic ideas for the entire piece; this unit occurs twice. Although this song does have one memorable melodic phrase, it is basically rhythmic, and provides a background for a pop rap tune.

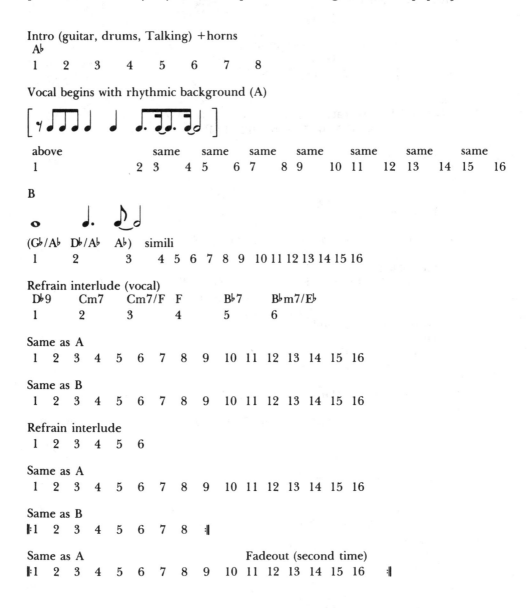

Intro (guitar, drums, Talking) +horns
A♭

1   2   3   4   5   6   7   8

Vocal begins with rhythmic background (A)

above   same   same   same   same   same   same   same
1   2   3   4   5   6   7   8   9   10   11   12   13   14   15   16

B

(G♭/A♭   D♭/A♭   A♭)   simili
1   2   3   4 5 6 7 8 9 10 11 12 13 14 15 16

Refrain interlude (vocal)
D♭9   Cm7   Cm7/F   F   B♭7   B♭m7/E♭
1   2   3   4   5   6

Same as A
1   2   3   4   5   6   7   8   9   10   11   12   13   14   15   16

Same as B
1   2   3   4   5   6   7   8   9   10   11   12   13   14   15   16

Refrain interlude
1   2   3   4   5   6

Same as A
1   2   3   4   5   6   7   8   9   10   11   12   13   14   15   16

Same as B
:1   2   3   4   5   6   7   8   :

Same as A   Fadeout (second time)
:1   2   3   4   5   6   7   8   9   10   11   12   13   14   15   16   :

Dr. Funkenstein by Parliament   **1/4 = 90**   **E**

This is a good example of rap/funk, where the polyrhythmic character of the background instruments essentially provides a fairly consistent framework. You will notice that there are no chord changes listed in this piece, except for one interlude section (which, interestingly, is always three-and-a-half measures long). Otherwise, the whole piece is funk in E. There is a rather interesting jazz-influenced trombone solo toward the end. However, the main focus of this piece is the rap of the singer.

Instrumental intro (horns)
G7/A D7   G7/A7
```
                    2/4
  1     2     3     4(2 beats)
```

Solo rap   +higher voice
```
  1  2  3  4  5  6  7  8  9  10 11 12
```

Refrain—Chorus
```
  1  2  3  4  5  6  7  8
```

Individual voices + horns
```
  1  2  3  4  5  6  7  8
```

Instrumental interlude
```
  1  2  3  4(2 beats)
```

Individual voices
```
  1  2  3  4
```

Chorus
```
  1  2  3  4  5  6  7  8
```

Individual voices Instrumental
```
  1  2  3  4  5  6  7  8
```

Chorus   Individual voices
```
  1  2  3  4  5  6  7  8
```

Soloist—Vocal
```
  1  2
```

Instrumental interlude
```
  1  2  3  4(2 beats)
```

Trombone solo/Chorus/Chorus/Individual voices/Rhythm section/Chorus
6 times   Chorus (fourth and fifth time)
```
‖:1  2  3  4  5  6  7  8 :‖
```

```
               fade out
  1  2  3  4
```

Purple Haze by Jimi Hendrix   1/4 = 128   E

To try to classify Jimi Hendrix's playing style would be an exercise in futility. He was truly unique, and the structure of his music is no exception. Commonly thought to be quintessential blues style, "Purple Haze" has little blues-progression logic to it. Although the playing style makes use of blues-like lines, harmonics, and sliding notes, the chord changes and structural phrases are definitely non-blues.

You will notice that the opening guitar solo is like a lead melody and that it is completely in E; the two-measure intro sets an E against a B♭. There is a short four-measure phrase, which sets up the chord progression for the three verses. There is a slightly unsusual set of chord progression following verses 2 and 3 in which Hendrix talks and then plays guitar. The last time this particular progression is used, Hendrix sets up a feedback chain that is supposed to have been the beginning of heavy metal. The song ends in a fade out.

Guitar intro
B♭/E
1   2

Guitar solo
E
1   2   3   4   5   6   7   8

Instrumental intro to vocal
E7♯9 G   A E7♯9 G A
1   2   3   4

Verse 1/Verse 2 |inst. out| bass + guitar together
E7♯9 G   A E7♯9 G A   E7♯9 G   A E7♯9
‖:1   2   3   4   5   6   7   8   9   :‖

Interlude (talking)   guitar solo
A   ~B   D   E   F♯m DE   F♯m DE   F♯m DE   F♯m D
1   2   3   4   5   6   7   8   9   10   11

Introductory guitar melody
E
1   2   3   4   5   6   7   8

Verse 3 |inst. out| bass + guitar
E7♯9 G A   E7♯9 G   A E7♯9 G   A E7♯9
1   2   3   4   5   6   7   8   9

Interlude (talking)   guitar solo
A   B   D   E   F♯m DE   F♯m DE   F♯m DE   F♯m D
1   2   3   4   5   6   7   8   9   10   11

Conclusion to fade out

E		F♯m D	E		F♯m D E ....
1	2	3	4	5	

Whole Lotta Love by Led Zeppelin   1/4 = 114   E

This piece is included because it illustrates the heavy metal style of Led Zeppelin; one might also want to analyze "Stairway to Heaven," which is not heavy metal. There is one rhythmic device predominant throughout the piece (notated in Verse 1). There is extensive used of distortion and feedback, and they also experiment with stereo separation as a call-and-response device. Toward the conclusion there is an old-style blues vocal solo that ends with a downward vocal slide. The fade-out ending is based on the standard changes between E and D. You will notice that except for the E to A chords concluding the blues vocal solo mentioned previously, there are no other chord changes in the entire piece.

Instrumental intro

E			D
‖: 1	2	3 :‖	4

Verse/Verse 2/Refrain/Verse 3/Refrain
5 times

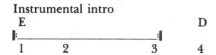

distortion (third time) strong drums (fifth time)

E	D	E	D	E	D	E	D	
‖:1	2	3	4	5	6	7	8	:‖

free drums	tempo guitar	voices	elec. distortion	drums
8 ms.	8 ms.	8 ms.	8 ms.	8 ms.

Guitar solo   drum pick-up
regular tempo with rhythm section—everyone rhythmically on E

1	2	3	4	5	6

Verse 4/Refrain

E		D	E		D	E		D E		D	
‖:1	2		3	4		5	6	7	8		:‖

Blues solo singing in indeterminate time crash chords drum pick-up

E   A   slide

original tempo/refrain-like/experimenting with call and response/fade out
6 times

E		D	E		D	
‖:1	2		3	4		:‖

Trooper by Iron Maiden   1/4 = 152   E

This piece illustrates the tight structuring and virtuosic showmanship displayed by a power ensemble like Iron Maiden. One also sees that the instrumental interludes have some structural integrity to them; for instance, the piece begins and ends with the same instrumental figure. That figure is contrasted with the double-guitar figure that follows it. The verse chord changes have a distinctive rhythmic quality, and there is a contrast in style between the verse singing and the harmony singing of the refrain. The guitar solo illustrates many of the heavy metal guitar techniques that have evolved over the years.

A—Instrumental intro

E	D		C	D		....		
1		2		3	4	5	6	7	8

B—Instrumental melody/Instrumental melody/Verse 1/Verse 2
4 times

E		DE		DC		DE		D
‖:1	2	3	4	5	6	7	8	:‖

Refrain

D		E		D		E	
	2	3	4	5	6	7	8

B—Instrumental melody/Instrumental melody/Verse 3/Verse 4
4 times

E		DE		DC		DE	
‖:1	2	3	4	5	6	7	8 :‖

Refrain

D		E		D		E	
1	2	3	4	5	6	7	8

Guitar solo

E		D	Bm		C	D	E		D	Bm		C	D
‖:1	2		3		4		5	6		7		8 :‖

Guitar cont.

A		G	Em		F	G	A		G	Em		F	G
1	2		3		4		5	6		7		8

Guitar cont.

A		G	E		F	G	A		G	E		D	F♯	D
1	2		3		4		5	6		7		8

B—Instrumental melody/Instrumental melody/Verse 5/Verse 6
4 times

E		DE		DC		DE		D
‖:1	2	3	4	5	6	7	8	:‖

Refrain

D		E		D		E		
1	2	3	4	5	6	7	8	

A—Instrumental intro

													stop(1)
E	D	C	D	E	D	C	D	E	D	C	D	E	D	E
1		2		3		4		5		6		7		8		9

I'm So Bored with the U.S.A. by the Clash   1/4 = 160   E major

This is a good example of punk, and it is fairly clear in structure as well. It fits nicely into two verses and a refrain; there is one ending and then a reprise of the refrain and concluding phrases from before. Please note the rhythmic structure notated for verse 1. For punk this is very musical; that is to say punk usually does not bother with meaningful rhythms.

Guitar octave E   Drums

1	2	3	4

Instrumental intro

E

1	2	3	4	5	6	7	8

Verse 1/Verse 2

E D	E D E	E D	E D E A			E D	E D E	
‖:1	2	3	4	5	6	7	8	:‖

Refrain—unison singing

C		A		C		A	
1	2	3	4	5	6	7	8

Instrumental interlude

E

1	2	3	4

Verse 3/Verse 4

E D	E D E	E D	E D E A			E D	E D E	
‖:1	2	3	4	5	6	7	8	:‖

Refrain

C		A		C		A	
1	2	3	4	5	6	7	8

Instrumental interlude   drums

E

1	2	3	4	5	6	7	8

Refrain

C		A		C		A	
1	2	3	4	5	6	7	8

Instrumental conclusion   held

E	A	E	A	E	A	E	A	E
1	2	3	4	5	6	7	8	9

Refrain

C		A		C		A	
1	2	3	4	5	6	7	8

Refrain continues   Instrumental conclusion

C		A		E	A	E	A
1	2	3	4	5	6	7	8

                                                    ⌒
                                                   held

E	A	E	A	E	A	E	A	E
1	2	3	4	5	6	7	8	9

Canary in a Coal Mine by the Police   1/4 = 140   E

This piece has a relatively easy structure to follow, with a verse and refrain concept similar to the previous piece. The most obvious musical characteristics are a very clear reggae influence and polyrhythmic texture. The short acoustic piano solo prior to verse 4 stands out demonstrably against the electronic and percussion sounds of the rest of the piece. The refrain is interesting because it features instrumental and choral responses on the title of the piece. The piece concludes in a fade out.

Instrumental intro

E C#m7 simili						C	Am F#m7♭5
1	2	3	4	5 6		7	8

Verse 1/Verse 2

E C#m7	E C#m7	E C#m7	E C#m7	C	Am F#7♭5	E C#m7	C C#m7	
‖:1	2	3	4	5 6		7	8	:‖

Refrain—instrumental then vocal

E C#m7	....				C	Am F#m7♭5	E C#m7	E C#m7
1	2	3	4	5 6	7	8	9	10

Verse 3

E C#m7	E C#m7	E C#m7	E C#m7	C	Am F#m7♭5	E C#m7	C C#m7
1	2	3	4	5 6		7	8

Refrain
E C♯m7 C   Am F♯7♭5   E C♯m7 E C♯m7
1   2   3   4   5 6   7   8   9   10

Instrumental interlude
acoustic piano
A7   E C♯m7 E C♯m7
1   2   3   4

Verse 4/Refrain/Refrain
3 times   fade out (third time)
E C♯m7 E C♯m7 E C♯m7 E C♯m7 C Am F♯m7♭5 E C♯m7 C C♯m7
‖:1   2   3   4   5 6   7   8   :‖

Burning Down the House by the Talking Heads   1/4 = 106   G

Although from 1983, this group and composition is mainstream new wave, making extensive use of polyrhythms and a current lyric. The composition is not complicated from a harmonic point of view; in fact the entire composition goes back and fourth between G and F except for the choral refrain on the title at the ends of some verses (beats 3 and 4 of measure seven and beat 1 of measure eight). Note the use of synthesizer, choral antiphony (call-and-response style), and African-influenced polyrhythms.

Intro fades in from nothing   drums
1   2   3   4   5   6   7   8

Verse 1/Verse 2   Refrain

G   F   G   F   G   F
‖:1   2   3   4   5   6

G   A   F
7   8   :‖

Verse 3   (no refrain)
G   F   G   F   G   F   G   F
1   2   3   4   5   6   7   8

Verse 4   refrain
G   F   G   F   G   F   G   A   F
1   2   3   4   5   6   7   8

Verse 5

G	F	G	F	G	F	G	F
1	2	3	4	5	6	7	8

Instrumental interlude   refrain (sung)

G	F	G	F	G	F	G	A	F
1	2	3	4	5	6	7		8

Choral call and response (antiphony)   refrain

G	F	G	F	G	F	G	A	F
1	2	3	4	5	6	7		8

Verse 6

G	F	G	F	G	F	G	F
1	2	3	4	5	6	7	8

Synthesizer solo

G	F	G	F	G	F	G	F
1	2	3	4	5	6	7	8

Stronger rhythm and added textures   played refrain

G	F	G	F	G	F	G	A	F
1	2	3	4	5	6	7		8

Continued rhythm changes

G	F	G	F	G	F	G	F
1	2	3	4	5	6	7	8

to fade out

1	2	3	4	5	6	7	8

Billy Jean by Michael Jackson   1/4 = 112   **F# minor**

"Billy Jean" and "Beat It" were Michael Jackson's big tunes of 1984. He represents a continuation of the funk evolution, and certainly reflects the techno-pop or
techno-funk of the mid-1980s. This particular song depends upon a funk background for the solo singing of Michael Jackson and for background vocals. The
funk style is fairly choked and quite rhythmic; in that sense there is a rap quality to
this piece although it is clearly a pop song. The chord changes are blues changes of
the eight-bar variety (I to IV back to I). Some verses use a twelve-bar structure of
the I-IV-I-IV-I variety. So it is not standard blues but it is still derived from that
tradition. Obviously, the dance steps and choreographed performance of this piece
are important to its impact, however, you can see that the structure is intelligent,
and the refrain-type use of verse 3 is the hook.

Instrumental intro (2 measure units)
DrumsBass   More percussion synthesizer
                              F♯m G♯m/F♯ F♯m7 G♯m7/F♯

1	2	3	4	5	6	7	8	9	10	11	12			13	14

Verse 1

F♯m..........				Bm7		F♯m		Bm7		F♯m7	
1	2	3	4	5	6	7	8	9	10	11	12

Verse 2

F♯m				Bm7		F♯m7	
1	2	3	4	5	6	7	8

Refrain—background singers + horns in smooth style (does not
use rhythm)

D	F♯m	D	F♯m	D	F♯m	D	C♯7
1	2	3	4	5	6	7	8

Verse 3 (harmony)/Verse 4
Refrain-like

F♯m				Bm7		F♯m		Bm7		F♯m7	
‖:1	2	3	4	5	6	7	8	9	10	11	12 :‖

Verse 5

F♯m				Bm7		F♯m7	
1	2	3	4	5	6	7	8

Refrain

D	F♯m	D	F♯m	D	F♯m	D	C♯7
1	2	3	4	5	6	7	8

Verse 6/Verse 7

F♯m				Bm7		F♯m7		
‖:1	2	3	4	5	6	7	8	:‖

Instrumental   Vocal

F♯m rhythm								Bm7		F♯m	
1	2	3	4	5	6	7	8	9	10	11	12

Verse 8

F♯m				Bm7		F♯m		Bm7		F♯m7	
1	2	3	4	5	6	7	8	9	10	11	12

Refrain fragments

F♯m rhythm changes										to fade out.....................					
1	2	3	4	5	6	7	8	9	10	11	12	13	14	15	16

Born in the U.S.A. by Bruce Springsteen   1/4 = 122   **B**

This was a mid-80s hit by the "Boss," and represents current techniques in pop/ hard rock. You will notice that there are essentially no chord changes in this piece. Everything is based on an open B chord (B and F# only). Each eight-measure phrase starts with four measures of the open B chord and then four measures of the same open chord against an E in the bass. Therefore, the chord changes will only be given for the first phrase. The song's textural density increases toward the middle of the piece, then becomes less dense toward the end. A loose, free-form refrain, and then a fade-out ending on the refrain conclude the piece. Another dominant feature is a very strong drum beat on beats 2 and 4 of virtually every measure.

Instrumental intro/V1/ Ref./V2/Ref./V3/Inst. ref./V4/V5/V6/Ref./Ref./IR/IR/IR
15 times

B(no third)				B(no third)/E			
‖:1	2	3	4	5	6	7	8 :‖

free form on refrain instrumental melody   fade out(second time)

B(no third)				B(no third)/E			
‖:1	2	3	4	5	6	7	8 :‖

refrain to fade out ....

I Wanna Dance With Somebody by Whitney Houston   1/4 = 124   **G♭**

This was a 1987 hit by Whitney Houston on the album *Whitney*. Light funk in style, it fits the Dance Music category perfectly. It starts with an introduction with drums only, adding the funk bass in measure three. It has essentially three verses to the song, with the third verse modulating to the key of A♭, which is pretty typical of 70s and 80s pop music. Notice the concluding section in which there is response type singing with one male vocalist and Whitney Houston. It fades out to an ending. The style is slightly contrasting, in that it goes back and forth between extremely smooth singing and stronger singing. This is an excellent example of Dance Music and it is done very well.

Introduction

Drums		Bass G♭							
1	2	3	4	5	6				

Introduction with Brass

G♭				E♭m		C♭	A♭m7 G♭/B♭C♭D♭7(+4) / / / /		G♭ ////
1	2	3	4	5	6	7	8	9	10

Verse 1

Db		Ebm	EbmAbmCb Db			Ebm	EbmBbm7
			// / /				// //
1	2	3	4	5	6	7	8

Abm7	Db	Gb/Bb	Cb	AbmBbmEbm		CbGb/BbCbDbDrum Fill
				// / / ////		(♩ ♩ ♩) / /
1	2	3	4	5	6	7

Refrain

Gb				Ebm		Cb	Db7
1	2	3	4	5	6	7	8

Gb				Ebm		Cb	AbmGb/BbCbDb7+4
							/ / / /
1	2	3	4	5	6	7	8

Gb	
1	2

Verse 2

Db		Ebm	EbmAbmCb Db			Ebm	EbmBbm7
			// / /				// //
1	2	3	4	5	6	7	8

Abm7	Db	Gb/Bb	Cb	AbmBbmEbm		CbGb/BbCbDbDrum Fill
				// / / ////		(♩ ♩ ♩) / /
1	2	3	4	5	6	7

Refrain

Gb				Ebm		Cb	Db7
						////	// //
1	2	3	4	5	6	7	8

Gb				Ebm		Cb	AbmGb/BbCbDb7+4
						////	/ / / /
1	2	3	4	5	6	7	8

Interlude

E♭m		D♭	D♭ A♭mC♭ E♭m	D♭			
			// / ////				

| 1 | 2 | 3 | 4 | 5 | 6 | 7 | 8 |

| A♭m7 | D♭ | G♭/B♭ | C♭ | A♭mB♭mE♭m | | C♭G♭/B♭C♭D♭Drum Fill | |
| | | | | // / / //// | | (♩ ♩ ♩♩) / / | |

| 1 | 2 | 3 | 4 | 5 | 6 | 7 |

Modulation
Verse 3

A♭				Fm		D♭	D♭ E♭

| 1 | 2 | 3 | 4 | 5 | 6 | 7 | 8 |

| A♭ | | | | Fm | | D♭ | B♭mA♭/CD♭E♭7+4 |
| | | | | | | | / / / / |

| 1 | 2 | 3 | 4 | 5 | 6 | 7 | 8 |

Concluding Section

A♭							

| 1 | 2 | 3 | 4 | 5 | 6 | 7 | 8 |

| A♭ | | | | Fm | | D♭ | B♭mA♭/CD♭E♭7+4 |
| | | | | | | | / / / / |

| 1 | 2 | 3 | 4 | 5 | 6 | 7 | 8 |

| A♭ | | | | Fm | | D♭ | D♭ E♭7 |

| 1 | 2 | 3 | 4 | 5 | 6 | 7 | 8 |

| A♭ | | | | Fm | to fade out | | |

| 1 | 2 | 3 | 4 | 5 | 6 | 7 | 8 |

U Can't Touch This by M. C. Hammer   **1/4 = 135**   **Am**

This commercial rap tune is from his *Please Hammer Don't Hurt 'Em* album discussed in the last chapter. Like many Rap tunes, the chord changes are implied only by the melody and bass line and in this case the changes are represented by a two-measure phrase, as indicated below. Structurally the composition is fairly easy to follow and is quite regular. This would be an excellent tune for a beginning student to analyze. It is broken up by three Instrumental Breakdown sections in which there is a distinctive synthesizer melody.

The chord changes from the bass line repeat in a two measure phrase for the entire composition, as follows:

The only exceptions are the Instrumental Breakdown sections in which the entire section remains in Am.

Intro	8 Measures
Verse 1	8 Measures
Refrain	8 Measures
Verse 2	8 Measures
Refrain	8 Measures
Verse 3	8 Measures
Refrain	8 Measures
Instrumental Breakdown	8 Measures
Verse 4	8 Measures
Refrain	8 Measures
Instrumental Breakdown	8 Measures
Verse (no words)	8 Measures
Refrain	8 Measures
Instrumental Breakdown	8 Measures
Verse 5	8 Measures
Refrain	8 Measures
Refrain	8 Measures
Refrain to fade out	4 Measures

Step by Step by New Kids on the Block   1/4 = 132   Em

This composition is a funk dance tune from 1990. From a highly successful album of the same name, tour and video, this composition represents the style of this particular group, in that it has sections of pure singing without real chord changes and then other sections in which there are very clear chord changes. Please note that there are several repeats in the composition and we have notated a **D.S. al Coda** which means go back to the sign ⊕ and then when you come to the **To Coda** mark skip to the *Coda*. Please notice that some sections do not fit into neat 8 measure phrases but are rather extended phrases. It is not a blues composition but rather more similar to rap style based on two measure units. Careful analysis will reveal that the tune is very cleverly put together and although it sounds simple it is actually a bit more complicated and irregular than one might suspect.

Intro
No chords

| | | | | | | | Am7Bm7 |
							// / /
1	2	3	4	5	6	7	8

| Em Bm | EmAm7Bm7Em | | Am7Bm7Em | Bm | EmAm7Bm7Em | Bm | EmAm7Bm7 |
// //	// / / ////		// / / //	//	// / / //	//	// / /
1	2	3	4	5	6	7	8

⊕

| | | | | | | | **To Coda** |
| Em Bm | EmAm7Bm7EmBm | | EmAm7Bm7Em | Bm | EmAm7Bm7Em | Bm | EmAm7Bm7 |
// //	// / / // //		// / / //	//	// / / //	//	// / /
𝄆 1	2	3	4	5	6	7	8

No chords

| | | | | | | | | | Am7Bm7 |
									// / /
1	2	3	4	5	6	7	8	9	10

| | | | | | | | | 1. | 2. |
| Em | | AmBmEm | | AmBmEm | Am7Bm | CM7 | | | **D.S. al Coda** |
////		/ / ////	//	/ / //// // / /	////		////	𝄇	////
1	2	3	4	5 6		7	8	8

Coda

| Am | D | Am | D | Am | D | Am | | BM7 CM7 |
								// ////
1	2	3	4	5	6	7	8	9

Em		Bm7Em		Bm7 Em		Bm7 Em		Bm7
1	2	3	4	5	6	7	8

| Em | | Bm7Em | | | | Am7Bm7Em No Chords |
						/ / /
1	2	3	4	5	6	7 8 9 10 11 12 13 14

Em		Am7BmEm			Am7BmEm			Am7BmEm		Am7BmCM7	
1	2		3	4		5	6	7	8	9	10

Repeat until fade

Em	Bm7	EmAm7Bm	EmBm7	EmAm7Bm	Em	Bm7	EmAm7Bm	Em	Bm7	Em	Am7Bm
//	//	// / /	// //	// / /	//	// / /	// //	// /	//	//	/ /

‖: _____ :‖

1	2	3	4	5	6	7	8

DISCOGRAPHY

Anyone seeking additional records by the groups mentioned in this book should consult a Schwann Catalog, available at local record stores. Albums on which pieces for analysis can be found are preceded by an asterisk. Albums in cassette form have a (C) after the record number.

Chapters One through Four

Black Swing Tradition	2-Savoy 2246
Boogie Woogie Rarities (1927–1943)	Mile. 2009
Copulatin' Blues	Stash 101
From Spirituals to Swing	2-Van. T. ⁴⁷/₄₈
Gut Bucket Blues and Stomps	Her. 112
Jazz — Vols. 1–11	Folk. 2801–2811
*Atlantic Rhythm and Blues, Vols. 1–7	Atlantic 7-81293-1F, 7-81294-15, 7-81295-1F, 7-81296-1F, 7-81297-1F, 7-81298-F, 7-81299-1F

Oldies but Goodies, Vols. 1–10	OSR-LPS 8850, 8852–8860
Piano Ragtimes, Vols. 1–3	Her. 402, 405, 406
Smithsonian Collection of Classic Jazz	Col. P611891

Chapter Five

Haley, Bill
Golden Hits	2-MCA 4010
Greatest Hits	MCA 161E
Rock and Roll Revival	Pick. 3280

Chapter Six

Presley, Elvis
Elvis Aaron Presley (1955–1980)	8-RCA CPL8-3699
The Sun Sessions	RCA AFM1-1675
Golden, Vol. 1	RCA AFL1-1717E
Golden, Vol. 2	RCA AFL1-2075E
Golden, Vol. 3	RCA AFL1-2765
Golden, Vol. 4	RCA AFL1-3921

Cash, Johnny
Rockabilly Stars, Vol. 3	EPC EG-37984

Holly, Buddy
20 Greatest Hits	MCA 37244
Rock 'n' Roll Collection	2-MCA 4009E
20 Golden Hits	MCA 3040

Lewis, Jerry Lee
Original Rock Oldies, Vol. 1	Spec. 2129
Golden Rock and Roll	Sun 1000
Memories	Mer 5004

Orbison, Roy
Original Sound	Sun 113

Perkins, Carl
Original Golden Hits	Sun 111

Chapter Seven

Anka, Paul
Lonely Boy	Pick. 3523
21 Golden Hits	RCA AYL1-3808

Avalon, Frankie
Venus	De-lite 2020

Berry, Chuck
Echoes of Early Rock, Vol. 1	Roulette RE-111
Greatest Hits	Arc. Folk 321
Golden Hits	Mer. 61103

Boone, Pat
16 Great Performances	MCA AB-4006

Charles, Ray
Rock Begins, Vol. 1	Atco SD 33-314
Rock Begins, Vol. 2	Atco SD 33-315

Checker, Chubby
Greatest Hits	2-Abkco 4219

Cooke, Sam
Best	RCA ANL1-3466
2 Sides of Sam Cooke	Spec. 2119E

Curtis, King
  Best   Prest. 7709
  Soul Meeting   Prest. 7833

Diddley, Bo
  Two Great Guitars   Checker 2991

Dion and the Belmonts
  Greatest Hits   Col. C-31942

Domino, Fats
  Fats Domino   Arc. Folk 280

Eddy, Duane
  Have Twangy Guitar   Jamie 3000
  Pure Gold   RCA ANL1-2671

Little Richard
  *Original Rock Oldies, Vol. 1 Spec. 2129
  Fabulous Little Richard Spec. 2104

Nelson, Ricky
  Playing to Win   Cap. SO 0-12109
  Ricky   U Artists LM-1009

Various artists
  At the Hop   MCA DXS 528
  The Rock and Roll Stars Buddah BDS 7503

Chapter Eight

Agnew, Spiro
  2 Attacks on TV and Press Lava STA-235

Booker T. and the MGs
  Best of Booker T. and the MGs ATCO 8202

Brown, James
  The James Brown Story   Pol. 821231-1

James, Rick
  Glow   GOR 6135

Kennedy, John F.
  Inaugural Address   Sp. Arts 1034

King, Jr., Martin Luther
  Free at Last   Gor. 7-929
  Great March on Washington Gor. 7-908
  Great March to Freedom Gor. 7-906
  In Search of Freedom   Mer. 61170
  ————— , *McCarthy, Sen. Joseph R.* Folk 5450
  ————— , *The Motown Story: Anthology* MO MS 5-726

Nixon, Richard M.
  Checkers Speech   Lava RMN-235

Pickett, Wilson
  Wilson Pickett's Greatest Hits ATCO 2-501

Redding, Otis
  Best   ATCO 2-801

Richie, Lionel
  Can't Slow Down   MTN 6059

Robinson, Smokey
  Smokey Robinson   MTN M5-118

Ross, Diana
  Diana Ross and the Supremes   MTN M8-237
Temptations
  Temptations — Live   MTN 5306
Ventures
  The Very Best of the Ventures   LIB LN-10122
Wonder, Stevie
  Stevie Wonder's Greatest Hits   Tamla T7-282
——— , Un-American Activities Committee   Folk 5530

Chapter Nine

Beatles
  Abbey Road   Cap. SO-383
  Early Beatles   Cap. ST-2309
  1962-1966   2-Cap. SKBO-3403
  1966-1970   2-Cap. SKBO-3404
  Revolver   Cap. SW-2576
  Rubber Soul   Cap. SW-2442
  Yellow Submarine   Cap. SW-153

Chapter Ten

Beach Boys
  Best — Beach Boys   CAP 2545
  Dance, Dance, Dance   Cap. SN-16019
  Fun, Fun, Fun   Cap. SN-16018
  Good Vibrations   Reprise 2280
  Surf's Up   Reprise 6453
Big Brother and the Holding Company
  Cheap Thrills   Col. PC-9700
Grateful Dead
  Anthem of the Sun   War. 1749
  Grateful Dead   War. 1689
Jan and Dean
  Legendary Masters, No. 3   2-U Artists 9961
Jefferson Airplane
  Bless Its Pointed Little Head   RCA AYL1-3799
  Surrealistic Pillow   RCA AYL1-3738
  Worst of Jefferson Airplane   RCA LSP 4459
Moby Grape
  Great Grape   Col. C31098
  Wow / Grape Jams   2-Col. CXS3

Chapter Eleven

Crosby, Stills, Nash and Young
  Crosby, Stills and Nash   At. 19104
  Deja Vu   At. 19118
  Four Way Street   2-At. 2-902
Dylan, Bob
  Bob Dylan   Col. PC-8579
  Self Portrait   2-Col. P2X-30050
  Times They Are a-Changin'   Col. PC-8905
Dylan, Bob, with the Band
  Basement Tapes   2-Col. C2-33682

Fifth Dimension
  Up, Up and Away — Lib. SCM 91000
Peter, Paul and Mary
  Peter, Paul and Mary — War. 1449
  Peter, Paul and Mommy — War. 1785
  Reunion — War. 3231

Chapter Twelve

John, Elton
  Capt. Fantastic and the Brown Dirt Cowboy — MCA 3009
  Don't Shoot Me, I'm Only the Piano Player — MCA 3005
  Empty Sky — MCA 3008
  Madman Across the Water — MCA 3003
  Single Man — MCA 3065
  Tumbleweed Connection — MCA 3001
  Yellow Brick Road — 2-MCA 3001
  Live — Collection — Pick PDA 047
Rolling Stones
  At Their Satanic Majesties' Request — Lon. NPS-2(7)
  Beggar's Banquet — Lon. 539(7)
  Get Yer Ya-Ya's Out — Lon. NPS-5(7)
  Goat's Head Soup — Rol. 39106
  It's Only Rock and Roll — Rol. 79101
  Out of Our Heads — Lon. 429(7)
  Sticky Fingers — Rol. 59100
  Tattoo You — RLS 16052
The Who
  Magic Bus / My Generation — 2-MCA 4068
  Meaty, Beaty, Big and Bouncy — MCA 3025
  Quadrophenia — 2-MCA 10004
  Tommy — 2-MCA 10005
  Who Are You? — MCA 3050

Chapter Thirteen

Asia
  Asia — GFN GHS-2008
Captain Beefheart and His Magic Band
  Shiny Beast — War. 3256
  Trout Mask Replica — 2-Reprise 2027
Emerson, Lake and Palmer
  Pictures at an Exhibition — ATCO 19122
Fugs
  Golden Filth — Reprise 6396
  Virgin Fugs — ESP 1038
Genesis
  The Lamb Lies Down on Broadway — ATCO 2-401
Kinks
  Another Compleat Collection — CMP 2-2003
Mothers of Invention/Frank Zappa
  Fillmore East — Reprise 2042
  Freak Out — Verve 5005
  Joe's Garage — Zappa 1603
  Mothers of Invention — MGM GAS 112

Ruben and the Jets	Verve 5055
Ship arriving too late to save a drowning witch	BKP FW-38066
Uncle Meat	2-Rep. SMS-2024

Pink Floyd
The Dark Side of the Moon Cap. SMAS 11163

Procol Harum
Procol Harum AAM 3259

Rush
21 12 Mer SRM-1-1079

Styx
Styx VIC AYL1-4756

Yes
Close to the Edge ATC 19133

Chapter Fourteen

Alabama
My Home in Alabama RCA AHL1 3644
The Closer You Get RCA AHL1 4663

Byrds
Sweetheart of the Rodeo Col. PC-9670

Commander Cody and the Lost Planet Airmen
Lost in the Ozone Para 6017

Daniels, Charlie
Charlie Daniels Cap. SN-16039

Dirt Band
Will the Circle Be Unbroken UAS 9801

Eagles
The Long Run Asy 508

Flying Burrito Brothers
Close Up Honky Tonks A & M 4258

Lynyrd Skynyrd
Gimme Back My Bullets MCA 37070

New Riders of the Purple Sage
Best Col. PC-34367

ZZ Top
Best of ZZ Top War. 3273
Dequello War. HS-3361

Chapter Fifteen

Blood, Sweat and Tears
Blood, Sweat and Tears Col. PC-9720
Child Is Father to the Man Col. PC-9619

Brown, James
Original Disco Man Pol. 6212
Take a Look At Pol. 6181

Chicago
Chicago Transit Authority 2-Col. PG-8
Chicago III 2-Col. C2-30110
Best of Chicago Col. 33900
Chicago V Col. PC-31102
Chicago X Col. PC-34200

Clarke, Stanley
    Children of Forever (with Chick Corea)   Pol 5531
    School Days   Col. PE-36975
    Stanley Clarke   Col. PE-36973

Cobham, Billy
    Crosswinds   At. 7300
    Spectrum   At. 7268

Commodores
    Heroes   Mo. 8-939
    Midnight Magic   Mo. 8-926

Corea, Chick
    Chick Corea   2-Blue LA395-H
    Inner Space   2-At. 2-305
    Spanish Heart   2-Pol. 9003

Earth, Wind and Fire
    Head   Col. PC-32194
    Need of Love   War. 1958
    Way of the World   Col. PC-33280

Electric Flag
    Long Time Comin'   Col. CS-9597

Funkadelics
    Electric Spanking of Babies   War. 3482
    Uncle Jam Wants You   War. HS-3371

Hancock, Herbie
    An Evening with Chick Corea   2-Col. PG-34688
    Sextant   Col. C-32212
    V.S.O.P.   2-Col. PG-34688

Kool and the Gang
    Celebrate   De-Lite 9518

Mahavishnu Orchestra (John McLaughlin)
    Birds of Fire   Col. PC-31996
    Bitches Brew (Miles Davis)   2-Col. PG-26

Parliament
    Gloryhallastoopid   Casa. 7195
    Clones of Dr. Funkenstein   Casa. NBLP 7034

Ponty, Jean-Luc
    Cosmic Messenger   At. 19189
    A Taste for Passion   At. 19253

Santana
    Abraxas   Col. JC-30130
    Caravanserai   Col. PC-31619
    Santana   Col. PC-9781

Summer, Donna
    Bad Girls   2-Casa. 7150
    Love Trilogy   Casa. 5004N
    Walk Away   Casa. 7244

Stevie Wonder
    Songs in the Key of Life   2-Tam. 13-340C2

Weather Report
    Heavy Weather   Col. PC-34418

Chapter Sixteen

AC/DC
   Highway to Hell   ATCO 19244

Black Sabbath
   Paranoid   WB BSK 3104

Def Leppard
   Pyromania   Mer 810308-1

Grand Funk Railroad
   Grand Funk Hits   Cap. SN-16138

Iron Maiden
   Piece of Mind   Cap. St-12274

Jimi Hendrix Experience
   Essential Jimi Hendrix   REP 2R5 2245(C)

Judas Priest
   Screaming for Vengeance   Col. FC-38160

Kiss
   Double Platinum   Casa. 7100

Led Zeppelin
   Soundtrack from the Film   Swan Song SS2-201
   Led Zeppelin II   AT-CS19127(C)

Loudness
   Thunder in the East   ATCO 90246-1

Motley Crue
   Theatre of Pain   ELK 60418-1

Mountain
   Mountain   Col. PC-32079

Ozzy Osbourne
   Diary of a Madman   JET F2-37492

Quiet Riot
   Metal Health   PSH F2-38443

Chapter Seventeen

Adam and the Ants
   Kings of the Wild Frontier   Epic JE-37033

B-52's
   The B-52's   War. 3355
   Wild Planet   War. 3471

Blondie
   Eat to the Beat   Chrys. CHE-1225

Bowie, David
   Hunky Dory   RCA AFL1 4623
   The Rise and Fall of Ziggy Stardust   RCA AFL1 4702
   Live   RCA APL2 0771

Buzzcocks
   A Different Kind of Tension   A & M SP-009

Clash
   Give 'Em Enough Rope   Epic JE-35543
   Sandinista   3-Epic E3X-37037
   Clash   Epic PE 36060

Costello, Elvis
Taking Liberties   Col. JC-36839

Iggy and the Stooges
Raw Power   Col. PC-32111

Knack
. . . but the Litte Girls Understand   Cap. S00-12145
Get the Knack   Cap. S0-11948

Parker, Graham
Squeezing Out Sparks   Ari. 4223

Plimsouls
Plimsouls   Planet 13

The Police
*Zenyatta Mondatta   A & M SP 3720

Pop, Iggy
New Values   Ari. 4237
Soldier   Ari. 4259

Sex Pistols
Never Mind the Bollocks   War. K-3147

Stray Cats
Rant 'n' Rave with the Stray Cats   EIA SO-17102

Surf Punks
My Beach   Epic JE-36500

Talking Heads
Fear of Music   Sire 6076
*Speaking in Tongues   Sire 23883
Little Creatures   Sire 25305-4(C)

Chapter Eighteen

Abdul, Paula
Straight Up   Virgin 99256

Beastie Boys
Licensed to Ill   Def Jam FCT 40238(C)

Bell Biv Devoe
Poison   MCAC-6387(C)

Big Daddy Kane
Long Live the Kane   Cold Chillin' 25731

Collins, Phil
No Jacket Required   Atlantic 81240

D.J. Jazzy Jeff & The Fresh Prince
He's The DJ, I'm The Rapper   Jive 1091

Fat Boys
Fat Boys   Sutra 1015

Houston, Whitney
*Whitney   Arista AC-8405(C)

Ice-T
Power   Sire 25765

Jackson, Janet
Control   A & M CS 5106(C)

Jackson, Michael
*Thriller   Epic QE 38112

Joel, Billy
Glass Houses   Columbia 36384
The Bridge   Columbia 40402
Kool Moe Dee
Knowledge Is King   Jive 1182
L. L. Cool J
Bigger and Deffer   Def Jam 40793
Lauper, Cyndi
She's So Unusual   Portrait 38930
M. C. Hammer
Please Hammer Don't Hurt 'Em   Capitol CA-92857(C)
Madonna
Like a Virgin   Sire 25157
Like A Prayer   Sire 25844
Miami Sound Machine
Let It Loose   Epic 40769
Michael, George
Faith   Columbia 40867
N.W.A.
Straight Outta Compton   Ruthless 57102
New Kids on the Block
Step by Step   Columbia CT 45129(C)
Prince
Purple Rain   Warner 25110
Public Enemy
It Takes a Nation of Millions To Hold Us Back   Def Jam 44303
RUN-D.M.C.
Raising Hell   Profile 1217
Run-DMC   Profile 1212
Springsteen, Bruce
Born in the USA   Col. QCT 38653(C)
2 Live Crew
Move Somethin'   Luke Skywalker 101

BIBLIOGRAPHY

BACON, TONY, ED. *Rock Hardware: Instrument, Equipment and Technology of Rock.* New York: Harmony Books, 1981.

BEETHOVEN, JAN, AND CARMAN MOORE. *Rock-It.* Sherman Oaks, Calif.: Alfred Publishing Co., 1980.

BELZ, CARL. *The Story of Rock,* 2nd ed. New York: Oxford University Press, 1972.

BIRD, BRIAN. *Skiffle.* London: Robert Hale Ltd., 1958.

BROWN, CHARLES T. *Music U.S.A.: America's Country and Western Tradition.* Englewood Cliffs, N.J.: Prentice Hall, 1986.

——— ,ED. *Proceedings of NAJE,* Vol. 1. Manhattan, Kan.: NAJE Press, 1981.

CHARLES, RAY, AND DAVID RITZ. *Brother Ray.* New York: Dial Press, 1966.

CHRISTGAU, ROBERT. *Any Old Way You Choose It: Rock and Other Pop Music (1967–1973).* New York: Penguin Books, 1973.

CLIFFORD, MIKE, ED. *The Harmony Illustrated Encyclopedia of Rock,* 6th ed. New York: Harmony Books, 1988.

COHN, NIK. *Rock from the Beginning.* New York: Pocket Books, 1969.

——. *WopBopa LooBop LopBamBoom.* London: Paladin, 1970.

COON, CAROLINE. *1988: The New Wave Punk Rock Explosion.* New York: Hawthorn, 1978.

DAVIES, HUNTER. *The Beatles,.* New York: McGraw-Hill, 1968.

DENISOFF, R. SERGE, AND RICHARD A. PETERSON, EDS. *The Sounds of Social Change.* Chicago: Rand McNally, 1972.

DIXON, ROBERT, AND JOHN GODRICH. *Recording the Blues.* New York: Stein and Day, 1970.

EISEN, JONATHAN, ED. *The Age of Rock.* New York: Random House, 1969.

———. *The Age of Rock 2.* New York: Random House, 1970.

FRITH, SIMON. *The Sociology of Rock.* London: Constable, 1978.

———, *Sound Effects: Youth, Leisure, and the Politics of Rock 'n' Roll.* New York: Pantheon, 1984.

GABREE, JOHN. *The World of Rock.* Greenwich, Conn.: Fawcett Publications, 1968.

GILLETT, CHARLIE. *The Sound of the City—The Rise of Rock and Roll.* New York: Outerbridge and Dienstfrey, 1970.

GLEASON, RALPH J. *The Jefferson Airplane and the San Francisco Sound.* New York: Ballantine, 1969.

GOLDROSEN, JON. *Buddy Holly: His Life and Music.* Bowling Green, Ohio: Bowling Green University Press, 1975.

HOPKINS, JERRY. *Elvis.* New York: Simon & Schuster, 1971.

———. *The Rock Story.* New York: New American Library, 1970.

JONES, LEROI. *Blues People.* New York: William Morrow, 1967.

KEIL, CHARLES. *Urban Blues.* Chicago: University of Chicago Press, 1966.

LAZELL, BARRY, ED. *Rock Movers and Shakers.* New York: Billboard Publications, Inc., 1989.

LEAF, DAVID. *The Beach Boys and the California Myth.* New York: Grosset & Dunlap, 1978.

LOGAN, NICK, AND BOB WOFFINDEN. *The Illustrated Encyclopedia of Rock.* New York: Harmony Books, 1977.

MARCUS, GREIL. *Mystery Train.* New York: Dutton and Co., 1975.

MELLERS, WILFRED. *Twilight of the Gods: The Beatles in Retrospect.* New York: Viking Press, 1974.

MILLER, JIM, ED. *The Rolling Stone Illustrated History of Rock and Roll.* New York: Random House, 1980.

OBRECHT, JAS, ED. *Masters of Heavy Metal.* New York: Quill/Guitar Player, 1984.

ORLOFF, KATHERINE. *Rock 'n' Roll Woman.* Los Angeles: Nash Publishing, 1974.

PREISS, BYRON. *The Beach Boys.* New York: Ballantine, 1979.

The Rolling Stone Interviews. New York: Straight Arrow Publishers, 1971.

ROWE, MIKE. *Chicago Breakdown.* New York: Drake Publishers, 1975.

ROXON, LILLIAN. *Rock Encyclopedia.* New York: Grosset & Dunlap, 1969.

SCADUTO, ANTHONY. *Bob Dylan: An Intimate Biography.* New York: Grosset & Dunlap, 1971.

———. *The Beatles.* New York: New American Library, 1968.

———. *Schwann Record and Tape Guide.* Boston: ABC Schwann Publications, 1986.

WALLER, DON. *The Motown Story.* New York: Charles Scribner's Sons, 1985.

WENNER, JANN, ED. *Rolling Stone* (magazine). New York: Straight Arrow Publishers.

WHITBURN, JOEL. *The Billboard Book of Top 40 Hits, 4th Ed.* New York: Billboard Publications, Inc., 1990.

WHITE, ADAM. *The Billboard Book of Gold & Platinum Records.* New York: Billboard Books, 1990.

INDEX